Management Accounting

Management Accounting

Michael Jones

Cardiff Business School

John Wiley & Sons, Ltd

Other Wiley Editorial Offices

John Wiley & Sons Inc., 111 River Street, Hoboken, NJ 07030, USA

Jossey-Bass, 989 Market Street, San Francisco, CA 94103-1741, USA

Wiley-VCH Verlag GmbH, Boschstr. 12, D-69469 Weinheim, Germany

John Wiley & Sons Australia Ltd, 42 McDougall Street, Milton, Queensland 4064, Australia

John Wiley & Sons (Asia) Pte Ltd, 2 Clementi Loop #02-01, Jin Xing Distripark, Singapore 129809

John Wiley & Sons Canada Ltd, 6045 Freemont Blvd, Mississauga, ONT, L5R 4J3, Canada

Wiley also publishes its books in a variety of electronic formats. Some content that appears
in print may not be available in electronic books.

Library of Congress Cataloging-in-Publication Data

Jones, Michael.
  Management accounting / Michael Jones.
    p. cm.
  Includes bibliographical references and index.
  ISBN-13: 978-0-470-05770-4 (pbk.)
  ISBN-10: 0-470-05770-X (pbk. : alk. paper)
  1. Managerial accounting. I. Title.
HF5657.4.J66 2006
658.15′11 – dc22
                    2006019154

British Library Cataloguing in Publication Data

A catalogue record for this book is available from the British Library

ISBN-13: 978-0-470-05770-4 (PB)
ISBN-10: 0-470-05770-X (PB)

Typeset in 10/13 Sabon by Laserwords Private Limited, Chennai, India
Printed and bound in Great Britain by Scotprint, Haddington, East Lothian
This book is printed on acid-free paper responsibly manufactured from sustainable forestry
in which at least two trees are planted for each one used for paper production.

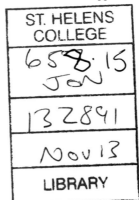

Dedication

I would like to dedicate this book to the following people who have made my life richer.

- My Father, Donald, who died in 2003
- My Mother
- My daughter, Katherine
- Tony Brinn (in memoriam)
- All my friends in Hereford, Cardiff and elsewhere
- All my colleagues
- And, finally, my past students!

Contents

About the Author

Michael Jones has taught accounting for 26 years, first at Hereford Technical College, then at Portsmouth Polytechnic (now University) and currently at Cardiff Business School. He has taught management accounting at all levels. He has published over 120 articles in both professional and academic journals. These articles cover a wide range of topics such as management accounting, financial accounting, the history of accounting and international accounting. The author is Professor of Financial Reporting at Cardiff Business School and Director of the Financial Reporting and Business Communication Unit. Michael has one daughter, Katherine.

About the Book

Background

Accounting is a key aspect of business. All those who work for, or deal with, businesses, therefore, need to understand accounting. Essentially, understanding accounting is a prerequisite for understanding business. This book aims to provide students with the necessary understanding of the theory and practice of management accounting. The book, therefore, is aimed primarily at students studying management accounting for the first time and seeks to be as understandable and readable as possible.

The Market

This book is intended as a primary text for students studying management accounting for the first time: either those following an undergraduate degree in a business school or non-business studies students studying an accounting course. Thus, this includes students on both accounting and non-accounting degrees and also MBA students. The book therefore covers, for example, accountants, business, engineers, physicists, hotel and catering, social studies and media-study students. The text aims to produce a self-contained, introductory, one-year course covering the major aspects of management accounting. However, it is also designed so that students can progress to more advanced follow-up courses in management accounting. The text is thus well-suited as an introduction for mainstream accounting graduates or MBA students as a basic text. The book should be particularly useful in reinforcing the fundamental theory and practice of introductory management accounting.

Scope

The book sets down my acquired wisdom (such as it is) over 26 years and interweaves context and technique. It aims to introduce the topic of management accounting to students in a student-friendly way. Not only are certain chapters devoted solely to context, but the key to each particular topic is seen as developing the student's understanding of the underlying concepts. This is a novel approach for this type of book.

The book is divided into 9 chapters and begins by setting out the broad context of accounting. In Chapter 1, we look at the nature of accounting and locate management accounting within a broader theoretical and practical framework. In particular, we look at the users of management accounting information, factors affecting accounting, the types of accountancy and the main professional institutes.

The book then explores the main concepts underpinning management accounting. In Chapter 2, we discuss the nature and importance of management accounting, the relationship between financial accounting and management accounting, explain the main branches of cost accounting and decision making and discuss cost minimisation and revenue maximisation. We also introduce important management accounting terminology. In the next seven chapters, seven main areas are covered: costing, budgeting, standard costing, short-term decision making, strategic management accounting, capital investment and sources of finance. We thus provide a good coverage of the basics of costing and management accounting as well as introducing strategic management accounting, a topic which has recently become more prominent. We also introduce students to a wide range of key concepts so that they gain a good knowledge base.

Special Features

A particular effort has been made to make management accounting as accessible as possible to students. There are thus several special features in this book which, taken together, distinguish it from other introductory textbooks.

Blend of Theory and Practice

I believe that the key to management accounting is understanding. As a result, the text stresses the underlying concepts of accounting and the context within which management accounting operates. The book, therefore, blends practice and theory. Worked examples are supplemented by explanation. In addition, the context of management accounting is explored. The aim is to contextualise management accounting within a wider framework.

Readable and Understandable Presentation

Much of my research has been into readable and understandable presentation. At all times, I have strived to achieve this. In particular, I have tried to present complicated materials in a simple way.

Innovative Presentation

I am very keen to focus on effective presentation. This book, therefore, includes many presentational features which aim to enliven the text. Quotations, extracts from newspapers and journals (real-life nuggets), and extracts from annual reports (the company camera) convey the day-to-day relevance of accounting. I also attempt to use realistic examples. This has not, however, always been easy or practical given the introductory nature of the material. In addition, I have attempted to inject some wit and humour into the text through the use of, among other things, cartoons and soundbites. The cartoons, in particular, are designed to present a sideways, irreverent look at accounting which hopefully students will find not only entertaining, but also thought-provoking. Finally, I have frequently used boxes and diagrams to simplify and clarify material. Throughout the text there are reflective questions (pause for thought). These are designed as places where students may pause briefly in their reading of the text to reflect on a particular aspect of accounting or to test their knowledge.

End-of-Chapter Questions and Answers

There are numerous questions and answers at the end of each chapter which test the student's knowledge. These comprise both numerical and discussion questions. The discussion questions are designed for group discussion between lecturer and students. At the end of the book an outline is provided to, at least, the first discussion question of each chapter. This answer provides some outline points for discussion and allows the students to gauge the level and depth of the answers required. However, it should not be taken as exhaustive or prescriptive. The other discussion answers are to be found on the lecturers' area of the website.

The answers to the numerical questions are divided roughly in two. Half of the answers are provided at the back of the book for students to practise the techniques and to test themselves. These questions are indicated by the number being in blue. The other numerical answers are to be found on the lecturer area of the website. A further extensive supplementary set of questions and answers is also available to lecturers on their website.

Websites

Access to the book companion site can be found at www.wileyeurope.com/college/jones. In addition to the supplementary questions, there are Powerpoint slides available on the lecturers' website. On the student's website, there are 90 multiple-choice questions (ten for each chapter) as well as additional questions with answers (one for each chapter).

The website also includes Wiley PLUS, which is a powerful online tool providing instructors and students with an integrated suite of teaching and learning resources, including an online version of the text, in one easy-to-use website.

Overall Effect

Taken together, I believe that the blend of theory and practice, focus on readable and understandable presentation, novel material, interpretative stance and innovative presentation make this a distinctive and useful introductory textbook. Hopefully, readers will find it useful and interesting! I have done my best. Enjoy!

Mike Jones
July 2006

Acknowledgements

In many ways writing a textbook of this nature is a team effort. Throughout the time it has taken to write this book I have consistently sought the help and advice of others in order to improve it. I am, therefore, extremely grateful to a great number of academic staff and students (no affiliation below) whose comments have helped me to improve this book. The errors, of course, remain mine.

Malcolm Anderson (Cardiff Business School)
Tony Brinn (Cardiff Business School)
Alex Brown
Peter Chidgey (BDO Binder, Hamlyn) Mark Clatworthy (Cardiff Business School)
Alpa Dhanani (Cardiff Business School)
Mahmoud Ezzamel (Cardiff Business School)
Charlotte Gladstone-Miller (Portsmouth Business School)
Paul Gordon (Heriot Watt University)
Tony Hincs (Portsmouth Business School)
Deborah Holywell
Carolyn Isaaks (Nottingham Trent University)
Tuomas Korppoo
Margaret Lamb (Warwick Business School)
Andrew Lennard (Accounting Standards Board)
Les Lumsdon (Manchester Metropolitan University)
Claire Lutwyche
Louise Macniven (Cardiff Business School)
Neil Marriott (University of Glamorgan)
Howard Mellett (Cardiff Business School)
Joanne Mitchell
Peter Morgan (Cardiff Business School)
Barry Morse (Cardiff Business School)
Simon Norton (Cardiff Business School)
Phillip O'Regan (Limerick University)
David Parker (Portsmouth Business School)
Roger Pegum (Liverpool John Moores University)
Maurice Pendlebury (Cardiff Business School)
Elaine Porter (Bournemouth University)
Neil Robson (University of the West of England)

Julia Smith (Cardiff Business School)
Aris Solomon (University of Exeter)
Jill Solomon (Cardiff Business School)
Tony Whitford (University of Westminster)
Jason Xiao (Cardiff Business School)

This book is hopefully enlivened by many extracts from books, newspapers and annual reports. This material should not be reproduced, copied or transmitted unless written permission is obtained from the original copyright owner. I am, therefore, grateful to all those who kindly granted the publisher permission to reproduce the copyright material. This includes the following companies and plcs: AstraZeneca, Heineken, HBOS, Hyder, Laing, Nokia, Manchester United, Marks & Spencer, Rentokil, Rolls-Royce, J. Sainsbury, Tesco, Vodafone, Volkswagen and J.D. Wetherspoon. In addition, *Accountancy Age*, the *Economist*, *The Financial Times*, *The Guardian*, *Management Accounting*, the *New Scientist*, *Sunday Business*, *The Daily Telegraph* and *The Sunday Telegraph*. Each source is also specifically mentioned in the text.

Many of the Soundbites are drawn from the following texts. The full references are: H. Ehrlich (1998), *The Wiley Book of Quotations* (John Wiley & Sons, Inc., New York); R. Flesch (1959), *The Book of Unusual Quotations* (Cassell, London); J. Vitullo-Martin and J. Robert Moskin (1994), *The Executive's Book of Quotations* (Oxford University Press, New York); and E. Weber (1991), *The Book of Business Quotations* (Business Books, London).

Every effort has been made to trace the original copyright owner; if we have accidentally infringed any copyright the publishers offer their apologies.

I am very appreciative of the help and support of my partner, Jill Solomon. I should also like to thank Steve Hardman and his team at John Wiley for their help and support. Finally, last but certainly not least, I should like to thank Jan Richards for her patience and hard work in turning my generally illegible scribbling into the final manuscript.

Preface to Management Accounting

Management accounting takes place within businesses and is essential to the running of a business. It can be usefully divided into (1) cost accounting, which includes costing (Chapter 3), and planning, control and performance (Chapters 4 and 5), and (2) decision making (Chapters 6–9).

In this book we investigate some major issues involved in management accounting. In Chapters 1 and 2, a brief introduction into the nature of management accounting is provided. Much of the terminology is introduced and an overview of the rest of the book is provided. Chapters 3, 4 and 5 look at cost accounting, one of the two main streams of management accounting. In Chapter 3, the role of costing in stock valuation and pricing is investigated. The cost allocation process is then outlined together with the use of different costing methods in different industries. Both traditional absorption costing and the more modern activity-based costing are discussed. Chapters 4 and 5 look at planning, control and performance. Chapter 4 sets out the cost control technique of budgeting. The different types of budget are also briefly discussed. Responsibility accounting is also discussed. Then in Chapter 5 standard costing is explored. The individual variances are explained and a worked example is shown.

Chapters 6–9 look at the decision-making aspects of management accounting. Chapter 6 investigates the managerial techniques (such as break-even analysis and contribution analysis) used for short-term operational decision making. Then Chapter 7 looks at the relatively new management accounting topic of strategic management accounting. This shows how management accounting influences strategic business decisions. In Chapter 8, we investigate capital budgeting. This chapter investigates the different techniques (such as payback and discounted cash flow) used to evaluate long-term investment decisions. Finally, Chapter 9 investigates two aspects of both internal and external sources of finance: short-term financing via the efficient management of working capital and long-term financing such as share capital and loan capital.

As most businesses are sole traders, partnerships or non-listed companies we use the accepted terminology for these businesses. However, when we are specifically referring to listed companies we use terminology as laid down by the International Accounting Standards Board in International Financial Reporting Standards. ■

Chapter 1

"One way to cheat death is to become an accountant, it seems. The Norfolk accountancy firm W.R. Kewley announces on its website that it was 'originally established in 1982 with 2 partners, one of whom died in 1993. After a short break he re-established in 1997, offering a personal service throughout.' He was, Feedback presumes, dead only for tax purposes."

New Scientist, 1 April 2000, p. 96

Learning Outcomes

After completing this chapter you should be able to:

✔ Explain the nature and importance of accounting.

✔ Outline the context which shapes accounting.

✔ Identify the main users of accounting and discuss their information needs.

✔ Distinguish between the different types of accountancy and accountant.

Introduction to Accounting

In a Nutshell

- *Accounting is the provision of financial information to managers or owners so that they can make business decisions.*

- *Accounting measures, monitors and controls business activities.*

- *Financial accounting supplies financial information to external users.*

- *Management accounting serves the needs of managers.*

- *Users of accounting information include shareholders and managers.*

- *Accounting theory and practice are affected by history, country, technology and organisation.*

- *Auditing, bookkeeping, financial accounting, financial management, insolvency, management accounting, taxation and management consultancy are all branches of accountancy.*

- *Accountants may be members of professional bodies, such as the Institute of Chartered Accountants in England and Wales.*

- *Although very useful, accounting has several limitations such as its historic nature and its failure to measure the non-financial aspects of business.*

Introduction

The key to understanding business is to understand accounting. Accounting is central to the operation of modern business. Accounting enables businesses to keep track of their money. If businesses cannot make enough profit or generate enough cash they will go bankrupt. Often accounting is called the 'language of business'. It provides a means of effective and understandable business communication. If you understand the language you will, therefore, understand business. However, like many languages, accounting needs to be learnt. The aim of this book is to teach the language of accounting, particularly management accounting.

Nature of Accounting

At its simplest, accounting is all about recording, preparing and interpreting business transactions. Accounting provides a key source of information about a business to those who need it, such as managers or owners. Management accounting, in particular, allows managers to monitor, plan and control the activities of a business. This enables managers to answer key questions such as:

- How much profit have we made?
- Have we enough cash to pay our employees' wages?
- What level of dividends can we pay to our shareholders?
- Should we expand our product range?

PAUSE FOR THOUGHT 1.1

Some Accounting Questions

You are thinking of manufacturing a new product, the superwhizzo. What are the main accounting questions you would ask?

The principal questions would relate to sales, costs and profit. They might be:

- What price are rival products selling at?
- How much raw material will I need? How much will it cost?
- How many hours will it take to make each superwhizzo and how much is labour per hour?
- How much will it cost to make the product in terms of items such as electricity?
- How should I recover general business costs such as business rates or the cost of machinery wearing out?
- How much profit should I aim to make on each superwhizzo?

In small businesses, managers and owners will often be the same people. However, in larger businesses, such as large companies, managers and owners will not be the same. Managers will run the companies on behalf of the owners. In such cases, accounting information serves a particularly useful role. Managers supply the owners with financial information in the form of a profit and loss account, a balance sheet and a cash flow statement. This enables the owners to see how well the business is performing. In companies, the owners of a business are called the shareholders.

Essentially, therefore, accounting is all about providing financial information to managers and owners so that they can make business decisions (see Definition 1.1). The formal definition (given below), although dating from 1966, has stood the test well as a comprehensive definition of accounting. In effect, management accounting is a subset of accounting.

DEFINITION 1.1

Accounting

Working definition
The provision of information to managers and owners so that they can make business decisions.

Formal definition
'The process of identifying, measuring and communicating economic information to permit informed judgments and decisions by users of the information.'

American Accounting Association (1966), *Statement of Basic Accounting Theory*, p. 1

Importance of Accounting

Accounting is essential to the running of any business or organisation. Organisations as diverse as ICI, Barclays Bank and Manchester United football club all need to keep a close check on their finances.

At its simplest, money makes the world go round and accounting keeps track of the money. Businesses depend on cash and profit. If businesses do not make enough cash or earn enough profit, they will get into financial difficulties, perhaps even go bankrupt. Accounting provides the framework by which cash and profit can be monitored, planned and controlled.

Unless you can understand accounting, you will never understand business. This does not mean everybody has to be an expert accountant. However, it is necessary to know the language of accounting and to be able to interpret accounting numbers. In some respects, there is a similarity between learning to drive a car and learning about accounting. When you are learning to drive a car you do not need to be a car mechanic. However, you have to understand the car's instruments, such as a speedometer or fuel gauge. Similarly, with accounting, you do not have to be a professional accountant. However, you do need to understand the basic terminology such as income, expenses, profit, assets, liabilities, capital, and cash flow. In addition, for management accounting we need to understand terms such as 'budgeting', 'costing' and 'decision making'.

Manchester United

What information might the board of directors of Manchester United find useful?

....

Manchester United is both a football club and a thriving business. Indeed, the two go hand in hand. Playing success generates financial success, and financial success generates playing success. Key issues for Manchester United might be:

- How much in gate receipts will we get from our league matches, cup matches and European fixtures?
- How much can we afford to pay our players?
- How much cash have we available to buy rising new stars and how much will our fading old stars bring us?
- How much will we get from television rights and commercial sponsorship?
- How much do we need to finance new capital expenditure, such as building a new stadium?
- What is our expected income and expenditure for the next twelve months?

Financial Accounting and Management Accounting

A basic distinction is between financial accounting and management accounting. Financial accounting is concerned with information on a business's performance and is targeted primarily at those outside the business (such as shareholders). However, it is also used internally by managers. By contrast, management accounting is internal to a business and used solely by managers. A brief overview is provided in Figure 1.1.

Figure 1.1   Overview of Financial and Management Accounting

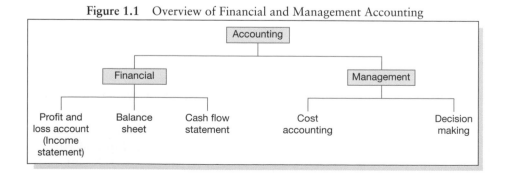

Financial Accounting

Financial accounting is the provision of financial information on a business's recent financial performance targeted at external users, such as shareholders. However, internal users, such as management, may also find it useful. It is required by law. Essentially, it is backward-looking, dealing with past events. Transactions are initially recorded using double-entry bookkeeping. Three major financial statements can then be prepared: the profit and loss account (also known as the income statement), the balance sheet and the cash flow statement. These are then interpreted using ratios by users such as shareholders and analysts.

Management Accounting

By contrast, management accounting serves only the internal needs of the business. It is not required by law. However, all organisations generate some sort of management accounting: if they did not they would not survive long. Management accounting can be divided into cost accounting and decision making. In turn, cost accounting can be split into costing (Chapter 3) and

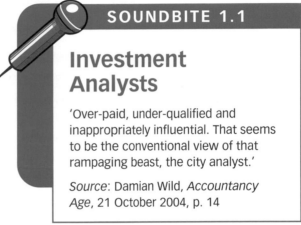

SOUNDBITE 1.1

Investment Analysts

'Over-paid, under-qualified and inappropriately influential. That seems to be the conventional view of that rampaging beast, the city analyst.'

Source: Damian Wild, *Accountancy Age*, 21 October 2004, p. 14

planning, control and performance: budgeting (Chapter 4) and standard costing (Chapter 5). Decision making is divided into short-term decisions (Chapter 6) and long-term decision making (Chapters 7–8). In Chapter 9 both short-term and long-term sources of finance are considered.

Users of Accounts

The users of accounting information may broadly be divided into insiders and outsiders (see Figure 1.2). The insiders are the management and the employees. However, employees are also outsiders in the sense that they often do not have direct access to the financial

Figure 1.2   Main Users of Accounting Information

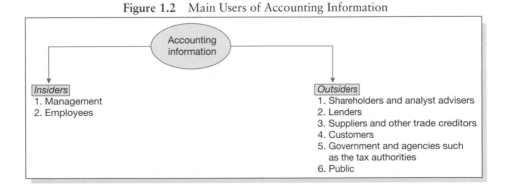

information. Management accounting is primarily concerned with providing information to internal users.

These users all need accounting information to help them make business decisions. Usually, the main information requirements for management and employees concern costing, decision making, and planning and control (see Figure 1.3). Management and employees being internal users may be less concerned with the company's prior year's profit and loss account, balance sheet and cash flow statement. However, this information will still be necessary – for example, when preparing next year's budgets.

Figure 1.3   User Information Requirements

User Group	Information Requirements
Internal Users	
1. Management	Information for costing, decision making, planning and control.
2. Employees	Information about job security and for collective bargaining.
External Users	
1. Shareholders and analyst advisers	Information for buying and selling shares.
2. Lenders	Information about assets and the company's cash position.
3. Suppliers and other trade creditors	Information about assets and the company's cash position.
4. Customers	Information about the long-term prospects and survival of the business.
5. Government and agencies such as tax authorities	Information to enable governmental planning. Information primarily on profits to use as a basis for calculating tax.
6. Public (e.g., individual citizens, or organisations such as Greenpeace)	Information about the social and environmental impact of corporate activities.

The information needs of each group differ slightly and, indeed may conflict (see Pause for Thought 1.3).

PAUSE FOR THOUGHT 1.3

Conflicting Interests of User Groups

Can you think of an example where the interests of users might actually conflict?

....

A good example would be in future budgeted information. Employees and managers may well have differing interests. If the company is budgeted to make a big profit, managers may wish to keep information secret. They might be scared that employees would use the information to press for higher wages through collective bargaining or industrial action. Alternatively, if a loss were forecast, managers might wish to plan for future redundancies while employees might seek to resist them.

Accounting Context

It is important to realise that accounting is more than just a mere technical subject. Although it is true that at the heart of accounting there are many techniques. For example, as we will see in Chapter 4, budgeting is a useful techniques when planning and controlling the future activities of a business. However, accounting is also determined by the context in which it operates. Accounting changes as society changes. Accounting in medieval England and accounting today, for example, are very different. There would be very different methods of controlling personnel and very different managerial activities. Similarly, there may be differences between accounting in Germany and in the United Kingdom. We can see the importance of context, if we look briefly at the effect of history, country, technology, and organisation (see Figure 1.4).

Figure 1.4 Importance of Accounting Context

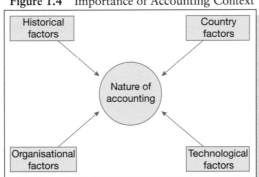

PAUSE FOR THOUGHT 1.4

The Term 'Accounting'

Why is accounting so called?

It is believed that accounting derives from the old thirteenth-century word *aconter*, to count. At its simplest, therefore, accounting means counting. This makes sense as the earliest accountants would have counted sheep or pigs!

History

Accounting is an integral part of human society. Early societies had accounting systems which although appearing primitive to us today, served their needs adequately. The Incas in South America, for example, used knotted ropes, called quipus, for accounting. In medieval England notched sticks called tally sticks were used to record transactions. Personal accountability was direct and visible.

Gradually, over time, human society became more sophisticated. As a result, accounting techniques gradually developed and became more complex.

International Accounting

Financial accounting techniques such as double-entry bookkeeping, the profit and loss account and balance sheet are now well-entrenched in most major countries. Management accounting is much more diverse. In some countries, management accountants represent an important progressive body operating within countries such as the UK and the USA. In other countries, such as Germany and Japan, management accountants are less important, with engineers and cost accountants performing the management accounting function.

Technology

A rapid change which has affected accounting is computerisation. Up until the advent of computers, accounting was done manually. This was labour-intensive work. Each transaction was entered into the books manually. The accounts were then prepared by hand. Costing, budgeting and decision making computations were all carried out manually.

Today, most businesses use computers. All complex management accounting techniques, such as budgeting, costing or break-even analysis, are likely to have stand alone customised computer packages. However, they must be used with caution. For the computer, GIGO rules. If you put garbage in, you get garbage out. To avoid GIGO, one needs to understand management accounting. In fact, computerisation probably makes it more, rather than less, important to understand the basics.

Organisations

The nature of accounting will vary from business to business. It will depend on the structure of the business and the nature of the business activity.

Structure

There are three main types of business enterprise: sole traders, partnerships, and companies. A sole trader's accounts will normally be a lot simpler than those of either a partnership or a company. Sole traders generally run smaller, less complicated businesses (for example, a small butcher's shop). Partnerships are multi-owned businesses typically larger in size than sole traders. The sole traders' and partnerships' accounts will normally be less complicated than company accounts as they are prepared for the benefit of active owner-managers rather than for owners who do not actually run the business.

Nature of the Business

Every organisation is different. Consequently, every organisation's accounts will differ in certain respects. For example, property companies will own predominantly more land and buildings than non-property companies. Manufacturing companies will have more stock than non-manufacturing companies. They may, for example, have more complicated budgetary systems.

It is clear from Figure 1.5 that the nature of sales varies from business to business. In some businesses, a service is provided (e.g., bank, football club, insurance company and plumber).

Figure 1.5   Nature of Sales

Business	Nature of Main Sales
Bank	Interest received from customers
Football club	Gate receipts
Insurance company	Premiums received
Manufacturing company	Sales of goods to retailers
Plumber	Sales of services and other goods
Shop	Sales of goods to customers

The nature of the sales will dictate, to a large extent, the nature of the management accounting techniques used. For example, a plumber might base his charge out rate on a notional hourly rate and charge materials on a cost plus basis. A manufacturing company, however, is likely to take a much more complicated and sophisticated system for determining the sales price of its goods.

The Company Camera 1.1 shows the sales (often termed turnover) of Manchester United plc, mainly gate receipts, television and merchandising, which are generated by entertaining its customers.

THE COMPANY CAMERA 1.1

Sales or Turnover

Turnover
Turnover, all of which arises from the Group's principal activity, can be analysed into its main components as follows:

	2004 £'000	2003 £'000
Matchday	61,206	70,593
Media	62,544	56,218
Commercial	45,330	46,190
	169,080	173,001

Turnover, all of which originates in the United Kingdom, can be analysed by destination as follows:

	2004 £'000	2003 £'000
United Kingdom	159,650	160,485
Rest of World	9,430	12,516
	169,080	173,001

Media income from European cup competitions is distributed by the Football Association and is therefore classified as being of United Kingdom origin and destination. Rest of World turnover includes an allocation of income receivable from Nike based on the geographical split of sales.

Source: Manchester United plc, 2004 Annual Report, p. 61

Types of Accountancy

We need to distinguish between the types of accountancy and the types of accountant. Accountancy refers to the process, while accountant refers to the person. In other words, accountancy is what accountants do! In this book, we primarily focus on management accounting. However, accountants perform other roles such as auditing, bookkeeping, financial accounting, financial management, insolvency, taxation and management consultancy. All of these are briefly covered below.

Auditing

Auditing is carried out by teams of staff headed by qualified accountants who are independent of the business. Essentially, auditors check that the financial statements, prepared by management, give a true and fair view of the accounts. Auditing is normally associated with company accounts. However, the tax authorities or the bank may request an audit of the accounts of sole traders or partnerships.

Bookkeeping

Bookkeeping is the preparation of the basic accounts. It involves entering monetary transactions into the books of account. A trial balance is then extracted, and a profit and loss account and balance sheet are prepared. Nowadays, most companies use computer packages for the basic bookkeeping function which is often performed by non-qualified accountants.

Financial Accounting

Financial accounting is a wider term than bookkeeping. It deals with not only the mechanistic bookkeeping process, but the preparation and interpretation of the financial accounts. For companies, financial accounting also includes the preparation of the annual report (a document sent annually to shareholders, comprising both financial and non-financial information). In orientation, financial accounting is primarily outward-looking and aimed at providing information for external users. However, monthly financial accounts are often prepared and used internally within a business. These would consist of the past month's profit and loss account, balance sheet and cash flow statement. They should be distinguished from the monthly management accounts, in which forecasted budgets are compared with actual results. However, in many businesses, the two sets of accounts are integrated.

Financial Management

An area of growing importance for accountants is financial management. Some aspects of financial management fall under the general heading of management accounting. Financial management, as its name suggests, is about managing the sources of finance of an organisation. It may, therefore, involve managing the working capital (i.e., short-term assets and liabilities) of a company or finding the cheapest form of borrowing. These topics are briefly examined in

Chapter 9. There is often a separate department of a company called the financial management or treasury department.

Insolvency

One of the main reasons for the rise to prominence of professional accountants in the UK was to wind up failed businesses. This is still part of a professional accountant's role. Professional accounting firms are often called in to manage the affairs of failed businesses, in particular to pay creditors who are owed money by the business.

Management Accounting

Management accounting covers the internal accounting of an organisation. There are several different areas of management accounting: costing (see Chapter 3), budgeting (see Chapter 4), standard costing (see Chapter 5), short-term decision making (see Chapter 6), strategic management accounting (see Chapter 7), capital investment appraisal (see Chapter 8), and management of working capital and sources of finance (Chapter 9). Essentially, these activities aim to monitor, control and plan the financial activities of organisations. Management uses such information for decisions such as determining a product's selling price or setting the sales budget.

Taxation

Taxation is a complicated area. Professional accountants advise businesses on a whole range of tax issues. Much of this involves tax planning (i.e., minimising the amount of tax that organisations have to pay by taking full advantage of the often complex tax regulations). This tax avoidance which operates within the law should be distinguished from tax evasion which is illegal. Professional accountants may also help individuals with a scourge of modern life, the preparation of their annual income tax assessment.

Management Consultancy

Management consultancy is a lucrative source of income for accountants (see Real-Life Nugget 1.1). However, as Soundbite 1.2 shows, management consultants are often viewed cynically. Management consultancy embraces a whole range of activities such as special efficiency audits, feasibility studies, and tax advice. Many professional accounting firms now make more money from management consultancy than from auditing. Examples of management consultancy are investigating the feasibility of a new football stadium, the costing of a local authority's school meals proposals, or the introduction of a new budgetary system.

REAL-LIFE NUGGET 1.1

Management Consultancy

To be fair, many of these issues were problems of success. The accountancy industry had kick-started phenomenal growth and change in the management consultancy services it offered its client base. It was natural to sell those services to its existing clients who eagerly purchased the IT, strategy and financial management consultancy on top of the bog-standard audit and tax services.

Suddenly audit became the poor relation, both in terms of excitement and financial return.

Audit became a commodity and we all know what happens then – the product becomes devalued and the price goes down.

Source: How the Brits started the Rot, Peter Williams, *Accountancy Age*, 11 November 2004, p. 28

Types of Accountant

There are several types of accountant. The most high-profile are those belonging to the six professionally qualified bodies. In addition to these six accountancy bodies, there are other accounting associations, the most important of which is probably the Association of Accounting Technicians. The web addresses for these institutes are listed at the end of the chapter.

Professionally Qualified Accountants

Chartered Accountants

There are six institutions of professionally qualified accountants currently operating in the UK (see Figure 1.6). All jealously guard their independence and the many attempts to merge over the past few years have all failed (see Real-Life Nugget 1.2). 'It's like proposing that Manchester United and Manchester City merge, suggests one indignant ICAEW member, illustrating the strength of feeling' (Michelle Perry, *Accountancy Age*, 22 July 2004, p. 6). Although they all have their individual specialisms, many of the members of these six institutions work in industry, many as management accountants.

Figure 1.6 Main UK Professional Accountancy Bodies

Body	Main Activities
Institute of Chartered Accountants in England and Wales (ICAEW)	Generally auditing, financial accounting, management consultancy, insolvency and tax advice. However, many work in industry.
Institute of Chartered Accountants in Ireland (ICAI)	Similar to ICAEW.
Institute of Chartered Accountants of Scotland (ICAS)	Similar to ICAEW.
Association of Chartered Certified Accountants (ACCA)	Auditing, financial accounting, insolvency, management consultancy, and tax advice. Many train or work in industry.
Chartered Institute of Management Accountants (CIMA)	Management accounting.
Chartered Institute of Public Finance and Accounting (CIPFA)	Accounting within the public sector and privatised industries.

REAL-LIFE NUGGET 1.2

Professional Accountancy Bodies

There have been several attempts to persuade the UK's accountancy bodies to merge over the past few years, all without much success. Six accountancy bodies is rather a lot and the government understandably gets exasperated from time to time by six (and sometimes seven) different responses to a consultation paper. But the bodies' members have consistently refused merger initiatives, always citing differing training requirements as a major consideration – and not without justification.

Source: Big Five Pressure Gets Results, Elizabeth Mackay, *Accountancy Age*, 9 March 2000, p. 18

There are three institutes of chartered accountants: the Institute of Chartered Accountants in England and Wales (ICAEW), the Institute of Chartered Accountants in Ireland (ICAI), and the Institute of Chartered Accountants of Scotland (ICAS). The largest of these three is the ICAEW. Its members were once mainly financial accountants and auditors, but now take part in a whole range of activities. Many leave the professional partnerships with which they train to join business organisations. In fact, qualifying as a chartered accountant is often seen as a route into a business career. Many ICAEW members thus end up performing management accounting functions within commercial companies.

Association of Chartered Certified Accountants (ACCA)

The ACCA's members are not so easy to pigeonhole as the other professionally qualified accountants. They work both in public practice as auditors and as financial accountants. They also have an enormous number of overseas students. Many certified accountants train for their qualification in industry and never work in public practice.

Chartered Institute of Management Accountants (CIMA)

This is an important body whose members generally train and work in industry. They are found in almost every industry, ranging, for example, from coal mining to computing. Originally, management accountants performed a primarily costing function. Nowadays they perform a great number of management accounting techniques.

Chartered Institute of Public Finance and Accountancy (CIPFA)

This institute is smaller than the ICAEW, ACCA or CIMA. It is also much more specialised with its members typically working in the public sector or the newly privatised industries, such as Railtrack. CIPFA members perform a wide range of financial activities within these organisations, such as budgeting in local government.

Second-Tier Bodies

The main second-tier body in the UK is the Association of Accounting Technicians. This body was set up by the major professional accountancy bodies. Accounting technicians help professional accountants, often doing the more routine bookkeeping and costing activities. Many accounting technicians go on to qualify as professional accountants.

The different accountancy bodies, therefore, all perform different functions. Members of different institution can be found in companies, in professional accountancy practices, and in the public sector. This diversity is highlighted in an original way in Real-Life Nugget 1.3.

REAL-LIFE NUGGET 1.3

A Sideways Look at the Accounting Profession

Thus, to take parallels from the Christian church, we have:

- **the lay priest:** the accountant working for a company;
- **the mendicant priest:** the professional accountant in a partnership;
- **the monastic priest:** the banker, who, while not strictly an accountant, serves much the same ends in a separate and semi-isolated unit;
- **the father confessor:** the auditing accountant to whom everything is (officially) revealed, and who then grants absolution.

Source: Graham Cleverly (1971) *Managers and Magic*, Longman Group Ltd, London, p. 47

SOUNDBITE 1.3

Limitations of Traditional Accounts

'Non-financial items like business opportunities, management strategies and risks have a big effect on company performance and need to be reflected in company reports.'

Mike Starr, Chairman of American Institute of Certified Public Accountants. Committee on Enhanced Business Reporting.

Source: Consortium Urges Reporting Reforms, Nicholas Neveling, *Accountancy Age*, 17 February 2005, p. 11

Limitations of Accounting

Accounting, therefore, measures business transactions in numerical terms. It thus provides useful information for managers and other users of accounts. It is, however, important to appreciate certain limitations of accounting. The first three limitations apply to accounting per se, the next two more particularly to management accounting. First, accounting tends to measure the cost of past expenditures rather than the current value of assets. Second, traditional accounting does not capture non-financial aspects of business. Thus, if an industry pollutes the air or the water this is not recorded in the conventional accounts. Third, traditional accounting does not measure the human resources of a business or its knowledge and skills base. Fourth, traditional management accounting is geared up to manufacturing rather than service industries. Fifth, traditional management accounting does not consider the strategic aspects of accounting (see Chapter 7).

Conclusion

Accounting is a key business activity. It provides information for a business so that managers or owners (for example, shareholders) can make business decisions. Accounting provides the framework by which cash and profit can be monitored and controlled. A basic distinction is between financial accounting (accounting targeted primarily at those outside the business, but also useful to managers) and management accounting (providing information solely to managers).

Accounting changes as society changes. In particular, it is contingent upon history, country, technology and the nature and type of the organisation. There are at least eight groups which use accounting information, the main ones being managers and shareholders. Managers and employees require information for, amongst other things, costing, budgeting and decision making. There are several types of accountancy and accountant. Besides management accounting, the types of accountancy include auditing, bookkeeping, financial accounting, financial management, insolvency, taxation and management consultancy. The six UK professional accountancy bodies are the Association of Chartered Certified Accountants, the Chartered Institute of Management Accountants, the Chartered Institute of Public Finance and Accountancy, and the Institute of Chartered Accountants in England and Wales, the Institute of Chartered Accountants in Ireland and the Institute of Chartered Accountants of Scotland. Members of any of the institutes may perform the management accounting functions. Although very useful, accounting has certain limitations, for example, its historic nature its failure to measure non-financial transactions, and its lack of a strategic management function.

Websites

A list of useful websites is included below for students interested in a career in accounting and who wish to find out more information.

i) Accountancy Institutes

www.**acca**global.com	=	Association of Chartered Certified Accountants (ACCA)
www.**cima**global.com	=	Chartered Institute of Management Accountants (CIMA)
www.**cipfa**.org.uk	=	Chartered Institute of Public Finance and Accounting (CIPFA)
www.**icaew**.co.uk	=	Institute of Chartered Accountants in England and Wales (ICAEW)

www.icai.ie	=	Institute of Chartered Accountants in Ireland (ICAI)
www.icas.org.uk	=	Institute of Chartered Accountants of Scotland (ICAS)
www.aat.co.uk	=	Association of Accounting Technicians (AAT)

ii) Accounting Firms

www.pwcglobal.com	=	PriceWaterhouseCoopers
www.ey.com	=	Ernst & Young
www.kpmg.com	=	KPMG
www.deloitte.com	=	Deloitte

Q&A   Discussion Questions

Questions with numbers in blue have answers at the back of the book.

Q1   What is the importance, if any, of accounting?

Q2   Can you think of three business decisions for which managers would need accounting information?

Q3   What do you consider to be the main differences between financial and management accounting?

Q4   Discuss the idea that as society changes so does accounting.

Chapter 2

"Jones was loyal to his staff, and diplomatic, but clearly had been bewildered by what he found when he arrived. 'Well, we've only just got an audited balance sheet for 1998', he said, 'We just don't have any contemporary operating or financial data on which to make management decisions in this airline at the moment. It's the old garbage-in, garbage-out syndrome.'"

Graham Jones commenting on the Greek airline company, *Olympic Airlines*
Source: Icarus Descending, Matthew Gwyther, *Management Today*, January 2000, pp. 52–53

Learning Outcomes

After completing this chapter you should be able to:

✔ **Explain the nature and importance of management accounting.**

✔ **Outline the relationship between financial accounting and management accounting.**

✔ **Explain the main branches of cost accounting and decision making.**

Introduction to Management Accounting

✔ Discuss cost minimisation and revenue maximisation.

✔ Understand some of the major terms used in management accounting.

In a Nutshell

■ *Management accounting is the provision of accounting information to management to help with costing, with planning, control and performance and with decision making.*

■ *Whereas the main focus of financial accounting is external, management accounting is internally focused.*

■ *Management accounting has its origins in costing; however, nowadays costing is less important as new areas such as strategic management accounting develop.*

■ *Management accounting can be broadly divided into cost accounting (costing; planning, control and performance) and decision making (short-term and long-term).*

■ *Costing consists of recovering costs for pricing and for the valuation of stock.*

■ *Planning, control and performance consists of planning and controlling future costs using budgeting and standard costing as well as evaluating performance.*

■ *Decision making involves short-term decision making, strategic management accounting, capital budgeting and sources of finance.*

■ *Traditionally, management accounting has been criticised for focusing on minimising costs rather than maximising revenue.*

Introduction

Management accounting is concerned with the internal accounting within a business. Essentially, it is the provision of both financial and non-financial information to managers so that they can manage costs and make decisions. In many ways, therefore, management accounting is less straightforward than financial accounting. Management accounting varies markedly from business to business and management accountants, in effect, carry around a toolkit of techniques, their 'tools of the trade'. The purpose of this section is to try to explain these techniques and to fit them into an overall picture of management accounting.

PAUSE FOR THOUGHT 2.1

Management Accounting

Why do you think management accounting is so called?

....

Management accounting is a relatively new term and has been in widespread use only since the 1950s. The term combines management and accounting. It suggests that accountants have a managerial role within the company. They are, in effect, more than just a functional specialist group. The term management accounting has come, therefore, to represent all the management and accounting activities carried out by accountants within a business. This involves not only costing, and planning, control and performance but also managerial decision making.

Context

The management accountant works within a business. The focus of management accounting is thus internal rather than external. In this book, we simplify the formal definition (see Definition 2.1 on the next page) and take the purpose of management accounting as being to provide managers with accounting information in order to help with costing, with planning, control and performance and with decision making. As the formal, official definition shows, management accounting concerns business strategy, planning and control, decision making, efficient resource usage, performance improvement, safeguarding assets, corporate governance and internal control.

DEFINITION 2.1

Management Accounting

Working definition

The provision of financial and non-financial information to management for costing, for planning, control and performance, and for decision making.

Formal definition

'The application of the principles of accounting and financial management to create, protect, preserve and increase value so as to deliver that value to the stakeholders of profit and not-for-profit enterprises, both public and private. Management accounting is an integral part of management, requiring the identification, generation, presentation, interpretation and use of information relevant to:

- formulating business strategy;
- planning and controlling activities;
- decision making;
- efficient resource usage;

- performance improvement and value enhancement;
- safeguarding tangible and intangible assets;
- corporate governance and internal control.'

Source: Chartered Institute of Management Accounting (2000), *Official Terminology*

In essence, costing concerns (1) setting a price for a product or service so that a profit is made and (2) arriving at a correct valuation for stock. Planning, control and performance involves planning and controlling future costs using budgeting and standard costing as well as performance evaluation. Decision making involves managers solving problems using various problem-solving techniques.

PAUSE FOR THOUGHT 2.2

Problem Solving

Can you think of five problems the management accountant may need to solve?

The list is potentially endless. However, here are ten.

1. What products or services should be sold?
2. How much should be sold?
3. Should a product be made in-house or bought in?
4. Should the firm continue manufacturing the product?
5. At what level of production will a profit be made?
6. Which products or services are most profitable?
7. How can the firm minimise its working capital?
8. How can the firm maximise revenue?
9. Which areas should the firm diversify into?
10. Should new finance be raised via debt or equity?

Relationship with Financial Accounting

The orientation of management accounting is completely different to that of financial accounting. As Figure 2.1 shows, financial accounting is concerned with providing information (such as the balance sheet and profit and loss account) to shareholders about past events. Management accountants will also be interested in such information, often on a monthly basis.

Figure 2.1 Relationship between Financial and Management Accounting

Financial Accounting	*Management Accounting*
1. Aims to provide information principally for external users, such as shareholders. 2. Concerned with recording information using double-entry bookkeeping. 3. Works within a statutory context. 4. Main statements are balance sheet and profit and loss account (income statement). 5. Basically looks back to the past. 6. The end product is the annual reporting package in a standardised format.	1. Aims to provide information for internal users such as management. 2. Not so concerned with recording. Information is needed for costing, for planning, control and performance, for decision making etc. 3. There is no statutory context. 4. Not so concerned with preparing these financial statements. 5. Looks to the future. 6. Different businesses produce very different management information.

However, management accountants will also require a broader range of internal management information for costing, for planning, control and performance, and for decision making. Importantly, whereas financial accounting works within a statutory context, management accounting does not. Management accounting is thus much more varied and customised than financial accounting.

Financial accounting, in fact, has influenced the development of management accounting. Management accounting emerged much later than financial accounting. Indeed, early management accountants were primarily cost accountants (see Figure 2.2).

Figure 2.2   The Cost Accountant

'The cost accountant is essentially a practical man and it is important for the registered student to have first-hand experience of works and factory practice and routine, including, for example, the following: operation of various machines; shop floor organisation; purchase; storage and control of materials; design, planning and progress of work; inspection; work study; maintenance; warehousing and distribution.'

Source: The Cost Accountant, December 1957, p. 280. As cited in P. Armstrong and C. Jones (1992), *Management Accounting Research*, pp. 53–75

Armstrong and Jones (1992) argue that management accountants have been involved in a 'collective mobility' project where cost accountants have redefined themselves as management accountants dealing with wider management accounting and strategic management issues. In part, this has been an attempt to move away from costing, which was perceived as low status, and to emulate the Institute of Chartered Accountants in England and Wales, which was considered as high status.

Perhaps because of its comparatively humble origins, management accounting has often been seen as subservient to financial accounting. Johnson and Kaplan (1987) argued in *Relevance Lost* that most management accounting practices had been developed by 1925 and that since then there has been comparatively little innovation. Under this view, management accounting has major problems. In particular, product costing is distorted, decision-making information becomes unreliable and management accounting reflects external reporting requirements rather than modern management needs.

Opinions differ on the current relevance of management accounting. However, it is true that management accounting has struggled to adapt to changes in the business environment. In particular, it has been relatively slow to adapt to the decline of manufacturing industry and the rise of service organisations (see Figure 2.3). These difficulties are likely to be exacerbated by the rise of knowledge-based companies. Management accounting is also struggling to adapt to globalisation and technological change. As we will see, however, new management techniques have arisen (such as activity-based costing, strategic management accounting and just-in-time stock valuation) which seek to address the criticisms of management accounting.

Figure 2.3   Service Industries

'There are many service organisations which do not have finished good stocks or work-in-progress. They require management accounting information to ascertain the cost of each service and its contribution to total company profits. These organisations do not have to conform to any financial accounting requirements for the purpose of tracing costs to various services. Nevertheless, most service organisations adopted traditional product cost accounting techniques based on arbitrary overhead allocation, to trace costs to the different business segments.'

Source: Drury, C. (1996), *Cost and Management Accounting*, pp. 833–34

Overview

The diversity of management accounting makes if difficult to separate out individual strands. However, this book broadly splits management accounting into two.

1. **Cost Accounting.** This involves:
   (i)   *Costing* (recovering costs as a basis for pricing and for stock valuation), and
   (ii) *Planning, control and performance* (i.e., planning and controlling future costs using budgeting and standard costing).
2. **Decision Making.** This involves:
   (i)   *Short-term decision making* (such as break-even analysis, contribution analysis and the efficient management of working capital), and
   (ii) *Long-term decision making* (i.e., strategic management accounting, capital budgeting, and management of sources of long-term finance).
These two major areas are shown in Figure 2.4 on the next page.

The major areas shown in Figure 2.4 are discussed briefly below and then more fully discussed in the chapters that follow. Key terms that underpin management accounting are introduced. These new terms are highlighted in **bold** in the text and a full definition is then provided

Figure 2.4 Overview of Management Accounting

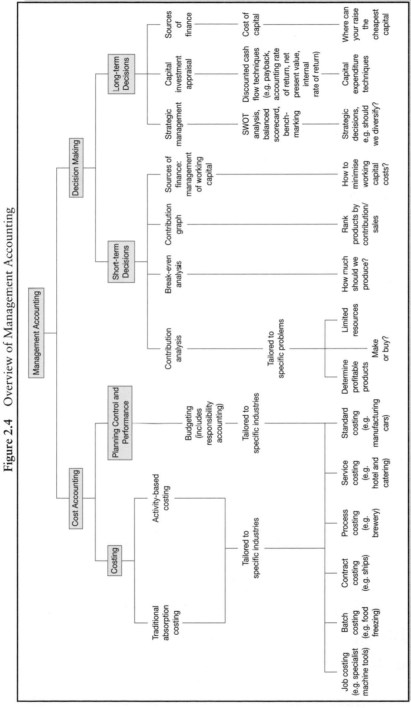

in Definitions 2.2 (below) and 2.3 (on page 31), which follow the same order as in the text. These terms are more fully discussed later in the book.

Cost Accounting

Costing (Chapter 3)

Costing has its origins in manufacturing industry. The basic idea underpinning costing is cost recovery (i.e. the need to recover all the **costs** of making a product into the price of the final product). Broadly, cost recovery is achieved using a technique called **total absorption costing**. Total absorption costing seeks to recover both **direct costs** and **indirect costs** into a product or service. This form of costing thus seeks to establish the total costs of a product so that they can be recovered in the final selling price. As well as costing for pricing, costing is used for stock valuation. In this case, either **absorption costing** or **marginal costing** is used.

Different industries will have different costing systems. For example, medicinal tablets will necessitate batch processing, while shipbuilding uses contract costing. A more modern technique called activity-based costing is often used.

Planning, Control and Performance (Chapters 4 and 5)

Planning, control and **performance** aims to control current costs and plan for the control of future costs as well as evaluating performance. Two essential **management control systems** (i.e. systems that provide information for managerial planning, control and performance evaluation are budgeting and standard costing.

- *Budgeting* (Chapter 4). Budgeting involves setting future targets. Actual results are then compared with these budgeted results. Any differences will be investigated. Budgets may be used as part of responsibility accounting. In such systems, a distinction is often made between **controllable costs** and **uncontrollable costs**.
- *Standard costing* (Chapter 5) is a standardised version of budgeting. Standard costing involves using preset costs for direct labour, direct materials and overheads. Actual costs are then compared with the **standard costs**. Any **variances** are then investigated.

DEFINITION 2.2

The Basic Building Blocks of Management Accounting: Some Key Cost Accounting Terms

i Costing

Cost. A cost is simply an item of expenditure (planned or actually incurred).

Total absorption costing. This form of costing is used to recover all the costs (both direct and indirect) incurred by a company into the price of the final product or service.

DEFINITION 2.2 (*continued*)

Direct costs. Direct costs are those costs that can be directly identified and attributed to a product or service, for example, the amount of direct labour that is incurred making a product. Sometimes these costs are called *product costs*.

Indirect costs. Indirect costs are those costs that cannot be directly identified and attributed to a product or service, examples are administrative, selling and distribution costs. These costs are totalled and then recovered into the product or service in an indirect way. For example, if there were £10,000 administrative costs and 10,000 products, each product might be allocated £1 of administrative costs. Indirect costs are often called *overheads* or *period costs*.

Absorption costing. Absorption costing is the form of costing used for valuing stock for external financial reporting. It recovers the costs of all the overheads that can be directly attributed to a product or service. However, unlike marginal costing, which can sometimes be used for stock valuation, it includes both fixed and variable production overheads.

Marginal costing. Marginal costing excludes fixed costs from the costing process. It focuses on sales, variable costs and contribution. Fixed costs are written off against contribution. It can be used for decision making or for valuing stock. When valuing stock only variable production overheads are included in the stock valuation. (See Definition 2.3 for explanations of *fixed costs, variable costs* and *contribution*.) Marginal costing is called contribution analysis when used for decision making.

ii Planning, Control and Performance Evaluation
Controllable costs. Costs that a manager can influence and that the manager can be held responsible for.

Uncontrollable Costs. Costs that a manager cannot influence and that the manager cannot be held responsible for.

Standard costs. Standard costs are individual cost elements (such as direct materials, direct labour and variable overheads) which are estimated in advance. Normally, the quantity and the price of each cost element is estimated separately. Actual costs are then compared with standard costs to determine variances.

Variances. Variances are the difference between the budgeted costs and the actual costs in both budgeting and standard costing. These variances are then investigated by management.

Decision Making

Decision making involves choosing between alternatives. When making a choice it is essential to consider only those costs that are relevant to the actual decision, i.e., *relevant costs*.

Short-Term Decisions (Chapter 6)

In many ways, distinguishing between short-term, operational decisions and long-term strategic decisions is somewhat arbitrary. However, it proves a useful basic distinction. Short-term decisions are dealt with in Chapter 6 and the first part of Chapter 9. Long-term decisions are covered in Chapters 7–8 and in the second half of Chapter 9.

Businesses face many short-term decisions. Essentially, as Soundbite 2.1 shows, decision making is about choice. Businesses need to make numerous decisions.

For example, should a business make a product itself or buy in the product? Should a business continue making or providing a product or service? At what price will a product break even (i.e., make neither a profit nor a loss)? These decisions are solved using various problem-solving techniques such as break-even analysis and contribution analysis. In such short-term decisions, it is essential to distinguish between **fixed costs** and **variable costs**.

A key aspect of short-term decision making is contribution. Contribution is sales less variable costs. In other words, fixed costs are excluded. Contribution is at the heart of two common management accounting techniques: **break-even analysis** and **contribution analysis**. This area of management accounting is sometimes called **cost-volume-profit analysis**.

DEFINITION 2.3

The Basic Building Blocks of Management Accounting: Some Key Decision-Making Terms

Short-Term Decisions

Fixed costs. Fixed costs are those costs that *will not vary* with production or sales (for example, insurance) in an accounting period. They will not, therefore, be affected by short-term decisions such as whether or not production is increased.

Variable costs. Variable costs, however, *will vary* with production and sales (for example, the metered cost of electricity). Short-term decision making is primarily concerned with variable costs. Sales less variable costs gives *contribution*, a useful concept in short-term decision making.

Break-even analysis. Break-even analysis involves calculating the point at which a product makes neither a profit nor a loss. Fixed costs are divided by the contribution per unit (i.e. sales less variable costs divided by number of products). This gives the break-even point.

DEFINITION 2.3 (continued)

Contribution analysis. When there is more than one product, this technique is useful in determining which product is the most profitable. It compares the relative contribution of each product. This can also be called cost-volume-profit analysis.

Long-Term Decisions
Discounted cash flow. Discounted cash flow discounts the future expected cash inflows and outflows of a potential project back to their present value today. Decisions can then be made on whether or not to go ahead with the project.

Strategic Management Accounting (Chapter 7)

Whereas costing represents the oldest branch of management accounting, strategic management accounting represents the newest. Strategic management accounting represents a response to criticisms that management accounting is outdated and lacking in innovation. Using strategic management accounting, the management accountant relates the activities of the firm to the wider external environment. Strategic management is thus concerned with the long-term strategic direction of the firm.

PAUSE FOR THOUGHT 2.3

Cost Accounting and Management Accounting

A distinction is sometimes made between cost accounting and management accounting. What do you see as the essential difference?

Management accounting has its origins in cost accounting. However, gradually cost accounting and management accounting have been seen as distinct. Cost accounting is seen, at its narrowest, as focusing on cost collection and cost recovery and more widely as cost recovery and control. However, management accounting is viewed as a much broader term which not only encompasses cost accounting, but also involves decision making and, more recently, strategic management accounting. Cost accounting is thus typically portrayed as routine and low-level, whereas management accounting is seen as a higher-level activity.

Capital Investment Appraisal (Chapter 8)

Capital budgeting involves the financial evaluation of future projects. This evaluation is carried out by using various techniques such as payback, the accounting rate of return, net present value and the internal rate of return. Under net present value and the internal rate of return, the technique of **discounted cash flow** analysis is used.

Sources of Finance (Chapter 9)

The topic of business finance is immense. The aspects covered in this book are the financing of the business in the short and the long term. This covers both the internal generation of funds and the raising of external finance. In the short term, the management of working capital involves the management accountant in a series of short-term decisions about the optimal level of stock and debtors. Meanwhile, the long-term financing of the business involves the choice between internal financing through retained profits and external financing through either leasing, loans or share capital.

PAUSE FOR THOUGHT 2.4

Short-Term vs Long-Term Decisions

What do you think are the essential differences between short-term and long-term decisions?

Short-term decisions are operational, day-to-day decisions which typically involve the firm's internal environment. For example, what quantity of a particular product should we make or what should be the price of a particular product.

By contrast, long-term decisions are strategic, non-operational decisions. These typically involve a firm's external environment. So, for example, they may involve the need to diversify or the need to make acquisitions and disposals. Alternatively, they might evaluate whether a long-term capital investment is worthwhile.

Cost Minimisation and Revenue Maximisation

The management accountant can make a business more efficient through cost minimisation or revenue maximisation. Cost minimisation attempts to reduce costs. This may be achieved by tight budgetary control or cutting back on expenditure.

Some authors argue strongly that management accounting needs to refocus on revenue maximisation. In part, revenue maximisation is achieved through the new focus on strategic management accounting which looks outwards to the external environment rather than inwards. Substantial opportunities arise to adopt new techniques such as customer database mining. This latter technique looks at customer databases and seeks to extract from them customer data which will expand the business's revenue.

Sales Maximisation

'Legend tells of the traveller who went into a county store and found the shelves lined with bags of salt. "You must sell a lot of salt", said the traveller, "Nah", said the storekeeper. "I can't sell no salt at all. But the feller who sells me salt – boy, can *he* sell salt".'

Martin Mayer, *The Bankers*, 1974

Source: *The Executive's Book of Quotations* (1994), p. 255

Management accountants have often been criticised for being overly concerned with cost cutting (see, for example, Lesley Jackson, H.P. Bulmer Holding plc's UK Finance Director, in Real-Life Nugget 2.1).

REAL-LIFE NUGGET 2.1

Cost minimisation

Jackson's time as general commercial manager gave her the opportunity to look at a business from a different angle. She says it made her a better accountant.

'A lot of accountants tend to look at cost minimalisation and low risk. They tend to have a more conservative mindset. I became slightly more maverick in this sense,' she says.

It was this broader outlook on business and varied skills-sets that gave Jackson the edge over other candidates for the role at Bulmers.

Source: Brewing up a Profit, Michelle Perry, *Accountancy Age*, 3 May 2001, p. 20

Use of Computers

The theory and practice of management accounting is shown in the next seven chapters. In practice, for most of the techniques shown, in practice, a dedicated computer program would be used. Alternatively, a spreadsheet could be set up so as to handle the calculations. These programs enable complicated and often complex real-life situations to be modelled. However, it is essential to be able to appreciate which figures should be input into the computer. As Peter Williams states.

'While it may be possible for any company with a PC to produce a set of management information using relatively low-cost accounting software, there is no guarantee that the output will be true and fair.'

Accountancy Age, 2 March, 2000, p. 23

Conclusion

Management accounting is the internal accounting function of a firm. It can be divided into cost accounting (costing; planning, control and performance) and decision making (short-term and long-term). In costing, the two main aspects are pricing and stock valuation. In planning, control, and performance budgeting and standard costing are used. Decision making has four main strands: short-term decision making; strategic management accounting; capital budgeting; and sources of finance. Management accountants are increasingly moving away from costing towards new areas such as strategic management accounting. In effect, this reflects the decline of manufacturing industry in developed countries.

Selected Reading

Armstrong, P. and C. Jones (1992), 'The decline of operational expertise in the knowledge-base of management accounting: An examination of some post-war trends in the qualifying requirements of the Chartered Institute of Management Accountants', *Management Accounting Research*, Vol. 3, pp. 53–75.

An interesting look at how the management accounting profession has gradually changed over time. Originally concerned with costing, it now has a much wider focus.

Drury, C. (2005), *Management and Cost Accounting* (Thomson Learning: London). This is a comprehensive text on management and cost accounting. Once students have mastered the basics, this represents a good book for future reading.

Johnson, T. and R.S. Kaplan (1987), *Relevance Lost: The Rise and Fall of Management Accounting* (Harvard University Press).

A benchmarking book which triggered a relook at management accounting. After this book a new management accounting emerged consisting of topics such as activity-based costing and strategic management accounting.

Kaplan, R.S. (1984), 'Yesterday's accounting undermines production', *Harvard Business Review*, July/August, pp. 95–101.

This provides a good overview of the problems with traditional management accounting.

Q&A   Discussion Questions

Questions with numbers in blue have answers at the back of the book.

Q1   What are the main branches of management accounting and what are their main functions?

Q2   Why do you think that management accounting has been so keen to lose its costing image?

Q3   What are the following types of cost and why are they important?
(a)   Direct cost   (d)   Variable cost
(b)   Indirect cost   (e)   Standard cost
(c)   Fixed cost

Q4   The management accountant has been described as a professional with a toolkit of techniques. How fair a description do you think this is?

Q5   Why have management accountants been criticised for being cost minimisers and how might they be revenue maximisers?

Q6   State whether the following statements are true or false. If false explain why.
(a) The two main branches of management accounting are cost accounting and decision making.
(b) Total absorption costing is where all the overheads incurred by a company are recovered in the valuation of stock.
(c) The difference between absorption costing and marginal costing as a form of costing for stock valuation is that absorption costing includes direct materials, direct labour and all production overheads. By contrast, marginal costing only includes direct materials, direct labour and all *variable* production overheads. Marginal costing, therefore, excludes fixed production overheads.
(d) Strategic management accounting is concerned principally with short-term operational decisions.
(e) Discounted cash flow discounts the future expected cash flows of a project back to their present-day monetary values.

Chapter 3

"Watch the costs and the profits will take care of themselves."

Andrew Carnegie, quoted in R. Sobel and D.B. Silicia, *The Entrepreneurs – An American Adventure* (Houghton Mifflin, 1986)
Source: *Wiley Book of Business Quotations* (1998), p. 89

Learning Outcomes

After completing this chapter you should be able to:

✔ Explain the nature and importance of costing.

✔ Discuss the process of traditional costing.

✔ Understand the nature of activity-based costing.

✔ Distinguish between different costing systems.

✔ Discuss target costing.

Costing

In a Nutshell

- *Costing is a subset of cost accounting and is used as a basis for stock valuation and for cost-plus pricing.*

- *There are direct costs and indirect costs or overheads.*

- *The six stages in traditional cost recovery are (1) recording costs, (2) classifying costs, (3) allocating indirect costs to departments, (4) reapportioning costs from service to productive departments, (5) calculating an overhead recovery rate, and (6) absorbing costs into products and services.*

- *Activity-based costing is a sophisticated version of cost recovery which uses cost allocation drivers based on activities to allocate costs.*

- *Different industries have different costing methods such as job costing, batch costing, standard costing, contract costing, process costing and service costing.*

- *Non-production overheads are included in cost-plus pricing, but not in stock valuation.*

- *In stock valuation, either all production costs (absorption costing) or only variable production costs (marginal costing) can be allocated.*

- *Target costing, developed by the Japanese, is based on market prices and set at the pre-production stage.*

- *Companies in trouble often cut costs, such as labour costs, in order to improve their profitability.*

Introduction

Management accounting can be broadly divided into cost accounting and decision making. In turn, cost accounting has two major strands: (1) costing, and (2) planning, control and performance. Costing involves ascertaining all the costs of a product or service so as to form the basis for pricing and for stock valuation. The first management accountants were essentially cost accountants. Their job was to make sure that manufactured products were priced so as fully to recover all the costs incurred in making them. This process of recording, classifying, allocating the costs and then absorbing those costs into individual products and services still remains the basis of cost recovery. However, the traditional methods of cost recovery were geared up for manufacturing industries and assumed that overhead costs were relatively small. The decline of manufacturing industry, the increasing importance of overhead costs, and the rise of service industries has caused a need to rethink some of the basics of cost recovery. In particular, the technique of activity-based costing has gained in popularity.

Importance of Cost Accounting

Cost accounting is a common term used to embrace both costing, and planning, control and performance. Definition 3.1 shows two formal definitions of cost accounting. The first is by

DEFINITION 3.1

Cost Accounting

Working definition
The determination of actual and standard costs, budgeting and standard costing.

Formal definition

1. 'The classification, recording and appropriate allocation of expenditure in order to determine the total cost of products or services.'

This earlier definition by ICMA is a good description of cost recovery.

2. 'The establishment of budgets, standard costs and actual costs of operations, processes, activities or products; and the analysis of variances, profitability or the social use of funds. The use of the term 'costing' is not recommended except with a qualifying adjective, e.g. standard costing.'

This CIMA (2000) definition embraces both cost accounting, and planning, control and performance.

the Institute of Cost and Management Accountants (ICMA), the predecessor body of the author of the second definition, the Chartered Institute of Management Accountants (CIMA). It is interesting to see that the definition has widened considerably. In particular, the more recent CIMA definition now explicitly mentions budgeting and standard costing.

In this book, we take cost accounting to involve two main parts. The first is costing, which is the process of determining the actual costs of products and service. This usually looks to the past. And, the second is costing for planning, control and performance where expected costs are determined for future periods either through budgeting or standard costing.

Costs are the essential building blocks for both financial and management accounting. In costing, costs represent *actual* items of expenditure. In budgeting and standard costing, costs represent *future* (expected) items of expenditure. Costs represent a major building block of management accounting. In financial accounting, it is important to match costs against revenue to determine profit.

An important part of this matching process in manufacturing industry is the allocation of production costs to stock. Either all production costs (absorption costing) or variable production costs (marginal costing) can be allocated. Sometimes marginal costing is termed variable costing. In Figure 3.1, we use absorption costing, in which all the production costs are allocated to stock. These costs will be included in the cost of opening stock in the next accounting period and then matched against sales to determine profit. Later on, in Figure 3.12, both absorption and marginal costing are shown for comparative purposes.

Figure 3.1   Allocation of Costs to Stock Using Absorption Costing

Stockco manufactures only toys. The direct costs of manufacturing 1,000 toys is £1,000. Total production overheads for the toys (for example, factory light and heat) are £500. At the end of the year 200 toys are in stock. What is the cost of the closing stock?

	1,000 units £	Per unit £
Direct costs	1,000	1.00
Production overheads	500	0.50
	1,500	1.50

The closing stock is thus 200 @ £1.50 = £300

Another extremely important function of costing is as a basis for pricing. The selling price of a product is key to making a profit. In many businesses, the fundamental economic law is that the cheaper the price of the goods, the more goods will be sold. This sentiment is expressed in Real-Life Nugget 3.1.

REAL-LIFE NUGGET 3.1

Pricing Policy

Retailing used to be so simple. If shopkeepers wanted to increase sales, they cut their prices, putting their goods within reach of people who previously could not afford them.

In developed countries, as incomes have risen, higher prices have become more affordable. But if retailers thought the need for discounting would fade, they were wrong.

Source: Marketing Value for Money, Richard Tomkins, *Financial Times*, 14 May 1999

In practice, there are two methods of pricing: market pricing and cost-plus pricing. In market pricing, the focus is external. The prices charged by competitors are examined together with the amount that customers are willing to pay. In cost-plus pricing, by contrast, the focus is internal. The total costs of making the product are established (i.e., all the direct costs and all the indirect costs or overheads) and then a profit percentage or profit mark-up is added. When setting prices, companies will bear in mind both the costs of making the product and also the amount for which competitor products are selling. At certain times firms will adopt different pricing strategies. For example, a company may discount its prices to boost sales.

PAUSE FOR THOUGHT 3.1

Cost-Plus Pricing

What is the purpose of cost-plus pricing and how can it prove dangerous in a competitive market?

....

Cost-plus pricing seeks to recover all the overheads into a product or service. However, it is only as good as the method chosen to recover the overheads, and the estimates made. The problem is that prices are often set by the market rather than by the company. A company may determine the cost of a product and then its selling price. However, in a competitive market, this price may be higher than competitors' prices or be more than customers wish to pay. When adopting cost-plus pricing it is always important to perform a reality check and ask: can we really sell the product or service at this price? In practice, therefore, it is advisable to use both cost-plus pricing and market pricing together.

In general, companies strive to keep their costs as low as possible. Those companies that can do this, such as Wal-Mart, the American retailer that purchased Asda, have a key competitive advantage (see Real-Life Nugget 3.2).

Types of Cost

A cost is simply an amount of expenditure which can be attributed to a product or service. It is possible to distinguish between two main types of cost: **direct costs** and **indirect costs**. Direct costs are simply those that **can** be directly attributed to a product or service. Indirect costs are those that **cannot** be directly attributed. Indirect costs are also known as overheads. In manufacturing industry, direct costs have declined over time while indirect costs have risen. This makes costing more difficult. Figures 3.2 (below) and 3.3 on page 45 demonstrate two cost structures, for

Figure 3.2 Cost Structure for a Manufactured Product (for Example, a Computer)

	£	Examples
Direct materials	50*	Plastics, steel
Direct labour	120*	Manufacturing labour
Direct expenses	10*	Royalties
Prime Cost	180	
Production overheads	60†	Supervisors' wages
Production Cost	240	
Administrative overheads	50†	Staff costs, office expenses
Selling and distribution overheads	60†	Advertising
Total Cost	350	
Profit	50	
Selling Price	400	

*Direct costs, i.e. those that can be directly attributed to the product
†Indirect costs, i.e. those that cannot be directly attributed to the product

a manufactured product and for a service product, respectively. In both cases, we are totalling all our costs so that we can recover them into the final selling price. This is known as **total absorption costing**. This should be distinguished from absorption costing and marginal costing which, as we have just discussed, are used for stock valuation not for pricing.

Essentially, a proportion of the cost of the manufactured product can be directly attributed. The direct materials are those such as the plastic, steel and glass that are actually used to make the product. The direct labour is the labour cost actually incurred in making the product. The direct expenses are royalties paid per product manufactured. These three costs (direct materials, direct labour and direct expenses) are known as the **prime cost. The remaining costs are all overheads**. The production overheads are those associated with the production process. Examples are supervisors' wages or the electricity used in the factory area. By contrast, administrative overheads (for example, staff costs, office expenses, accountants' fees) and selling and distribution overheads (for example, transport and advertising) are incurred outside the production area. An essential element of costing is that as we move further away from the direct provision of a product or service it becomes more difficult to allocate the costs fairly. Thus, it is easiest to allocate the direct costs, but most difficult to allocate the administrative costs. The Company Camera 3.1 provides an example of administrative overheads for the HBOS, a bank.

SOUNDBITE 3.1

Costs

'I haven't heard of anybody who wants to stop living on account of the cost.'

Ken Hubbard

Source: R. Flesch (1959) *The Book of Unusual Quotations*, p. 51

THE COMPANY CAMERA 3.1

Administrative Expenses

	Notes	2004 £million	2003 £million
Administrative expenses (excluding exceptional items) includes			
Staff costs	4	1,875	1,755
Property rentals		149	145
Hire of equipment		40	35

Source: HBOS, Annual Report and Accounts 2004, p. 10

In Figure 3.3, we use the example of a computer helpline, which callers phone to receive advice. In this case, the only direct costs will probably be direct labour. The administrative, selling and distribution costs will be proportionately higher. The key problem in cost recovery is thus how to recover the overheads. Direct costs can be directly allocated to a cost unit (i.e., an individual product or service unit, such as a customer's phone call). However, indirect costs have to be totalled and then divided up amongst all the cost units. This is much more problematic.

Figure 3.3 Cost Structure for a Service Product (for Example, the Cost per Customer Call for a Computer Helpline)

	£	Examples
Direct labour	4*	Telephone operator
Prime Cost	4	
Administrative expenses	5†	Management, office expenses
Selling and distribution costs	4†	Advertising, marketing
Total Cost	13	
Profit	2	
Selling Price	15	

*Direct costs, i.e. those that can be directly attributed to the service
†Indirect costs, i.e. those that cannot be directly attributed to the service

PAUSE FOR THOUGHT 3.2

Manufacturing a Television

From the following information can you work out the cost and selling price of each television using total absorption costing?

....

(i) *Direct materials £25; direct labour £50; direct expenses £3 per television.*
(ii) *£18,000 production overheads; £14,000 administrative expenses; and £15,000 selling and distribution costs.*
(iii) *1,000 televisions produced. Profit mark-up of 20% on total cost.*

We would thus have:	£
Direct materials	25
Direct labour	50
Direct expenses	3
Prime Cost	78
Production overheads (N1)	18
Production Cost	96
Administrative expenses (N1)	14
Selling and distribution costs (N1)	15
Total Cost	125
Profit (20% × £125, i.e. 20% mark-up on cost)	25
Selling Price	150

Traditional Costing

The aim of costing is simply to recover (also known as 'to absorb') the costs into an identifiable product or service so as to form the basis for pricing and stock valuation. In pricing, all the overheads are recovered. For stock valuation, only those overheads directly related to the production of stock can be recovered (i.e., direct costs and attributable production overheads). In the next two sections, we look at total absorption costing for pricing, using traditional costing and activity-based costing. In traditional cost recovery or cost absorption, there are six major steps. We will then look at activity-based costing, which is a more modern way of tackling cost recovery. Both traditional total absorption costing and activity-based costing can be used in manufacturing or non-manufacturing industries.

In manufacturing industry, total absorption costing means recovering all the costs from those departments in which products are manufactured (*production departments*) and from those that supply support activities such as catering, administration, or selling and distribution (*service support departments*) into the cost of the end product. In service industries, we recover all the costs from those departments that deliver the final service to customers (*service delivery departments*) and from the *service support departments*. We set out below the six steps for recovering costs into products (see Figure 3.4 on the next page). Diagrammatically, this process is illustrated in Figure 3.5 on the next page. **However, exactly the same process would be used for recovering costs into services.**

Figure 3.4   Six Steps in Traditional Total Absorption Costing

1. Record all the costs.
2. Classify all the costs.
3. Allocate all the indirect costs to the departments of a business.
4. Reallocate costs from service support departments to production departments.
5. Calculate an overhead recovery rate.
6. Absorb both the direct costs and the indirect costs (or overheads) into individual products.

Figure 3.5   Diagrammatic Representation of Traditional Total Absorption Costing

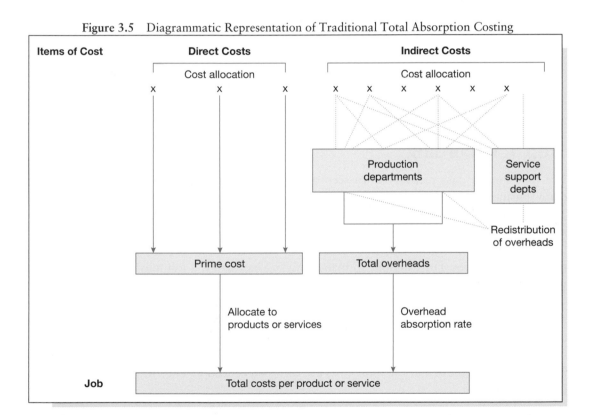

In essence, businesses need to make a profit. Revenue from sales, therefore, needs to exceed the total costs incurred in making a product. Businesses are thus very keen to ascertain their costs so that they can set a reasonable price for their products. Sometimes, especially for long-term contracts or one-off jobs, this can prove very difficult. For example, Cardiff's Millennium stadium, although a triumph of construction, was a financial disaster for John Laing (see Real-Life Nugget 3.3).

REAL-LIFE NUGGET 3.3

Pricing Long-Term Contracts

'Cardiff is the cause,' said Weir. 'The race to finish for the October kick-off has caused further unexpected costs.'

Weir blamed the tender process: 'It was a guaranteed maximum price job and we got the bidding wrong. We have delivered a super project, but a financial disaster.'

Last year John Laing had exceptional losses of £26 m on the stadium. There may be more to come, 'but not on the same scale', said Weir.

'We have a four-cylinder business firing on three. We are taking action to get construction right.'

Source: Cardiff Stadium a Penalty for Laing, Roger Nuttall, *The Express*, 10 September 1999

Step 1: Recording

The first step in cost recovery is to record all the costs. It is important to appreciate that many businesses have integrated financial accounting and management accounting systems. There is thus no need to keep separate records for both financial accounting and management accounting.

Direct costs, such as direct materials and direct labour, can be directly traced to individual products or services. For example, in manufacturing industries, a job may have a job card on which the direct material and direct labour incurred is recorded.

Indirect costs, such as rent or administrative costs, are much more difficult to record. There are two main problems: estimation and total amount. The first problem is that it is unlikely that the actual costs will be known until the end of a period. Transport costs, for example, may be known only after the journeys have been made. They will, therefore, have to be estimated. The second problem is that the total costs are recorded centrally. They must then be allocated to products.

Step 2: Classification

This involves categorising and grouping the costs before allocating them to departments. We may, for example, need to calculate the total rent or total costs for light and heat.

Step 3: Allocate indirect costs to departments

Direct costs can be directly traced to goods or services. For overheads, the process is indirect. The key to overhead allocation is to find an appropriate basis for allocation. These are called allocation bases or cost drivers. Figure 3.6 shows some possible allocation bases for various types of cost.

Figure 3.6   Departmental Allocation Bases

Types of Cost	Possible Allocation Bases
Power	Number of machine hours
Depreciation, insurance	Value of fixed assets
Canteen, office expenses	Relative area of floor space
Rent, business rates, light and heat	Number of employees

Step 4: Reallocate service support department costs to production departments

Once all the costs are allocated, we must reallocate them to the production departments. This is because we need to recover these costs into *specific products* which are *made* only in the *production departments*.

Step 5: Overhead recovery rate

Once we have allocated our costs to production departments, we need to absorb these costs into the final product. We must choose a suitable recovery rate. The choice of rate reflects the nature of the activity and could be any of the following (or even others):

- Rate per unit
- Rate per direct labour hour
- Rate per machine hour
- Rate per £ materials
- Rate per £ direct labour
- Rate per £ prime cost

Figure 3.7 illustrates this process

Figure 3.7   Overhead Recovery Rate

A firm has £12,000 indirect costs in department F. It also has the following data available:

	£	
Direct materials	30,000	240,000 units produced
Direct labour	70,000	6,000 direct labour hours are used
Prime Cost	100,000	50,000 machine hours are used

Calculate the various overhead recovery rates discussed above in step 5.
The various overhead recovery rates are:

1. Per unit $\quad = \dfrac{£12,000}{240,000} = $ £0.05 per unit

2. Per direct labour hour $\quad = \dfrac{£12,000}{6,000} = $ £2.00 per labour hour

3. Per machine hour $\quad = \dfrac{£12,000}{50,000} = $ £0.24 per machine hour

4. Per £ material $\quad = \dfrac{£12,000}{30,000} = $ £0.40 per £ material

5. Per £ labour $\quad = \dfrac{£12,000}{70,000} = $ £0.17 per £ labour

6. Per £ prime cost $\quad = \dfrac{£12,000}{100,000} = $ £0.12 per £ prime cost

In practice, only one of these six overhead recovery rates would be used, most likely direct labour hours.

Step 6: Absorption of costs into products

Once we have calculated an absorption rate we can absorb our costs. In practice, there will be many products of varying size and complexity. Figure 3.8 illustrates how we would now recover our costs into products.

Figure 3.8   Recovery into Specific Jobs

If, for example, the following Job X007 was one of the 200,000 units produced and we recover our overheads *per direct labour hour* then we might have the following situation.

Job X007		£
Direct materials	(10 kilos at £2)	20
Direct labour	(12 hours at £12)	144
Prime Cost		164

The direct materials are directly recovered into the job; we must now recover the indirect costs. We recover into our product 12 hours at £2.00 per hour (as calculated in Figure 16.7) = £24.00.

Our total cost is therefore	£
Prime Cost	164
Overheads	24
Total Cost	188
Profit: 25 % mark-up on cost	47
Selling Price	235

Comprehensive Example

In Figure 3.9, a comprehensive example of cost recovery looks at all six steps in the cost recovery process.

Figure 3.9 Comprehensive Cost Recovery Example

Millennium plc has the following three departments:

A. Production
B. Production
C. Service support

Type of Cost	Proposed Basis of Apportionment	£
Rent and business rates	Floor area	4,000
Repairs and maintenance	Amount actually spent	1,000
Canteen	Number of employees	500
Depreciation	Cost of fixed assets	2,100
		7,600

It is estimated that:

(i) Department A has a floor area of 4,000 sq.ft., Department B has a floor area of 3,000 sq.ft., and Department C has a floor area of 1,000 sq.ft.
(ii) The following direct labour hours will be used: A (2,000 hours), B (3,000 hours), and C (300 hours)
(iii) Department A has 50 employees, Department B 30 employees and Department C 20 employees
(iv) Department A has machinery costing £15,000, Department B has £25,000 machinery and Department C has £30,000 machinery
(v) The wage rates are £11 per hour for A, £12 per hour for B, and £10 per hour for C
(vi) Repairs are to be A £200; B £300; C £500.

It is estimated that 70% of Department C's facilities are used by Department A, and 30% by Department B, and that C's direct material and direct labour for the year will be £3,000 and £1,500. The overheads will be recovered by reference to the amount of direct labour hours used. Profit is to be at 25% on cost.

. . . .

Millennium plc wishes to prepare a quotation for the following job C206.

Direct material	£400
Direct labour	Department A 20 hours
	Department B 10 hours

We have already recorded (step 1), and classified (step 2) our information so the next stage (step 3) is to allocate our indirect costs (i.e. overheads) to departments.

Step 3: Overhead Allocation to Departments

Type of Cost	Allocation	Total £	A £	B £	C £
C's direct labour	Traced directly	3,000			3,000
C's direct material	Traced directly	1,500			1,500
Rent and business rates (calculation shown below in Helpnote point 1)	Area (4,000: 3,000: 1,000)	4,000	2,000	1,500	500
Repairs and maintenance	Actual	1,000	200	300	500
Canteen	No. of employees (50: 30: 20)	500	250	150	100
Depreciation	Cost of fixed assets (15,000: 25,000: 30,000)	2,100	450	750	900
Total		12,100	2,900	2,700	6,500

Figure 3.9   Comprehensive Cost Recovery Example (*continued*)

Helpnotes:

1. The allocations for each type of cost are made by allocating each cost across the departments in proportion to the total cost. For example, the rent and business rates total area is 8,000 sq.ft. Thus:

    A (4,000/8,000) × £4,000 = £2,000.

    B (3,000/8,000) × £4,000 = £1,500, and

    C (1,000/8,000) × £4,000 = £500

2. We must include our direct labour and direct materials for Department C in our calculations of the overhead absorption rate because although direct for Department C, they are indirect for Departments A and B, which are the production departments.

. . . .

Step 4: Reallocate Service Support Department Costs to Production Departments

The next stage is to reallocate the service support department costs to the production departments. Since 70 % of C is used by A, and 30 % by B, it is only fair to reallocate them in this proportion.

	Total £	A £	B £	C £
Total overheads	12,100	2,900	2,700	6,500
Reallocation %		70 %	30 %	(100 %)
		4,550	1,950	(6,500)
New total	12,100	7,450	4,650	

If there were more service support departments, we would have to continue to reallocate the costs until they were all absorbed into production departments. In this case the allocation is finished.

Step 5: Calculate an Overhead Recovery Rate

It is now time to work out an overhead recovery rate.

	Total £	A £	B £
Total overheads	12,100	7,450	4,650
Direct labour hours		2,000	3,000
Recovery rate		3.73	1.55

Step 6: Absorption of Costs into Products

Finally, we must absorb both our direct and indirect costs into our products as a basis for pricing.

Job C206

		£
Direct labour	A. 20 hours at £11	220.00
	B. 10 hours at £12	120.00
Direct material		400.00
Prime Cost		740.00
Overheads	A. 20 hours at £3.73	74.60
	B. 10 hours at £1.55	15.50
Total Cost		830.10
25 % mark-up on cost		207.52
Selling Price		1037.62

Total absorption costing (as we have just demonstrated in Figure 3.9) is where we try to recover all our overheads (direct and indirect) into a product or service. It forms the basis of job, contract, batch, process and service costing.

PAUSE FOR THOUGHT 3.3

Traditional Product Costing

Traditional product costing usually uses either direct machine hours or direct labour hours to determine its overhead recovery rate. Can you see any problems with this in a service and knowledge-based economy?

....

In manufacturing industry, products are made intensively using machines and direct labour. It makes sense, therefore, to recover overheads using those measures. However, in service industries or knowledge-based industries, products or services may have very little direct labour input and do not use machines. The financial services industry or Internet companies, for example, have very few industrial machines or direct labour. In this case, machine hours and labour hours become, at best, irrelevant and, at worst, very dangerous when pricing goods or services. In these and other industries new methods of allocating cost are necessary. The stimulus to find these new methods has led to the development of activity-based costing. This seeks to establish activities as a basis for allocating overheads.

Activity-Based Costing

Traditional total absorption costing was developed in manufacturing industries. In these industries, there are usually substantial quantities of machine hours or direct labour hours. These volume-related allocation bases are used to allocate overheads. However, recently traditional absorption costing has been criticised for failing to respond to the new post-manufacturing industrial environment and for lacking sophistication. Allocation using direct cost bases often, therefore, fails to reflect the true distribution of the costs. It is argued that this leads to inaccurate pricing.

Activity-based costing aims to remedy these defects. It is based on the premise that activities that occur within a firm cause overhead costs. By identifying these activities, a firm can achieve a range of benefits, including the ability to cost products more accurately. Essentially, activity-based costing is a more sophisticated version of the traditional product costing system. There is a six-stage process (see Figure 3.10 overleaf).

Figure 3.10   Six Steps in Activity-Based Costing

1. Record all the costs.
2. Classify all the costs.
3. Identify activities.
4. Identify cost drivers and allocate overheads to them.
5. Calculate activity-cost driver rates.
6. Absorb both the direct costs and indirect costs into a product or service.

We will now work through these six steps. The process is portrayed graphically in Figure 3.11.

Figure 3.11   Diagrammatic Representation of Activity-Based Costing

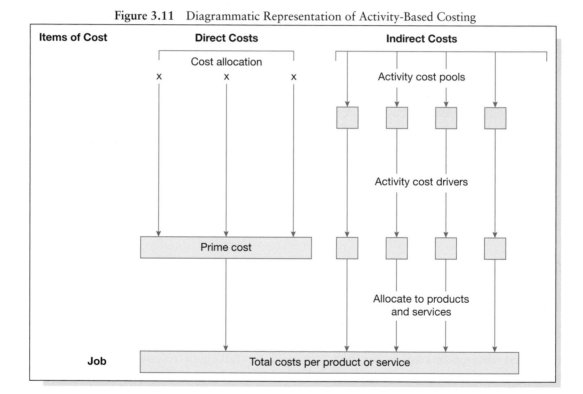

Steps 1 and 2

The first two steps are the same as for traditional costing.

Step 3: Identify activities

The firm identifies those activities that determine overhead costs. Production is one such activity.

Step 4: Identify cost drivers and allocate appropriate overheads to them

Activity-based accounting seeks to link cost recovery to cost behaviour. Activity-cost drivers determine cost behaviour. Activity-cost drivers for a production department, for example, might be the number of purchase orders, the number of set-ups, maintenance hours, the number of inspections, the number of despatches, machine hours or direct labour hours.

Step 5: Calculate activity-cost driver rates

Here, for each activity driver we calculate an appropriate cost driver rate. This is the total costs for a cost driver divided by the number of activities. An example might be £2,000 total costs for material inspections divided by 250 material inspections.

Step 6: Absorb both direct and indirect costs into a product or service

This process is similar to traditional product costing. The total costs are allocated to products using activity cost drivers; they are then divided by the number of products.

In Figure 3.12 an activity-based costing example is given for Fireco. This has two products

Figure 3.12   Activity-Based Costing Example

Fireco has the following costs: for setting up machinery £8,000, for ordering material £3,000, for inspecting the material £2,000 and sales ledger expenses £8,000. Selling price is cost plus 25%. There is also the following information:

	A £	B £
Direct materials	8,000	7,000
Direct labour	10,000	15,000
Number of set-ups	20	30
Number of purchase orders	4,000	1,000
Number of inspections	100	150
Number of sales invoices processed	7,000	3,000
Number of products	16,000	10,000

What would be the activity-cost driver rates, total cost and selling price?

As we have already completed steps 1–4 (recording, classifying, and identifying cost drivers with associated overheads), we can proceed to step 5, calculating the activity cost-driver rates.

Step 5: Calculation of Activity-Cost Driver Rates

Activity	Set-ups	Purchase orders	Inspections	Sales invoices
Cost	£8,000	£3,000	£2,000	£8,000
Cost driver	50 set-ups	5,000 purchase orders	250 inspections	10,000 sales invoices
Cost per unit of cost driver	£160	£0.60	£8.00	£0.80

Figure 3.12　Activity-Based Costing Example (*continued*)

Here we simply divided the total costs of each activity by the total number of the activities. There are, for example, 20 set-ups for A and 30 set-ups for B making 50 set-ups in total. We divide this into the total cost of £8,000 to arrive at £160 per set-up.

Step 6: Absorb both the Direct and Indirect Costs into the Products

Activity	Set-ups	Purchase orders	Inspections	Sales	Total costs*
A	20 × £160 = £3,200	4,000 × £0.60 = £2,400	100 × £8.00 = £800	7,000 × £0.80 = £5,600	£12,000
B	30 × £160 = £4,800	1,000 × £0.60 = £600	150 × £8.00 = £1,200	3,000 × £0.80 = £2,400	£9,000
Total	£8,000	£3,000	£2,000	£8,000	£21,000

Here, we multiplied the cost per unit of cost driver by the number of cost drivers. For example, we have 20 set-ups (i.e., number of cost drivers) for A and 30 set-ups (i.e., number of cost drivers) for B. Each set-up costs £160 (i.e., cost per unit of cost driver).

	A £	B £
Total overhead costs*	12,000	9,000
Number of products	16,000	10,000
Overhead per product	£0.75	£0.90

Here, we took the total overhead costs for A (£12,000) and for B (£9,000) and divided by the number of products to arrive at the overhead per product. We can now prepare the product cost statements for products A and B. Direct materials and direct labour are calculated by dividing the total costs for each product by the total number of products (i.e., for A's direct materials, we divide £8,000 by 16,000 products).

	A Product cost £	B Product cost £
Direct materials	0.50	0.70
Direct labour	0.62	1.50
Prime Cost	1.12	2.20
Overheads	0.75	0.90
Total Cost	1.87	3.10
Profit (25% mark-up on cost)	0.47	0.78
Sales Price	2.34	3.88

(A and B) and four activity-cost drivers have been identified (set-ups, purchase orders, inspections and sales invoices.

Activity-based costing is thus a more sophisticated version of traditional product costing. It can give more accurate and reliable information. It also significantly increases the company's ability to manage costs and is suitable for both manufacturing and service companies. However, importantly, it involves much more time and effort to set up than traditional product costing and may not be suitable for all companies.

Costing for Stock Valuation

Non-Production Overheads

It is important to distinguish between costing as a basis of pricing, which we have just looked at, and costing as the basis for stock valuation. The key difference is in the treatment of non-production overheads.

PAUSE FOR THOUGHT 3.4

Non-Production Overheads

Why are administrative, sales and marketing costs not included as overheads in stock valuation?

....

The problem of non-production overheads is a tricky one. The administrative, sales and marketing costs, for example, are required when calculating the total cost of a product as a basis for pricing. However, they should not be included when calculating a stock valuation. The reason is that these costs are not incurred in actually making the product. It would, therefore, be incorrect to include them in the cost of the product. These non-production costs are often called period costs. This is because they are allocated to the **period** *not* the **product**.

When valuing stock it is permissible to include production overheads, but not non-production overheads. However, for cost-plus pricing we need to take into account all overheads. These include non-production overheads such as sales, administrative and marketing expenses. As Figure 3.13 on the next page shows, there can be quite a difference.

Different stock valuation measures: FIFO, LIFO, AVCO

The inclusion of production overheads in finished goods stock is one key problem in stock valuation. Another difficulty, which primarily concerns raw material stock, is the choice of stock valuation methods. There are three main methods: FIFO, LIFO and AVCO. All three are permitted in management accounting and for stock valuation in the financial accounts in the US. However, in the UK only FIFO and AVCO are permitted for stock valuation in financial accounting.

Figure 3.13 Costing for Stock Valuation and for Cost-Plus Pricing

A product has the following cost structure. 100,000 products are manufactured.

	Stock valuation (Marginal costing)	Stock valuation (Absorption costing)	Cost-plus pricing (Total absorption costing)
	£000	£000	£000
Direct materials	10	10	10
Direct labour	25	25	25
Prime Cost	35	35	35
Variable production overheads	10	10	10
Fixed production overheads	–	5	5
Total Production Costs	45	50	50
Administrative costs			10
Marketing costs			8
Sales costs			7
Total Cost			75
Profit: 33.3% mark-up on cost			25
Selling Price			100

At what value should each item be recorded in stock and what is the selling price per item?

i. *Stock* using marginal costing

$$\frac{£45,000}{100,000} = 0.45p$$

ii. *Stock* using absorption costing

$$\frac{£50,000}{100,000} = 0.50p$$

iii. *Selling price* using total absorption costing

$$\frac{£100,000}{100,000} = £1.00$$

Helpnote: Using **marginal costing,** only the **variable production overheads** that can be attributed are included in the stock valuation. In **absorption costing,** we include **all the production overheads.** It is absorption costing that is used for stock valuation in *financial reporting*. In **total absorption costing,** we recover **all the costs** into the product's final selling price.

Stock valuation is not quite as easy as it may at first seem. It depends on which assumptions you make about the stock sold. Is the stock you buy in first, the first to be sold (first-in-first out (FIFO))? Or is the stock you buy in last, sold first (last-in-first-out (LIFO))? If the purchase price of stock changes then this assumption matters.

In Figure 3.14, we investigate an example of the impact that using FIFO or LIFO has upon the valuation of raw materials stock. We also include a third method, AVCO (average cost), which takes the average purchase price of the goods as their cost of sale.

Figure 3.14   FIFO, LIFO and AVCO Stock Valuation Methods

Stockco purchases its stock on the first day of the month. It starts with no stock. Its purchases and sales over the first three months are as follows:

		Kilos	Cost per kilo	Total cost
January 1	Purchases	10,000	£1.00	£10,000
February 1	Purchases	15,000	£1.50	£22,500
March 1	Purchases	20,000	£2.00	£40,000
		45,000		£72,500
March 30	Sales	(35,000)		
March 30	Closing stock	10,000		

What is the closing stock valuation using FIFO, LIFO and AVCO?

- -

(i) **FIFO:** Here, the first stock purchased is the first sold. The 35,000 kilos sold therefore, used up all the January stock (10,000 kilos), and the February stock (15,000 kilos), and (10,000 kilos) of the March stock. We, therefore, have left in stock 10,000 kilos of material valued at the March purchase price of £2.00 per kilo. Closing stock is, therefore, $10,000 \times £2 = £20,000$.

(ii) **LIFO:** Here the last stock purchased is assumed to be the first to be sold. The 35,000 kilos sold, therefore, used up:

20,000	kilos from March
15,000	kilos from February
35,000	

We, therefore, have remaining 10,000 kilos from January at £1 per kilo $= £10,000$.

(iii) **AVCO:** Here the stock value is pooled and the average cost of purchase is taken as the cost of the goods sold. We purchased 45,000 kilos for £72,500 (i.e. £1.611 per kilo). The cost of our stock, is therefore, 10,000 kilos $\times$ average cost £1.611 $= £16,110$.

We can, therefore, see that our *stock valuations* vary considerably.

	£
FIFO	20,000
LIFO	10,000
AVCO	16,110

It should be appreciated that stock valuation is distinct from physical stock management. In most businesses, good business practice dictates that you usually physically issue the oldest stock first (i.e., adopt FIFO). However, in stock valuation you are allowed to choose what is acceptable under the regulations.

PAUSE FOR THOUGHT 3.5

FIFO, LIFO and AVCO and Cost of Sales

Do you think that using a different stock valuation method in Figure 3.14 would affect cost of sales or profit?

....

Yes!! Whichever valuation method is used, both cost of sales and profit are affected. Essentially, the cost of purchases will be split between stock and cost of sales.

	Total cost £	Cost of sales £	Stock £
FIFO	72,500	52,500 (N1)	20,000
LIFO	72,500	62,400 (N2)	10,000
AVCO	72,500	56,390 (N3)	16,110

(N1) FIFO represents:			£
	January	10,000 kilos at £1.00	10,000
	February	15,000 kilos at £1.50	22,500
	March	10,000 kilos at £2.00	20,000
			52,500

(N2) LIFO represents:			£
	February	15,000 kilos at £1.50	22,500
	March	20,000 kilos at £2.00	40,000
			62,500

(N3) AVCO represents:		£
	35,000 kilos at £1.611	56,390

Profit is affected because if cost of sales is less, stock, and thus profit, is higher and vice versa. In this case, using FIFO will show the greatest profit as its cost of sales is lowest. LIFO will show the lowest profit. AVCO is in the middle!

Different Costing Methods for Different Industries

So far we have focused mainly on allocating costs to individual jobs in manufacturing. However, job costing is not appropriate in many situations. Different industries have different costing problems. To solve these problems different types of costing have evolved. In order to give a flavour of this, we look below at four industries (see Figure 3.15).

Figure 3.15   Overview of Different Industries' Costing Methods

	Industry	Costing Method
1	Manufacturing in batches	Batch costing
2	Shipbuilding	Contract costing
3	Brewery	Process costing
4	Hotel and catering	Service costing

1. Batch Costing

Batch costing is where a number of items of a similar nature are processed together. There is thus not one discrete job. Batch costing can be used in a variety of situations, such as manufacture of medicinal tablets.

Figure 3.16   Batch Costing

A run of 50,000 tablets are made for batch number x1.11. There are 2,000 defective tablets and 50 tablets per box. Overheads are recovered on the basis of £6 per labour hour. The material was 3 kg at £5.00 per kg, and labour rate A 6 hours at £9.00, and rate B 7 hours at £10.00.

	£
The costing statement might look as follows:	
Direct materials (3 kg at £5.00)	15.00
Direct labour (13 hours: A 6 at £9	54.00
B 7 at £10)	70.00
Prime Cost	139.00
Overheads (13 hours at £6)	78.00
Total Cost	217.00
Boxes (48,000 ÷ 50)	960
Cost per box	22.6p

2. Contract Costing

A contract can be looked at as a very long job, or a job lasting more than one year. It occurs in big construction industries such as shipbuilding and aircraft building. A long-term contract extends over more than one year and creates the problem of when to take profit. If we have a three-year contract do we take all our profit at the start of our contract, at the end, or equally throughout the three years?

The answer has gradually evolved over the years, and there are now certain recognised guidelines for taking a profit or loss. Generally, losses should be taken as soon as it is realised they will occur. By contrast, profits should be taken so as to reflect the proportion of the work carried out. This is shown in The Company Camera 3.2, which shows John Laing's accounting policy for long-term contracts.

THE COMPANY CAMERA 3.2

Long-Term Contracts

Profits on long-term contracts are calculated in accordance with industry standard accounting practice and do not therefore relate directly to turnover. Profit on current contracts is only taken at a stage near enough to completion for that profit to be reasonably certain. Provision is made for all losses incurred to the accounting date together with any further losses that are foreseen in bringing contracts to completion.

Source: John Laing plc, Annual Report 2003, p. 67

In practice, allocating profits can be very complex. We will use a simplified formula: **Profit to be taken = %contractcomplete × total estimated contract profit × 2/3**. Usually, the customer and the supplier will negotiate and set a price for a contract in advance. Figure 3.17 provides an illustrative example.

Figure 3.17   Contract Costing

O&P Ferries requires a new ferry to be built. It asks Londonside Shipbuilders for a quotation. Londonside looks at its costs and decides that the ship will cost £4 million direct materials, £4 million direct labour and £5 million indirect overheads. They then quote O&P Ferries £19 million for the job. The aim to complete the job in 3 years. Londonside therefore estimate a £6 million profit (£19 million less £13 million). When should they take the profit?

Figure 3.17   Contract Costing (*continued*)

The answer is that the situation is reviewed as the contract progresses, and profit taken according to the formula given earlier. For example, if we have the following costs:

In £ millions	Year 1		Year 2		Year 3	
	£	£	£	£	£	£
Contract Price		19		19		19
(Remains fixed)						
Costs Incurred to Date						
Direct materials	2		3		5	
Direct labour	2		2		5	
Indirect overheads	2		3		6	
Total costs incurred to date	6		8		16	
Estimated future costs	8		5		–	
Total Costs (estimated and incurred)		14		13		16
Estimated Profit		5		6		3
% Contract complete		6/14ths		8/13ths		Complete

At the end of year 3 the contract is finished, therefore, the estimated profit will be the actual profit.

So if we apply our formula we can see how it works:

	% contract complete	×	Total estimated contract profit	×	$\frac{2}{3}$		This year's profit £	Total estimated profit to date £
Year 1	$\frac{6}{14}$	×	£5m	×	$\frac{2}{3}$ = £1.43m		£1.43m	£1.43m
Year 2	$\frac{8}{13}$	×	£6m	×	$\frac{2}{3}$ = £2.46m		£1.03m	£2.46m

We take an additional £1.03 million in year 2 (i.e., the profit to date, £2.46m, less year 1's profit, £1.43m).

| **Year 3** | | | | | | | £0.54m | £3.0m |

In year 3, we know the actual profit is £3 million. We can therefore take all the profit not taken so far. This is £3 million – £2.46 (already taken) = £0.54 million.

3. Process Costing

Process costing is used in industries with a continuous production process, e.g., beer brewing. Products are passed from one department to another, and then processed further. At any one point in time, therefore, many of the products will only be partially complete. To deal with this problem of partially completed products, the concept of equivalent units has developed. At the end of a process if we partially finish units then we take the percentage of completion and convert to fully completed equivalent units. If, for example, we have 1,000 litres of beer that are half way through the beer-making process this would equal 500 litres fully complete (i.e., there would be the equivalent of 500 litres).

Figure 3.18   Process Costing

A firm manufactures beer. There are two processes A and B. There are 1,000 litres of opening stock of beer for process B, the fermentation stage (the product has already been through process A). They are 50% complete. During the year 650 litres are finished and transferred (i.e., completed). The closing work in progress consists of 800 litres, 75% completed. The costs incurred in that process during that year are £15,000.

To find out the cost per litre, we must first find out how many litres are effectively produced during the period. We can do this by deduction. First of all we can establish the total stock that was completed by the end of the year. This will equal the stock we have finished and transferred (650 litres) plus the closing stock (800 litres, 75% complete, equals 600 litres). From this 1,250 litres we need to take the opening stock (1,000 litres, 50% complete, equals 500 litres). We have, therefore, our effective production of 750 litres.* The cost is then £15,000 divided by the 750 equivalent litres, equals £20 per litre

	Equivalent litres
Finished and transferred	650
Closing stock (800 × 75%)	600
Total completed	1,250
Opening stock (1,000 × 50%)	(500)
Effective production	750

Therefore, using 'equivalent' litres our cost per litre for process B is:

$$\frac{£15,000}{750} = £20$$

4. Service Costing

Service costing concerns services such as canteens. In large businesses, for example, canteens might be run as independent operating units that have to make a profit. The cost of a particular service is simply the total costs for the service divided by the number of services provided. Service costing uses the same principles as job costing.

Figure 3.19 Service Costing for Canteens

A canteen serves 10,000 meals: 6,000 are roast dinners and 4,000 salads. The roast dinners are bought in for £2.50 each and the salads for £1.25. The canteen costs are £1,000. They are apportioned across the number of meals served. What is the cost of each meal?

	Roast Dinners £	Salads £
Bought-in price	2.50	1.25
Overheads per meal $\left(\dfrac{£1,000}{10,000} = 0.10\text{p} \right)$	0.10	0.10
	2.60	1.35

Target Costing

So far we have focused principally on cost-plus pricing. However, the Japanese have introduced a concept called target costing, which focuses on market prices. Essentially, a price is set with reference to market conditions and customer purchasing patterns. A target profit is then deducted to arrive at a target cost. This target cost is set in order to allow a company to achieve a certain market share and a certain profit. The target profit is set before the product is manufactured.

The costs are then examined and re-examined in order to make the target cost. Often this is done by breaking down the product into many individual components and costing them separately. The product may be divided into many functions using 'functional analysis'. Functions may include attractiveness, durability, reliability, and style among other things. Each function is priced. Target costing may also be used in conjunction with life cycle costing. Life cycle costing (see Chapter 7) involves tracing all the costs of a product over their entire life cycle. Target costing will be the first stage in this process.

Cost-Cutting

A final key reason why it is essential for a business to have a good knowledge of its costs is for cost-cutting. As we mentioned in Chapter 2, the two major ways to improve profitability are by improving sales or by cutting costs. Whereas improving sales is a long-term solution, cost-cutting is a short-term solution. It is particularly useful when a business is in trouble. By announcing cost-cutting measures, the business signals to the City and to its investors that it is serious about improving its profitability. Unfortunately, one of the most important elements of most companies costs is labour. Therefore, companies often shed labour. When doing this companies may run into trouble with trade unions or with politicians. Centrica's reduction of the number of staff in its gas showrooms is a good example of this (see Real-Life Nugget 3.4).

REAL-LIFE NUGGET 3.4

Cutting Labour Costs

Centrica, Britain's largest gas retailer, plans to axe almost 1,500 jobs in its underperforming high street energy stores, drawing the wrath of unions who claimed the act was a 'betrayal of staff'.

The company said it would close its 243 British Gas Energy Centres and incur £60 m in costs to be charged this financial year.

Centrica chief executive Roy Gardner revealed the operating losses for those stores had grown to an estimated £25 m in the June half, compared with £33 m for the whole 1998 year.

Source: Centrica Faces Anger over Store Job Cuts, Anne Hyland, *Daily Telegraph*, 20 July 1999

As an alternative to cutting labour costs, companies sometimes attempt to cut other costs such as training or research and development. By doing this, companies may sacrifice long-term profitability for short-term profitability.

Conclusion

Costing is an important part of management accounting. It involves recording, classifying, allocating and absorbing costs into individual products and services. Cost recovery is used to value stock by including production overheads and for cost-plus pricing by determining the total costs of a product or service. Traditionally, overheads have been allocated to products or services primarily using volume-based measures such as direct labour hours or machine hours. However, more recently, activity-based measures such as number of purchase orders processed have been used. Different industries use different costing systems such as batch costing, contract costing, process costing and service costing. Target costing, based on a product's market price, has been developed in Japan. Businesses in trouble often cut costs, such as labour, in order to try to improve their profitability.

Q&A Discussion Questions

Questions with numbers in blue have answers at the back of the book.

Q1 What is costing and why is it important?

Q2 Compare and contrast the traditional and the more modern activity-based approaches to costing.

Q3 Overhead recovery is the most difficult part of cost recovery. Discuss.

Q4 Target costing combines the advantages of both market pricing and cost-plus pricing. Discuss.

Q5 State whether the following statements are true or false. If false, explain why.

(a) A cost is an actual past expenditure.

(b) When recovering costs for pricing we use total absorption costing. However, for stock valuation we use absorption costing or marginal costing.

(c) When using traditional total absorption costing it is important to identify activity cost drivers.

(d) In batch costing if we had 100 units that were 50 % complete this would equal 50 equivalent units.

(e) In stock valuation, marginal costing is normally used in valuing stock in financial reporting.

Q&A Numerical Questions

Questions with numbers in blue have answers at the back of the book.

Q1 Sorter has the following costs:

(a)	Machine workers' wages	(i)	Depreciation on office furniture
(b)	Cost clerks' wages	(j)	Computer running expenses for office
(c)	Purchase of raw materials	(k)	Loan interest
(d)	Machine repairs	(l)	Auditors' fees
(e)	Finance director's salary	(m)	Depreciation on machinery
(f)	Office cleaners	(n)	Advertising costs
(g)	Delivery van staff's wages	(o)	Electricity for machines
(h)	Managing director's car expenses	(p)	Bank charges

Required: An analysis of Sorter's costs between:

(i)	Direct materials	(iv)	Administrative expenses
(ii)	Direct labour	(v)	Selling and distribution costs
(iii)	Production overheads		

Q2   Costa has the following costs:

	£
Salaries of administrative employees	90,800
Wages of factory supervisors	120,000
Computer overhead expenses	
(^{2}/$_3$ in factory, ^{1}/$_3$ in administration)	9,000
Interest on loans	3,000
Wages: selling and distribution	18,300
Salaries: marketing	25,000
Royalties	3,600
Raw materials used in production	320,000
Depreciation: Machinery used for production	8,000
Office fixtures and fittings	4,200
Delivery vans	3,500
Buildings (^{1}/$_2$ factory; ^{1}/$_4$ office; ^{1}/$_4$ sales)	10,000
Labour costs directly connected with production	200,000
Other production overheads	70,000
Commission paid to sales force	1,200

Required: A determination of Costa's:
(i)   prime cost
(ii)   production cost
(iii) total cost

Q3   Makemore has three departments: Departments A and B are production and Department C is a service support department. It apportions its overheads as follows (see brackets):

		£
Supervisors' salaries	(number of employees)	25,000
Computer advisory	(number of employees)	18,000
Rent and business rates	(floor area)	20,000
Depreciation on machinery	(cost)	21,000
Repairs	(actual spend)	4,000
		84,000

You have the following information:
(a) Department A 1,000 employees, B 2,000 employees, C 500 employees.
(b) Department A 10,000 sq.feet, B 6,000 sq.feet, and C 4,000 sq.feet.
(c) Department A machinery costs £30,000, B machinery costs £15,000.

(d) Repairs are £2, 800, £1,100 and £100, respectively, for departments A, B and C.

(e) Department C's facilities will be reallocated 60 % for A and 40 % for B.

(f)

	Department A	Department B
Direct labour hours	80,000	40,000
Machine hours	100,000	200,000

Required: An apportionment of the overheads to products A and B

(i) using direct labour hours, and

(ii) using machine hours.

Q4 Flight has two products, the 'Takeoff' and the 'Landing'. They go through two departments and incur the following costs:

		Takeoff		*Landing*	
Dept. A –	Direct labour	10 hours	£10 per hour	9 hours	£7 per hour
	Direct materials	10 kilos	£5 per kilo	7 kilos	£12 per kilo
Dept. B –	Direct labour	8 hours	£12 per hour	5 hours	£8 per hour
	Direct materials	5 kilos	£15 per kilo	6 kilos	£10 per kilo

Takeoff's indirect overheads are absorbed at £7 per labour hour for Dept. A and £5 per hour Dept. B.

Landing's indirect overheads are absorbed at £6 per labour hour for Dept. A and £4 per hour for Dept. B.

Selling price is to be 20 % on cost.

Required: The prices for which Flight should sell 'Takeoff' and 'Landing'.

Q5 An up-market catering company, Spicemeals, organises banquets and high-class catering functions. A particular function for the Blue Devils university drinking club has the following costs for 100 guests.

100 starters	at	£1.00 each
50 main meals	at	£3.00 each
50 main meals	at	£2.50 each
200 sweets	at	£1.50 each
200 bottles of wine	at	£5.00 each
100 coffees	at	£0.20 each

Direct labour:	Supervisory	8 hours	at	£15.00
	Food preparation	30 hours	at	£8.00
	Waitressing	200 hours	at	£5.00

Overheads relating to this job based on total hours are recovered at £1.10 per hour. There are £180,000 general overheads within the business and about 300 functions. Profit is to be 15 % on cost.

Required: The price Spicemeals should charge for this function and the amount for each guest.

Q6   A medicinal product 'Supertab' is produced in batches. Batch number x308 has the following costs:

Direct labour: Grade	1	200 hours	at	£5.00
	2	50 hours	at	£8.00
	3	25 hours	at	£15.00
Direct materials: Type	A	10 kilos	at	£8.00
	B	5 kilos	at	£10.00
	C	3 kilos	at	£15.00

Production overheads are based on labour hours at £3 per hour. 20,000 tablets are produced, but there is a wastage of 10 %. Non-production overheads are £15,000 for the month. There are usually 250 batches produced per month. There are 50 tablets in a container. The selling price will be 25 % on cost.

Required: What is the selling price of each container?

Q7   Dodo Airways has agreed a tender for a new aircraft at £20 m. The company making the product has the following cost structure for this long-term contract.

	Tender		Year 1		Year 2		Year 3	
	£m	£m	£m	£m	£m	£m	£m	£m
Sales price		20		20		20		20
Direct materials	3		1		2		4.5	
Direct labour	8		2		5		8.0	
Overheads	4	15	1	4	2	9	4.5	17
Profit		5		16		11		3
Estimated costs to complete				12		7		–

Required: What is the profit Dodo should take every year? Use the formula given in this chapter (see page 63).

Q8 Serveco is a home-service computer company. There are two levels of computer service offered: basic and enhanced service. You have the following details on each.

	Basic	Enhanced
Total basic call out time	25,000 hours	37,500 hours
Total travelling time	25,000 hours	5,000 hours
Parts serviced/replaced	50,000	100,000
Technical support (mins)	75,000	100,000
Service documentation (units)	100,000	25,000
Number of call outs	50,000	10,000

You have the following costs:

	Basic	Enhanced	Total
Basic computer operatives' labour	£20 per hour	£25 per hour	
Spare parts installed			£100,000
Technical support cost			£125,000
Service documentation cost			£300,000

Serveco requires a profit mark-up of cost plus 25 %.

Required: Calculate an appropriate standard call out charge for the basic and enhanced services using activity-based costing.

Q9 A company, Rugger, manufactures two products: the Try and the Conversion. The company has traditionally allocated its production overhead costs on the basis of the 100,000 direct hours used in the manufacturing department. Direct labour costs £5 per hour. The company is now considering using activity-based costing. Details of the overheads and cost drivers are as follows:

Production Overheads	Total Cost (£)	Cost Driver	Total
(a) Manufacturing	10,000	Assembly-line hours	100,000 hours
(b) Materials handling	60,000	Number of stores notes	1,500 notes
(c) Inspection	40,000	Number of inspections	600 inspections
(d) Set-ups	5,000	Number of set-ups	500 set-ups

You have the following information about the products.

	Try	Conversion
Number of units	15,000	2,500
Assembly-line hours (direct labour) per unit	6 hours	4 hours
Direct materials per unit	£8	£100
Number of stores notes	600	900
Number of inspections	257	343
Number of set-ups	200	300

Required: Calculate a product cost using
(i)   traditional total absorption costing, recovering overheads using direct labour hours;
(ii) activity-based costing, and then
(iii) comment on any differences.

Chapter 4

"The budget is God."

Slogan at Japanese Company, Topcom (*Economist*, January 13, 1996)
Source: *The Wiley Book of Business Quotations* (1998), p. 90

Learning Outcomes

After completing this chapter you should be able to:

✔ **Explain the nature and importance of budgeting.**

✔ **Outline the most important budgets.**

✔ **Prepare the major budgets and a master budget.**

✔ **Discuss the behavioural implications of budgets.**

Planning, Control and Performance: Budgeting

In a Nutshell

- *The two major branches of cost accounting are costing, and planning, control and performance.*

- *Budgeting is a key element of planning, control and performance.*

- *Budgets are ways of turning a firm's strategic objectives into practical reality.*

- *Most businesses prepare, at the minimum, a cash budget.*

- *Large businesses may also prepare a sales, a debtors and a creditors budget.*

- *Manufacturing businesses may prepare a raw materials, a production cost, and a finished goods budget.*

- *Individual budgets fit into a budgeted trading and profit and loss account and a budgeted balance sheet.*

- *Budgeting has behavioural implications for the motivation of employees.*

- *Some behavioural aspects of budgets are spending to budget, padding the budget and creative budgeting.*

- *Responsibility accounting may involve budget centres and performance measurement.*

Introduction

Cost accounting can be divided into costing, and planning, control and performance. Budgeting and standard costing are the major parts of planning, control and performance. Budgeting, or budgetary control, is a key part of businesses' planning for the future. A budget is essentially a plan for the future. Budgets are thus set in advance as a way to quantify a firm's objectives. Actual performance is then monitored against budgeted performance. For small businesses, the cash budget is often the only budget. Larger businesses, by contrast, are likely to have a complex set of interrelating budgets. These build up into a budgeted trading and profit and loss account, and budgeted balance sheet. Although usually set for a year, budgets are also linked to the longer-term strategic objectives of an organisation.

Management Accounting Control Systems

A business needs systems to control its activities. Budgeting and standard costing are two essential management control systems that enable a business to run effectively. They represent an assemblage of management accounting techniques which enable a business to plan, monitor and control ongoing financial activities. A particular aspect of a management accounting control system is that it is often set up to facilitate performance evaluation. Performance evaluation involves evaluating the performance of either individuals or departments. A key facet of performance evaluation is whether it is possible to allocate responsibility and whether the costs are controllable or uncontrollable.

Nature of Budgeting

In many ways, it would be surprising if businesses did not budget. For budgeting is part of our normal everyday lives. Whether it is a shopping trip, a university term or a night out on the town, we all generally have an informal budget of the amount we wish to spend. Businesses merely have a more formal version of this 'informal' personal budget.

PAUSE FOR THOUGHT 4.1

Personal Budgets

You are planning to jet off for an Easter break in the Mediterranean sun. What sort of items would you include in your holiday budget?

....

There would be a range of items, for example,

- transport costs to and from the airport
- cost of flight to Mediterranean
- cost of hotel
- cost of meals
- spending money
- entertainment money
- money for gifts

All these together would contribute to your holiday budget.

Planning, control and performance is one of the two major branches of cost accounting. This is shown in Figure 4.1. Standard costing is, in reality, a more tightly controlled and specialised type of budget. Although often associated with manufacturing industry, standard costs can, in fact, be used in a wide range of businesses.

Figure 4.1   Main Branches of Cost Accounting

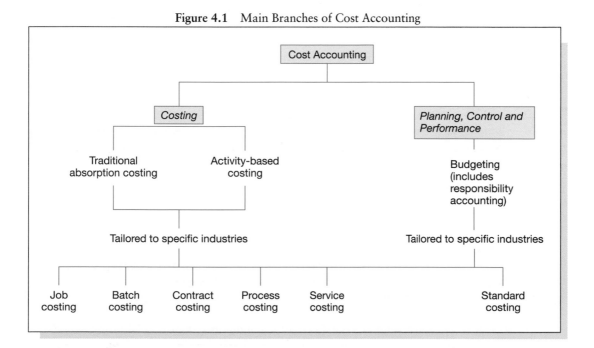

Budgeting can be viewed as a way of turning a firm's long-term strategic objectives into reality. As Figure 4.2 shows, a business's objectives are turned into forecasts and plans. These plans are then compared with the actual results and performance is evaluated.

Figure 4.2   The Budgeting Process

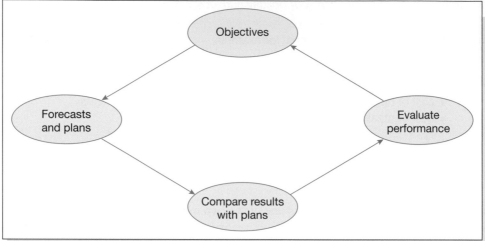

In small businesses, this process may be relatively informal. However, for large businesses there will be a complex budgeting process. The period of a budget varies. Often there is an annual budget broken down into smaller periods such as months or even weeks.

As Definition 4.1 shows, a budget is a quantitative financial plan, which sets out a business's targets.

DEFINITION 4.1

Budget

Working definition
A future plan which sets out a business's financial targets.

Formal definition
'A quantitative statement, for a defined period of time, which may include planned revenues, expenses, assets, liabilities and cash flows. A budget provides a focus for the organisation, aids the co-ordination of activities, and facilitates control.'

Source: Chartered Institute of Management Accountants (2000), *Official Terminology*

Four major aspects of budgets are planning, coordinating, motivation and control. Budgets, therefore, combine both technical and behavioural features. Budgets can be used for performance evaluation. These behavioural aspects and performance evaluation are discussed more fully later in the chapter.

(i) Planning

This involves setting out a comprehensive plan appropriate to the business. For small businesses, this may mean a cash budget. For larger businesses, there will probably be a formalised and sophisticated budgeting system.

(ii) Coordinating

A key aspect of the budgetary process is that it relates the various activities of a company to each other. Therefore, sales are related to purchases, and purchases to production. The business can be viewed as an interlocking whole.

(iii) Motivation

By setting targets the budget has important motivational aspects. If the targets are too hard, they can be demotivating. If too easy, they will not provide any motivation at all.

(iv) Control

This is achieved through a system of making individual managers responsible for individual budgets. When actual results are compared against target results, individual managers will be asked to explain any differences (or variances). The manager's performance is then evaluated. Budgets, as Real-Life Nugget 4.1 shows, are an indispensable form of administrative control. Formal performance evaluation mechanisms such as responsibility accounting are often introduced.

REAL-LIFE NUGGET 4.1

Budgeting

Budgeting now occupies a central position in the design and operation of most management accounting systems. Almost regardless of the type of organisation, the nature of its problems and the other means for influencing behaviour, the preparation of a quantitative statement of expectations regarding the allocation of the organisation's resources tends to be seen as an essential, indeed indispensable, feature of the battery of administrative controls. Nevertheless, despite its wide acceptance, budgeting remains one of the most intriguing and perplexing of management accounting procedures.

Source: A. Hopwood (1974), *Accounting and Human Behaviour*, p. 39

In large businesses, budgets are generally set by a budgetary committee. This will normally involve managers from many different departments. The sales manager, for example, may provide information on likely future sales, which will form the basis of the sales budget. However, it is important that individual budgets are meshed together to provide a coordinated and coherent plan. As Soundbite 4.1 shows, the starting point for this year's budget is usually last year's budget. A form of budgeting called *zero based budgeting* assumes the activities are being incurred for the first time. The budgetary process is normally ongoing, however, with meetings during the year to review progress against the current budget and to set future budgets.

SOUNDBITE 4.1

Last Year's Budget

'The largest determining factor of the size and content of this year's budget is last year's budget.'

Aaron Wildavsky, The Politics of the Budgetary Process, 1964

Source: The Executive's Book of Quotations (1994), p. 39

Although budgets are set within the business, external factors will often constrain them. A key external constraint is demand. It is futile for a company to plan to make ten million motorised skateboards if there is demand for only five million. Indeed, potential sales are the principal factor that limits the expansion of many businesses. Usually, the sales budget is determined first. Some businesses employ a *materials requirement planning* (MRP) system. Based on sales demand, MRP coordinates production and purchasing to ensure the optimal flow of raw materials and optimal level of raw material stocks. Another important budgetary constraint in manufacturing industry is production capacity. It is useless planning to sell ten million motorised skateboards if the production capacity is only five million. A key element of the budgetary process is thus harmonising demand and supply.

Nowadays, it is rare for businesses not to have budgets. As Figure 4.3 shows, budgets have many advantages. The chief disadvantages are that budgets can be inflexible and create behavioural problems. Budgets can be inflexible if set for a year. It is common to revise budgets regularly to take account of new circumstances. This is easier when they are prepared using spreadsheets. The behavioural problems may be created, for example, when individuals attempt to manipulate the budgeting process in their own interest. This is discussed later.

Figure 4.3   The Benefits of Budgeting

- Strategic planning can be more easily linked to management decisions
- Standards can be set to aid performance evaluation
- Plans can be set in financial terms
- Managers can be made responsible for budgets
- Budgets encourage cooperation and coordination

Cash Budget

The cash budget is probably the most important of all budgets. Almost all companies prepare one. Indeed, banks will often insist on a cash budget before they lend money to small businesses. For a sole trader, the cash budget is often as important as the trading and profit and loss account and balance sheet. It reflects the need to balance profitability and liquidity. There are similarities, but also differences, between the cash budget and the cash flow statement that we see in Chapter 8.

PAUSE FOR THOUGHT 4.2

Budgets

Budgets are often said to create inflexibility as they are typically set for a year in advance. Can you think of any ways to overcome this inflexibility?

....

This inflexibility can be dealt with in two ways: rolling budgets and flexible budgets. With rolling budgets the budget is updated every month. There is then a new twelve-month budget. The problem with rolling budgets is that it takes a lot of time and effort to update budgets regularly. Flexible budgets attempt to deal with inflexibility by setting a range of budgets with different activity levels. So a company might budget for servicing 100,000, 150,000 or 200,000 customers. In this case, there would, in effect, be three budgets for three different levels of business activity.

They are similar in that both the cash budget and cash flow statement chart the flows of cash within a business. The differences arise in that the cash flow statement is normally prepared in a standardised format in accordance with accounting regulations and looks backwards in time. By contrast, the cash budget is not in a standardised format and looks forward in time.

Essentially, the cash budget looks into the future. Figure 4.4 gives the format of the cash budget. We start with the opening cash balance. Receipts are then recorded, for example, cash received from cash sales, from debtors or from the sale of fixed assets. Cash payments are then listed, for example, cash purchases of goods, payments to creditors or expenses paid. Receipts less payments provide the monthly cash flow. Opening cash and cash flow determine the closing cash balance.

Figure 4.4   The Format of a Cash Budget

	Jan. £	Feb. £	March £	April £	May £	June £	Total £
Opening cash	X	X	X	X	X	X	X
Add *Receipts*							
Debtors	X	X	X	X	X	X	X
	X	X	X	X	X	X	X
Less *Payments*							
Payments for goods	X	X	X	X	X	X	X
Expenses	X	X	X	X	X	X	X
Other payments	X	X	X	X	X	X	X
	X	X	X	X	X	X	X
Cash flow	Y	Y	Y	Y	Y	Y	Y
Closing cash	X	X	X	X	X	X	X

In Figure 4.5, we show an actual example of how in practice a cash budget is constructed.

Figure 4.5   Illustrative Example of a Cash Budget

Jason Chan has £12,000 in a business bank account. His projections for the first six months trading are as follows.
(i)   Credit sales will be: January £8,800, February £8,800, March £9,000, April £12,500, May £20,200, June £30,000. Debtors pay in the month following sale.
(ii)   Goods supplied on credit will be: January £7,000, February £10,000, March £9,800, April £10,400, May £7,000, June £8,000. Creditors are paid one month in arrears.
(iii) Loan receivable 1 March £4,000 to be repaid in full plus £400 interest on 1 June.
(iv)   Drawing £500 per month.
Prepare the cash budget.

	Jan. £	Feb. £	March £	April £	May £	June £	Total £
Opening cash	12,000	11,500	12,800	15,100	13,800	15,400	12,000
Add *Receipts*							
Debtors		8,800	8,800	9,000	12,500	20,200	59,300
Loan received			4,000				4,000
	–	8,800	12,800	9,000	12,500	20,200	63,300
Less *Payments*							
Payments for goods		7,000	10,000	9,800	10,400	7,000	44,200
Loan repayment						4,400	4,400
Drawings	500	500	500	500	500	500	3,000
	500	7,500	10,500	10,300	10,900	11,900	51,600
Cash flow	*(500)*	*1,300*	*2,300*	*(1,300)*	*1,600*	*8,300*	*11,700*
Closing cash	11,500	12,800	15,100	13,800	15,400	23,700	23,700

Helpnotes:
(i) The receipts from debtors and payments by creditors are thus running one month behind actual sales and actual purchases, respectively. Thus, for example, the debtors will pay the £30,000 of sales made in June in July and they are, therefore, not recorded in this budget.
(ii) The cash flow column is simply total receipts less total payments. Cash outflows (where receipts are less than payments) are recorded in brackets.

Other Budgets

A business may have numerous other budgets. Indeed, each department of a large business is likely to have a budget. In this section, we will look at three key budgets common to many businesses: sales budget; debtors budget and creditors budget.

In the next section, we will look at three additional budgets that are commonly found in manufacturing businesses: raw materials budget, finished goods budget and production cost budget. Finally, we will bring the budgets together in a comprehensive example.

(i) Sales Budget

The sales budget is determined by examining how much the business is likely to sell during the forthcoming period. Figure 4.6 provides an example. Sales budgets like many other budgets can be initially expressed in units before being converted to £s. In many businesses, the sales budget is the key budget as it determines the other budgets. The sales budget is, therefore, often set first.

Figure 4.6   Example of a Sales Budget

A business has two products, Alpha and Omega. It is anticipated that sales of the Alpha will run at 500 units throughout January to June. However, the Omega will start at 1,000 units and rise by 100 units per month. Each Alpha sells at £35, each Omega sells at £50. Prepare the sales budget.

	Jan. £	Feb. £	March £	April £	May £	June £	Total £
Alpha	17,500	17,500	17,500	17,500	17,500	17,500	105,000
Omega	50,000	55,000	60,000	65,000	70,000	75,000	375,000
Total sales	67,500	72,500	77,500	82,500	87,500	92,500	480,000

(ii) Debtors Budget

The debtors budget begins with opening debtors (often taken from the opening balance sheet) to which are added credit sales (often taken from the sales budget). Cash receipts are then deducted, leaving closing debtors. An example of the format for a debtors budget is provided in Figure 4.7, while Figure 4.8 on the next page provides an illustrative example.

Figure 4.7   Format of a Debtors Budget

	Jan. £	Feb. £	March £	April £	May £	June £	Total £
Opening debtors	X	X	X	X	X	X	X
Credit sales	X	X	X	X	X	X	X
	X	X	X	X	X	X	X
Cash received from debtors	(X)	(X)	(X)	(X)	(X)	(X)	(X)
Closing debtors	X	X	X	X	X	X	X

Figure 4.8   Example of a Debtors Budget

Sara Peters has opening debtors of £800. Debtors pay one month in arrears. Sales are forecast to be £900 in January rising by £200 per month. Prepare the debtors budget.

	Jan. £	Feb. £	March £	April £	May £	June £	Total £
Opening debtors	800	900	1,100	1,300	1,500	1,700	800
Credit sales	900	1,100	1,300	1,500	1,700	1,900	8,400
	1,700	2,000	2,400	2,800	3,200	3,600	9,200
Cash received	(800)	(900)	(1,100)	(1,300)	(1,500)	(1,700)	(7,300)
Closing debtors	900	1,100	1,300	1,500	1,700	1,900	1,900

(iii) Creditors Budget

In many ways, the creditors budget is the mirror image of the debtors budget. It starts with opening creditors (often taken from the opening balance sheet), adds credit purchases and then deducts cash paid. The result is closing creditors. The format for the creditors budget is given in Figure 4.9, while Figure 4.10 provides an illustrative example.

Figure 4.9   Format of a Creditors Budget

	Jan. £	Feb. £	March £	April £	May £	June £	Total £
Opening creditors	X	X	X	X	X	X	X
Credit purchases	X	X	X	X	X	X	X
	X	X	X	X	X	X	X
Cash paid to creditors	(X)	(X)	(X)	(X)	(X)	(X)	(X)
Closing creditors	X	X	X	X	X	X	X

Figure 4.10   Example of a Creditors Budget

Jon Matthews has opening creditors of £1,200. Creditors are expected to pay one month in arrears. In January, purchases are forecast to be £9,000 rising by £100 per month. Prepare the creditors budget.

	Jan. £	Feb. £	March £	April £	May £	June £	Total £
Opening creditors	1,200	9,000	9,100	9,200	9,300	9,400	1,200
Credit purchases	9,000	9,100	9,200	9,300	9,400	9,500	55,500
	10,200	18,100	18,300	18,500	18,700	18,900	56,700
Cash paid	(1,200)	(9,000)	(9,100)	(9,200)	(9,300)	(9,400)	(47,200)
Closing creditors	9,000	9,100	9,200	9,300	9,400	9,500	9,500

Manufacturing Budgets

Manufacturing companies normally hold more stock than other businesses. It is, therefore, common to find three additional budgets: a production cost budget; a raw materials budget; and a finished goods budget. Often these budgets are expressed in units, which are then converted into £s. For ease of understanding, we express them here only in financial terms.

(i) Production Cost Budget

The production cost budget, as its name suggests, estimates the cost of production. This involves direct labour, direct materials and production overheads. There may often be sub-budgets for each of these items. The production cost format is shown in Figure 4.11, while Figure 4.12 shows an example. Once the production cost is determined, the finished goods budget can be prepared. It is important to realise that the budgeted production levels are generally determined by the amount the business can sell.

Figure 4.11   Format of a Production Cost Budget

	Jan. £	Feb. £	March £	April £	May £	June £	Total £
Direct materials	X	X	X	X	X	X	X
Direct labour	X	X	X	X	X	X	X
Production overheads	X	X	X	X	X	X	X
	X	X	X	X	X	X	X

Figure 4.12   Example of a Production Cost Budget

Ray Anderson has the following forecast details from his production department. Direct materials are £6 per unit, direct labour is £8 per unit and production overheads are £4 per unit. 1,000 units will be made in January rising by 100 units per month. Prepare the production cost budget.

	Jan. £	Feb. £	March £	April £	May £	June £	Total £
Direct materials	6,000	6,600	7,200	7,800	8,400	9,000	45,000
Direct labour	8,000	8,800	9,600	10,400	11,200	12,000	60,000
Production overheads	4,000	4,400	4,800	5,200	5,600	6,000	30,000
	18,000	19,800	21,600	23,400	25,200	27,000	135,000
Units	1,000	1,100	1,200	1,300	1,400	1,500	7,500

(ii) Raw Materials Budget

The raw materials budget is particularly useful as it provides a forecast of how much raw material the company needs to buy. This can supply the purchases figure for the creditors budget. The raw materials budget format is shown in Figure 4.13. It starts with opening stock of raw materials (often taken from the opening balance sheet); purchases are then added. The amount used in production is then subtracted, arriving at closing stock. An example is shown in Figure 4.14.

Figure 4.13   Format of a Raw Materials Budget

	Jan. £	Feb. £	March £	April £	May £	June £	Total £
Opening stock of raw materials	X	X	X	X	X	X	X
Purchases	X	X	X	X	X	X	X
	X	X	X	X	X	X	X
Used in production	(X)	(X)	(X)	(X)	(X)	(X)	(X)
Closing stock of raw materials	X	X	X	X	X	X	X

Figure 4.14   Example of a Raw Materials Budget

Dai Jones has opening raw materials stock of £1,200. Purchases of raw materials will be £600 in January, increasing by £75 per month. Production will be 400 units per month using £2 raw material per unit. Prepare the raw materials budget.

	Jan. £	Feb. £	March £	April £	May £	June £	Total £
Opening stock of raw materials	1,200	1,000	875	825	850	950	1,200
Purchases	600	675	750	825	900	975	4,725
	1,800	1,675	1,625	1,650	1,750	1,925	5,925
Used in production	(800)	(800)	(800)	(800)	(800)	(800)	(4,800)
Closing stock of raw materials	1,000	875	825	850	950	1,125	1,125

(iii) Finished Goods Budget

The finished goods budget is similar to the raw materials budget except it deals with finished goods. As Figure 4.15 shows, it starts with the opening stock of finished goods (often taken from the balance sheet), the amount produced is then added (from the production cost budget). The cost of sales (i.e., cost of the goods sold) is then deducted. Finally, it finishes with the closing stock of finished goods. The finished goods budget is useful for keeping a check on whether the business is producing sufficient goods to meet demand. Figure 4.16 gives an example of a finished goods budget.

Figure 4.15   Format of a Finished Goods Budget

	Jan. £	Feb. £	March £	April £	May £	June £	Total £
Opening stock of finished goods	X	X	X	X	X	X	X
Produced	X	X	X	X	X	X	X
	X	X	X	X	X	X	X
Cost of sales	(X)	(X)	(X)	(X)	(X)	(X)	(X)
Closing stock of finished goods	X	X	X	X	X	X	X

Figure 4.16   Example of a Finished Goods Budget

Ranjit Patel has £8,000 of finished good stocks in January. 1,000 units per month will be produced at a product cost of £10 each. Sales will be £10,000 in January rising by £1,000 per month. Gross profit is 25% of sales. Prepare the finished goods budget.

	Jan. £	Feb. £	March £	April £	May £	June £	Total £
Opening stock of finished goods	8,000	10,500	12,250	13,250	13,500	13,000	8,000
Produced	10,000	10,000	10,000	10,000	10,000	10,000	60,000
	18,000	20,500	22,250	23,250	23,500	23,000	68,000
Cost of sales*	(7,500)	(8,250)	(9,000)	(9,750)	(10,500)	(11,250)	(56,250)
Closing stock of finished goods	10,500	12,250	13,250	13,500	13,000	11,750	11,750
*Cost of sales is 75% of sales	10,000	1,000	12,000	13,000	14,000	15,000	75,000

Comprehensive Budgeting Example

Once all the budget have been prepared, it is important to gain an overview of how the business is expected to perform. Normally, a budgeted trading and profit and loss account and budgeted balance sheet are drawn up. This is often called a master budget. The full process is now illustrated using the example of Jacobs Engineering (see Figure 4.17), a manufacturing company. A manufacturing company is used so as to illustrate the full range of budgets

Figure 4.17   Comprehensive Budgeting Example

Jacobs Engineering is a small manufacturing company. There are the following forecast summarised details.

Jacobs Engineering Ltd
Balance Sheet (Abridged) as at 31 December 2005

	£	£	£
Fixed Assets			100,000
Current Assets			
Debtors (Nov. £13,000, Dec £14,000)	27,000		
Stock of raw materials	10,000		
Stock of finished goods	15,000	52,000	
Current Liabilities			
Creditors (Nov. £12,000, Dec. £13,000)	(25,000)		
Bank overdraft	(7,000)	(32,000)	
Net current assets			20,000
Total net assets			120,000

			£
Share Capital and Reserves			
Share Capital			
Ordinary share capital			90,000
Reserves			
Profit and loss account			30,000
Total shareholders' funds			120,000

Notes:

1. Depreciation is 10 % straight line basis per year.
2. Purchases will be £10,000 in January, increasing by £300 per month. They are payable two months after purchase.
3. Sales will be 450 units of product A at average production cost plus 25 % and 500 units of product B at average production cost plus 20 %. Debtors will pay two months in arrears.
4. Average production cost *per unit* remains the same as last year and is the same for product A and product B. It consists of direct materials £10, direct labour £7, production overheads £3. Both direct labour and production overheads will be paid in the month used. Production 1,000 units per month.
5. Non-production expenses are £4,000 per month, and will be paid in the month incurred.

Required: Prepare the sales budget, cash budget, debtors budget, creditors budget, production cost budget, finished goods budget, raw materials budget, budgeted trading, profit and loss account and budgeted balance sheet for six months ending 30 June, 2006.

Figure 4.17 Comprehensive Budgeting Example (*continued*)

Sales Budget

	Jan.	Feb.	March	April	May	June	Total
	£	£	£	£	£	£	£
Product A*	11,250	11,250	11,250	11,250	11,250	11,250	67,500
Product B**	12,000	12,000	12,000	12,000	12,000	12,000	72,000
	23,250	23,250	23,250	23,250	23,250	23,250	139,500

*　(450 units × (£20 average production cost, i.e. direct materials £10, direct labour £7 and production overheads £3) plus 25 %
**　(500 units × (£20 average production cost, i.e. direct materials £10, direct labour £7 and production overheads £3) plus 20 %

Cash Budget

	Jan.	Feb.	March	April	May	June	Total
	£	£	£	£	£	£	£
Opening cash	(7,000)	(20,000)	(33,000)	(33,750)	(34,800)	(36,150)	(7,000)
Add Receipts							
Debtors	13,000	14,000	23,250	23,250	23,250	23,250	120,000
	13,000	14,000	23,250	23,250	23,250	23,250	120,000
Less Payments							
Payment for goods	12,000	13,000	10,000	10,300	10,600	10,900	66,800
Non-production expenses	4,000	4,000	4,000	4,000	4,000	4,000	24,000
Direct labour	7,000	7,000	7,000	7,000	7,000	7,000	42,000
Production overheads	3,000	3,000	3,000	3,000	3,000	3,000	18,000
	26,000	27,000	24,000	24,300	24,600	24,900	150,800
Cash flow	(13,000)	(13,000)	(750)	(1,050)	(1,350)	(1,650)	(30,800)
Closing cash	(20,000)	(33,000)	(33,750)	(34,800)	(36,150)	(37,800)	(37,800)

Debtors Budget

	Jan.	Feb.	March	April	May	June	Total
	£	£	£	£	£	£	£
Opening debtors	27,000	37,250	46,500	46,500	46,500	46,500	27,000
Credit sales	23,250	23,250	23,250	23,250	23,250	23,250	139,500
	50,250	60,500	69,750	69,750	69,750	69,750	166,500
Cash received	(13,000)	(14,000)	(23,250)	(23,250)	(23,250)	(23,250)	(120,000)
Closing debtors	37,250	46,500	46,500	46,500	46,500	46,500	46,500

Figure 4.17   Comprehensive Budgeting Example (*continued*)

Creditors Budget

	Jan. £	Feb. £	March £	April £	May £	June £	Total £
Opening creditors	25,000	23,000	20,300	20,900	21,500	22,100	25,000
Credit purchases	10,000	10,300	10,600	10,900	11,200	11,500	64,500
	35,000	33,300	30,900	31,800	32,700	33,600	89,500
Cash paid	(12,000)	(13,000)	(10,000)	(10,300)	(10,600)	(10,900)	(66,800)
Closing creditors	23,000	20,300	20,900	21,500	22,100	22,700	22,700

Production Cost Budget

	Jan. £	Feb. £	March £	April £	May £	June £	Total £
Direct materials	10,000	10,000	10,000	10,000	10,000	10,000	60,000
Direct labour	7,000	7,000	7,000	7,000	7,000	7,000	42,000
Production overheads	3,000	3,000	3,000	3,000	3,000	3,000	18,000
	20,000	20,000	20,000	20,000	20,000	20,000	120,000

Finished Goods Budget

	Jan. £	Feb. £	March £	April £	May £	June £	Total £
Opening stock of finished goods	15,000	16,000	17,000	18,000	19,000	20,000	15,000
Produced	20,000	20,000	20,000	20,000	20,000	20,000	120,000
	35,000	36,000	37,000	38,000	39,000	40,000	135,000
Cost of sales*	(19,000)	(19,000)	(19,000)	(19,000)	(19,000)	(19,000)	(114,000)
Closing stock of finished goods	16,000	17,000	18,000	19,000	20,000	21,000	21,000

*(950 units × £20)

Raw Materials Budget

	Jan. £	Feb. £	March £	April £	May £	June £	Total £
Opening stock of raw materials	10,000	10,000	10,300	10,900	11,800	13,000	10,000
Purchases	10,000	10,300	10,600	10,900	11,200	11,500	64,500
	20,000	20,300	20,900	21,800	23,000	24,500	74,500
Used in production*	(10,000)	(10,000)	(10,000)	(10,000)	(10,000)	(10,000)	(60,000)
Closing stock of raw materials	10,000	10,300	10,900	11,800	13,000	14,500	14,500

*1,000 units per month × £10 direct materials.

Figure 4.17   Comprehensive Budgeting Example (*continued*)

Jacobs Ltd Engineering
Budgeted Trading and Profit and Loss Account
for Year Ending 30 June 2006

	£	£	Source budget
Sales		139,500	Sales
Less *Cost of Sales*		114,000	Finished goods
Gross Profit		25,500	
Less *Expenses*			
Depreciation	10,000		–
Expenses	24,000	34,000	
Net Loss		(8,500)	–

Jacobs Ltd Engineering
Budgeted Balance Sheet as at 30 June 2006

	£ Cost	£ Accumulated depreciation	£ Net book value	Source Budget
Fixed Assets	100,000	(10,000)	90,000	
Current Assets				
Debtors	46,500			Debtors
Stock of raw materials	14,500			Raw materials
Stock of finished goods	21,000	82,000		Finished goods
Current Liabilities				
Creditors	(22,700)			Creditors
Bank overdraft	(37,800)	(60,500)		Cash
Net current assets			21,500	
Total net assets			111,500	
Share Capital and Reserves				
Share Capital			£	Opening balance
Ordinary share capital			90,000	sheet
Reserves				
Opening profit and loss account		30,000		Opening balance sheet
Less: Loss for year		(8,500)	21,500	Trading and
Total shareholders' funds			111,500	profit and loss account

discussed in this chapter. An overview of the whole process is presented in Figure 4.18. It must be appreciated that Figure 4.18 does not include all possible budgets (for example, many businesses have labour, selling and administration budgets). However, Figure 4.18 does give a good appreciation of the basic budgetary flows.

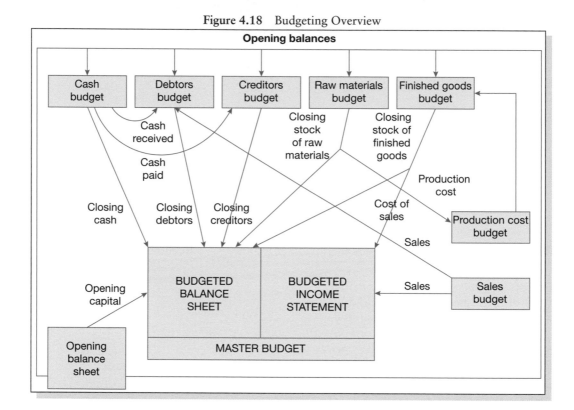

Figure 4.18   Budgeting Overview

After the budgetary period, the actual results are compared against the budgeted results. Any differences between the two sets of results will be investigated and action taken, if appropriate. This basic principle of investigating why any variances have occurred is common in both budgeting and standard costing.

Behavioural Aspects of Budgeting

It is important to realise that there are several, sometimes competing, functions of budgets, for example, planning, coordinating, motivation and control. Budgeting is thus a mixture of technical (planning and coordinating) and behavioural (motivation and control) aspects. In short, budgets affect the behaviour of individuals within firms.

The budgetary process is all about setting targets and individuals meeting those targets. The problem is that an optimal target for the business is not necessarily optimal for the individual employee. Conflicts of interest, therefore, arise between the individual and the company. It may, for example, be in a company's interests to set a very demanding budget. However, it is not necessarily in the employee's interests. Budgets can, therefore, have powerful motivational or demotivational effects. For employees, in particular, budgets are often treated with great suspicion. Managers often use budgets deliberately as a motivational tool (see Real-Life Nugget 4.2).

REAL-LIFE NUGGET 4.2

Budgetary Optimism

Where senior managers and accountants use a single budget and are reluctant to relinquish it as a motivational tool, which they often are, the problem gives rise to the 'bottom drawer phenomenon'. The main budget is designed to include some reflection of aspired performance levels, but the senior accountants keep another version in the bottom drawer of their desks which tries to make some allowance for the prevailing corporate optimism. Sometimes this merely takes the form of an overall 5 per cent or 10 per cent, but in other organisations, it is done on a departmental basis, with 5 per cent off Fred's budget and possibly 15 per cent off Joe's, depending on estimates of the aspirational element in each case. This is obviously done because senior management required a more realistic statement of expected performance for decision and planning purposes.

Source: A. Hopwood (1974), *Accounting and Human Behaviour*, p. 63

To demonstrate the behavioural impact of budgeting, we look below at three behavioural practices associated with budgeting: spending to budget; padding the budget; and creative budgeting.

(i) Spending to Budget

Many companies allocate their expense budget for the year. If the budget is not spent, then the department loses the money. This is a double whammy as often next year's budget is based on

SOUNDBITE 4.2

Spending to Budget

'People spend what's in a budget, whether they need it or not.'

George W. Sztykiel, *Fortune* (December 28, 1992)

Source: *The Wiley Book of Business Quotations* (1998), p. 90

this year's. So an underspend this year will also result in less to spend next year. It is in managers' individual interests (but not necessarily in the firm's interests) to avoid this. Managers, therefore, will spend money at the last-minute on items such as recarpeting of offices. This is the idea behind the cartoon at the start of this chapter!

PAUSE FOR THOUGHT 4.3

Spending to Budget

Jane Morris has a department and was allocated £120,000 to spend for year ended 31 December 2005. In 2006, the budget is based on the 2005 budget plus 10% inflation. She spends prudently so that by 1 December she has spent £90,000. Normal expenditure would be a further £10,000. Thus, she would have spent £100,000 in total. What might she do?

....

Well, it is possible she might give the £20,000 unspent back to head office. However, this will result in only £110,000 (£100,000 + 10%) next year. More likely she will try to spend the surplus. For example, buy

- a new computer
- new office furniture
- new carpets

REAL-LIFE NUGGET 4.3

Padding the Budget

Managers seek out and receive facts and opinions in order to arrive at an estimate of what they should ask for in the light of what they can expect to get and then, with due '*padding*' made to allow for anticipated cuts, they seek to market their budgetary demands. As in the initial example, the support of other parties can be actively canvassed and demands packaged in the most appealing form. Tangible results can be given undue weight and complex activities described in either the simplest or the most complex of terms ...
Emphasis can be placed on the qualitative rather than measurable advantages, the forthcoming rather than current results, and the procedures rather than the outcome.

Source: A. Hopwood (1974), *Accounting and Human Behaviour*, p. 56

(ii) Padding the Budget

Budgets are set by people. Therefore, there is a great temptation for individuals to try to create slack in the system to give themselves some leeway. For example, *you might think* that your department's sales next year will be £120,000 and the expenses will be £90,000. Therefore, you think you will make £30,000 profit. However, at the budgetary committee *you might argue* that your sales will be only £110,000 and your expenses will be £100,000. You are, therefore, attempting to set the budget so that your profit is £10,000 (i.e., £110,000 – £100,000). You have, therefore, built in £20,000 budgetary slack (£30,000 profit [true position] less £10,000 profit [argued position]). Real-Life Nugget 4.3 demonstrates the negotiating process involved in padding the budget.

(iii) Creative Budgeting

If departmental managers are rewarded on the basis of the profit their department makes, then they may indulge in creative budgeting. Creative budgeting may, for example, involve deferring expenditure planned for this year until next year (see, for example, Figure 4.19).

Figure 4.19   Creative Budgeting

Jasper Grant gets a bonus of £1,000 if he meets his budgeted profit of £100,000 for the year ending in December. At the end of November, he has the following information.

	£
Sales commission to date	200,000
Extra sales commission for December	25,000
Expenses to date	97,000
Expenses to be incurred	
: Weekly press advertising	3,000
: Repairs	8,000
: Necessary expenses	25,000

How can Jasper meet budget?

At the moment, Jasper's situation is as follows:

	£
Sales commission (£200,000 + £25,000)	225,000
Less: *Expenses* (£97,000 incurred + £36,000 anticipated)	133,000
Actual Profit	92,000
Budgeted Profit	100,000
Budgetary Shortfall	(8,000)

Jasper would, therefore, fail to meet his budgeted profit.

However, if the advertising and repairs were deferred until the next period, Jasper would make the budget. So he might be tempted to defer them.

	£
Sales commission	225,000
Less: Expenses to date	97,000
Necessary expenses	25,000
Actual Profit	103,000
Budgeted Profit	100,000
Surplus over Budget	3,000

Jasper would, therefore, gain his bonus as he would meet his target. However, what is good for Jasper is not necessarily good for his firm. By not advertising or having repairs done quickly it is likely that the long-term productivity of the firm will suffer.

Responsibility Accounting

The behavioural aspects of budgeting can be utilised when designing responsibility accounting systems. In such systems, organisations are divided into budgetary areas, known as responsibility centres. Managers are held accountable for the activities within these centres. As Figure 4.20 shows there are different sorts of responsibility centre.

Figure 4.20   Responsibility Centres and Managerial Accountability

Responsibility Centre	Managerial Accountability
Revenue Centre	Revenues
Cost Centre	Costs
Profit Centre	Revenues, costs and thus profits
Investment Centre	Revenues and costs (i.e., profits) and investment

Managers of investment centres thus have more responsibility than those of profit centres who in turn have more responsibility than managers of cost or revenue centres. A key aspect of responsibility accounting is that the manager is responsible for controllable costs, but not uncontrollable costs. Controllable costs are simply those costs that a manager can be expected to influence.

Responsibility accounting is a way of monitoring the activities of managers and judging their performance. The budgeted costs, revenues and profits are compared with the actual results. Managers can be rewarded or penalised accordingly often by the payment or non-payment of bonuses.

Investment centres are often evaluated using specific performance measures. Three of the most common are Return on Investment (ROI), Residual Income (RI) and Return on Sales (ROS). These three ratios are outlined in Figure 4.21.

Figure 4.21   Three Performance Measures

Ratio	Definition	Comments
i. Return on Investment (ROI)	$\dfrac{\text{Income}}{\text{Investment}}$	Simple, but often investment difficult to determine. Does not take size into account. Similar to return on capital employed.
ii. Residual Income (RI)	Income – (required rate of return × investment)	Quite simple; can use quite an arbitrary rate of return.
iii. Return on Sales (ROS)	$\dfrac{\text{Operating profit}}{\text{Sales}}$	Quite simple. Definition of profit may be difficult. Similar to net profit ratio.

Below, in Figure 4.22, is an example of how these particular measures may be used in practice. The example of three divisions of an international car hire firm is used, HireCarCo. These are based in London, Paris and Berlin.

Figure 4.22   Performance Measures for Three Divisions

HireCarCo has three operating divisions in London, Paris and Berlin. Each acts as a broadly independent investment centre. The key figures are set out below

	London	Paris	Berlin
	£m	£m	£m
Investment	1,000,000	800,000	600,000
	£m	£m	£m
Sales	500,000	350,000	200,000
Costs	(300,000)	(180,000)	(120,000)
Operating profit	200,000	170,000	80,000

Required:

Calculate   a) Return on Investment (ROI)
            b) Residual Income (RI) – assuming the required rate of return is 10 %
            c) Return on Sales (ROS)

	London	Paris	Berlin
i) Return on Investment			
$\dfrac{\text{Income}}{\text{Investment}}$	$\dfrac{£200,000}{£1,000,000} = 20\%$	$\dfrac{£170,000}{£800,000} = 21.2\%$	$\dfrac{£80,000}{£600,000} = 13.3\%$
ii) Residual Income			
Income – (Required Rate of Return × Investment)	£200,000 – (£1,000,000 × 10%) = £100,000	£170,000 – (£800,000 × 10%) = £90,000	£80,000 – (£600,000 × 10%) = £20,000
iii) Return on Sales			
$\dfrac{\text{Operating Profit}}{\text{Sales}}$	$\dfrac{£200,000}{£600,000} = 33.3\%$	$\dfrac{£170,000}{£350,000} = 48.6\%$	$\dfrac{£80,000}{£200,000} = 40\%$

From the results, it can be seen that measured by return on investment and return on sales the manager of the Paris branch would be judged to be performing the best. However, in absolute terms, the London manager has done best having the highest residual income.

Conclusion

Budgeting is planning for the future. This is important as a business needs to compare its actual performance against its targets. Most businesses prepare a cash budget and large businesses often prepare a complex set of interlocking budgets which culminate in a budgeted trading and profit and loss account and a budgeted balance sheet. Budgets have a human as well as a technical side. As well as being useful for planning and coordination, budgets are used to motivate and monitor individuals. Budgets are often used as the basis for performance evaluation. Sometimes, therefore, the interests of individuals and businesses may conflict.

Q&A   Discussion Questions

Questions with numbers in blue have answers at the back of the book.

Q1   What are the advantages and disadvantages of budgeting?

Q2   Why do some people think that the cash budget is the most important budget?

Q3   The behavioural aspects of budgeting are often overlooked, but are extremely important. Do you agree?

Q4   State whether the following statements are true or false? If false, explain why.
   (a) The four main aspects of budgets are planning, coordinating, control and motivation.
   (b) The commonest limiting factor on the budgeting process is production.
   (c) A master budget is formed by feeding in the results from all the other budgets.
   (d) Depreciation is commonly found in a cash budget.
   (e) Spending to budget, padding the budget and creative budgeting are all common behavioural responses to budgeting.

Q&A   Numerical Questions

Questions with numbers in blue have answers at the back of the book.

Q1   Jill Lee starts her business on 1 January with £15,000 in the bank. Her plans for the first six months are as follows.
   (a) Payments for goods will be made one month after purchase:

January	February	March	April	May	June
£21,000	£19,500	£18,500	£23,400	£25,900	£31,100

(b) All sales will be cash sales:

January	February	March	April	May	June
£25,200	£27,100	£21,200	£20,250	£48,300	£37,500

(c) Expenses will be £12,000 in January and will rise by 10 % per month. They will be paid in the month incurred.

Required: Prepare Jill Lee's cash budget from 1 January to 30 June.

Q2 John Rees has the following information for the six months 1 July to 31 December.
(a) Opening cash balance 1 July £8,600
(b) Sales at £25 per unit:

	April	May	June	July	Aug.	Sept.	Oct.	Nov.	Dec.
Units	100	130	150	180	200	210	220	240	280

Debtors will pay two months after they have bought the goods.
(c) Production in units:

	April	May	June	July	Aug.	Sept.	Oct.	Nov.	Dec.	Jan.
Units	140	140	140	180	200	190	200	210	260	200

(d) Raw materials costing £10 per unit are delivered in the month of production and will be paid for three months after the goods are used in production.
(e) Direct labour of £6 per unit will be payable in the same month as production.
(f) Other variable production expenses will be £6 per unit. Two-thirds of this cost will be paid for in the same month as production and one-third in the month following production.
(g) Other expenses of £200 per month will be paid one month in arrears. These expenses have been at this rate for the past two years.
(h) A machine will be bought and paid for in September for £8,000.
(i) John Rees plans to borrow £4,500 from a relative in December. This will be banked immediately.

Required: Prepare John Rees's cash budget from 1 July to 31 December.

Q3 Fly-by-Night plc has the following sales forecasts for two products: the Moon and the Star.
(a) The Moon will sell at 1,000 units in January, rising by 50 units per month. From January to March each Moon will sell at £20, with the price rising to £25 from April to June.
(b) The Star will sell 2,000 units in January rising by 100 units per month. Each Star will sell at £10.

Required: Prepare the sales budget for Fly-by-Night from January to June.

Q4 David Ingo has opening debtors of £2,400 (November £1,400, December £1,000). The debtors will pay two months in arrears. Credit sales in January will be £1,000 rising by 10 % per month.

Required: Prepare D. Ingo's debtors budget for January to June.

Q5 Thomas Iger has opening creditors of £2,900 (£400 October, £1,200 November, £1,300 December). Creditors will be paid three months in arrears. Credit purchases in January will be £2,000 rising by £200 per month until March and then suffering a 10 % decline in April and remaining constant.

Required: Prepare T. Iger's creditors budget for January to June.

Q6 Brenda Ear will have production costs per unit of £5 raw materials, £5.50 direct labour and £2 variable overheads. Production will be 700 units in January rising by 50 units per month.

Required: Prepare B. Ear's production cost budget for January to June.

Q7 Roger Abbit has £1,000 opening stocks of raw materials. Purchases will be £900 in January rising by £200 per month. Production will be 240 units from January to March at £4 raw materials per unit, rising to 250 units per month at £5 raw materials per unit from April to June.

Required: Prepare R. Abbit's raw materials budget for January to June.

Q8 Freddie Ox has £9,000 of opening finished goods stocks. In July, 1,500 units will be produced at a production cost of £10 each. Production will increase at 100 units per month; production cost remains steady. Sales will be £15,000 in July rising by £1,500 per month. Gross profit is 20 % of sales.

Required: Prepare F. Ox's finished goods budget for July–December.

Q9 Asia is a small non-listed manufacturing company. There are the following details.

Asia Ltd
Abridged Balance Sheet as at 31 December 2005

	£	£	£
Fixed Assets			99,500
Current Assets			
Debtors (Nov. £10,000, Dec. £11,000)	21,000		
Stock (raw materials)	10,000		
Stock (finished goods)	9,500	40,500	
Current Liabilities			
Creditors (Nov. £3,500, Dec. £3,500)	(7,000)		
Bank	(8,000)	(15,000)	
Net current assets			25,500
Total net assets			125,000
Share Capital and Reserves			£
Share Capital			
Ordinary share capital			103,000
Reserves			
Profit and loss account			22,000
Total shareholders' funds			125,000

Notes

1. Fixed assets are at cost. Depreciation is at 10 % straight line basis per year.
2. Purchases will be £4,800 in January increasing by £200 per month. They will be paid two months after purchase.
3. Sales will be £15,000 in January increasing by £400 per month. Debtors pay two months in arrears. They will be based on market price with no formal mark-up from gross profit.
4. Production cost per unit will be: direct materials £12; direct labour £10; production overheads £2 (direct labour and production overheads will be paid in the month incurred). Production 400 units per month. Sales 380 units per month.
5. Expenses will run at £6,000 per month. They will be paid in the month incurred.

Required: Prepare sales budget, cash budget, debtors budget, creditors budget, production cost budget, raw materials budget, finished goods budget, trading and profit and loss account and balance sheet for six months ending 30 June 2005.

Q10 Peter Jenkins manages a department and has the following budget for the year.

	£	£
Sales	100,000	
Discretionary costs:		
Purchases	(20,000)	
Advertising	(10,000)	
Training	(8,000)	
Repairs	(19,000)	(57,000)
		43,000
Non-discretionary costs:		
Labour (split equally throughout the year)		(18,000)
Profit		25,000

Peter receives a budget of 10 % of profit for any quarter in which he makes a minimum profit of £8,000. If he makes less than £8,000 profit, he receives no bonus. Any quarter in which he makes a loss he will earn no profit, but will not incur a penalty.

Required: Calculate the maximum and minimum bonuses Peter could expect. Assume Peter has *complete discretion* about when the sales will be earned and when the discretionary costs will be incurred.

Q11 All Sunshine Enterprises runs a hire car service in three locations: London, Oslo and Stockholm. The three operating divisions have the following results for the year.

	London	Oslo	Stockholm
	£m	£m	£m
Investment	2,000,000	1,000,000	500,000
	£m	£m	£m
Sales	1,500,000	800,000	300,000
Costs	(800,000)	(400,000)	(135,000)
Operating profit	700,000	400,000	165,000

Required:
Calculate
    a) Return on Investment (ROI)
    b) Residual Income (RI) – assuming the required rate of return is 12 %
    c) Return on Sales (ROS)

Which is the best relative measure for each division?

Chapter 5

"No amount of planning will ever replace dumb luck."

Anonymous

Source: *The Executive's Book of Quotations* (1994), p. 217

Learning Outcomes

After completing this chapter you should be able to:

✔ Explain the nature and importance of standard costing.

✔ Outline the most important variances.

✔ Calculate variances and prepare a standard costing operating statement.

✔ Interpret the variances.

Planning, Control and Performance: Standard Costing

In a Nutshell

- *Costing, and planning, control and performance are the two main branches of cost accounting.*

- *Standard costing, along with budgeting, is one of the key aspects of planning, control and performance.*

- *Standard costing is a sophisticated form of budgeting based on predetermined costs for cost elements such as direct labour or direct materials.*

- *There are sales and cost variances.*

- *Variances are deviations of the actual results from the standard results.*

- *Standard cost variances can be divided into quantity variances and price variances.*

- *There are direct materials, direct labour, variable overheads and fixed overheads cost variances.*

- *Standard cost variances are investigated to see why they have occurred.*

Introduction

Cost accounting has two main branches: costing, and planning, control and performance. Standard costing, along with budgeting, is one of the two parts of planning, control and performance. Standard costing can be seen as a more specialised and formal type of budgeting. A particular feature of standard costing is the breakdown of costs into various cost components such as direct labour, direct materials, variable overheads and fixed overheads. In standard costing, **expected (or standard) sales or costs are compared against actual sales or costs**. Any differences between them (called **variances**) are then investigated. Variances are divided into those based on quantity and those based on prices. Standard costing, therefore, links the future (i.e., expected costs) to the past (i.e., costs that were actually incurred). Standard costing has proved a useful planning and control tool in many industries.

Nature of Standard Costing

Standard costing is a sophisticated form of budgeting. Standard costing was originally developed in manufacturing industries in order to control costs. Essentially, standard costing involves investigating, often in some detail, the distinct costing elements which make up a product such as direct materials, direct labour, variable overheads and fixed overheads. After this investigation the costs which should be incurred in making a product or service are determined. For example, a table might be expected to be made using eight hours of direct labour and three metres of wood. These become the standard quantities for making a table.

DEFINITION 5.1

Standard Cost

Working definition
A predetermined calculation of the costs that *should* be incurred in making a product.

Formal definition
'The planned unit cost of the products, components or services produced in a period. The standard cost may be determined on a number of bases. The main uses of standard costs are in performance measurement, control, stock valuation and in the establishment of selling prices.'

Source: Chartered Institute of Management Accounting (2000), *Official Terminology*

After a table is made the direct labour and direct materials actually used are compared with the standard. For example, if nine hours are taken rather than eight, this is one hour worse than standard. However, if two metres of wood rather than three metres are used, this is one metre better than standard.

These differences from standard are called variances, which may be favourable (i.e., we have performed better than expected) or unfavourable (i.e., we have performed worse than expected). Unfavourable variances are sometimes called adverse variances. The essence of a good standard costing system is to establish the reason for any variances. Although standard costing is associated with manufacturing industry, it can be adopted in other industries, such as hotel and catering.

Setting standards involves making a decision about whether you are aiming for ideal, attainable or normal standards. They are all different. As Real-Life Nugget 5.1 shows, there is no such thing as a perfect standard. Ideal standards are those which would be attained in an ideal world. Unfortunately, the real world differs from the ideal world. Attainable standards are more realistic and can be reached with effort. Normal standards are those which a business usually attains. Attainable standards are the standards most often used by organisations.

REAL-LIFE NUGGET 5.1

A Manager under Pressure

'We had unrealistic production allowances in the budget last year, but I got them adjusted a bit. It's done by the industrial engineers and the accountants, but I have a bit of a say in it. Some are too slack now, but they are very workable. There is never a perfect standard. The industrial engineers are back in the caveman era. Well, if there is going to be some imperfections, why not have them in my favour? We can modify them and we have done quite well. Why should I beat myself'

Source: A. Hopwood, *Accounting and Human Behaviour* (1974), p. 82

Standards are usually set by industrial engineers in conjunction with accountants. This often causes friction with the workers who are actually monitored by the standards. Real-Life

Nugget 5.2 gives a flavour of these tensions.

REAL-LIFE NUGGET 5.2

Setting the Standards

'Remember those bastards are out to screw you, and that's all they got to think about. They'll stay up half the night figuring out how to beat you out of a dime. They figure you're going to try to fool them, so they make allowances for that. They set [rates] low enough to allow for what you do. It's up to you to figure out how to fool them more than they allow for....'

Source: W.P. Whyte, *Money and Motivation* (1955), pp. 15–16, as quoted in A. Hopwood, *Accounting and Human Behaviour* (1974), p. 6

Standard Cost Variances

In order to explain how standard costing works, the illustration of manufacturing a table is continued. In a succession of examples, more detail is gradually introduced. Figure 5.1 introduces the basic overview information for Alan Carpenter who is setting up a furniture business. In May, he makes a prototype table. To simplify the presentation in the figures *favourable* variances are shorted to 'Fav'. and *unfavourable* variances to 'Unfav'.

Figure 5.1   Overview of Standard Costs for Alan Carpenter for May

	Standard £	Actual £	Variance £	
Sales	30	33	3	Fav.
Costs	20	22	(2)	Unfav.
Profit	10	11	1	Fav.

Before the prototype table was actually made, Alan Carpenter thought it would cost £20 and that he could sell it for £30. He, therefore, anticipated a profit of £10. In actual fact, the table was sold for £33. Carpenter thus made £3 more sales than anticipated. However, the table cost £22 (£2 more than anticipated). Overall, therefore, actual profit is £11 rather than the predicted standard profit of £10. Carpenter benefits £3 from selling well, but loses £2 through excessive costs. There is an overall favourable sales variance of £3, and an overall unfavourable cost variance of £2 which gives a £1 favourable profit variance.

We now expand the example and look at Alan Carpenter's operations for June. In June he anticipates making and selling 10 tables. In actual fact, he makes and sells only 9 tables (see Figure 5.2).

Figure 5.2   Standard Costs for Alan Carpenter for June

	Budget 10 Tables £	Actual 9 Tables £
Sales	300	290
Costs	200	170
Profit	100	120

Calculation of variances

i. Flex the Budget

	Budget 10 Tables £	Flexed Budget 9 Tables £	Actual 9 Tables £	Variance £	
Sales	300	270	290	20	Fav.
Costs	200	180	170	10	Fav.
Profit	100	90	120	30	Fav.

ii. Calculate Variances

	£	
Budgeted Profit	100	
Sales quantity variance (1 table at £10 profit)	(10)	Unfav.
Budgeted profit for actual production	90	
Sales price variance	20	Fav.
Cost variance	10	Fav.
Actual Profit	120	

Before calculating the variances, we must flex the budget. Flexing the budget simply means adjusting the budget to take into account the *actual quantity produced*. We need to do this because we need to calculate the costs *which would have been incurred if we actually made nine tables*. If we made only nine tables, we would logically expect to incur costs for nine rather than ten tables. In addition, we would expect to sell nine not ten tables. The budget must, therefore, be calculated on the basis of the nine actual tables made rather than the ten predicted.

PAUSE FOR THOUGHT 5.1

Flexing the Budget

Why would it be so misleading if we failed to flex our budget?

....

If we failed to flex our budget then we would not compare like with like. For example, we would be trying to compare costs based on an output of ten tables with costs incurred actually making nine tables. We need to adjust for this, otherwise the budget will be distorted.

By making nine rather than ten tables, the profit for one table is lost. This was £10 (as there was £100 profit for ten tables). There is thus a £10 drop in profits. This is called a **sales quantity variance**. (Note that we are *assuming*, at this stage, that all the *costs will vary in direct relation to the number of tables*.)

We can now compare the sales and costs actually earned and incurred for nine tables with those that were expected to be earned and incurred. As Figure 5.2 shows, the nine tables were expected to sell for £270, but were actually sold for £290. In other words, we received £20 more than we had anticipated for our tables. This was the **sales price variance**. Note that the sales quantity variance is caused by lost profit. By contrast, the sales price variance is caused by the fact we are selling the tables for more than we anticipated. There is thus a **favourable sales price variance** of £20.

The budgeted cost for nine tables was £180. However, the actual cost incurred is only £170. There is thus a favourable cost variance of £10. The difference between the budgeted profit of £100 and the actual profit of £120 can be explained by these three variances (unfavourable sales quantity variance (£10), favourable sales price variance (£20), and favourable cost variance (£10)).

So far, we have seen that it is important to flex the budget, and looked at the sales volume variance and the sales price variance. It is now time to look in more detail at the cost variances. When looking at cost variances, it is important to distinguish between variable and fixed costs. As we saw in Chapter 2, variable costs are those costs that directly vary with a product or service (for example, direct materials, direct labour or production overheads). The more products made, the more the variable costs. Thus, if it costs £20 to make one table, it will cost £200 to make ten tables. Fixed costs, however, do not vary. You will pay the building's insurance of £10 per month whether you make one table or 100 tables. In continuing the Alan Carpenter example, the costs are now divided into fixed and variable.

Essentially, *all the variable costs* (direct materials, direct labour, and variable overheads) *have two elements – price and quantity*. For example, when making a table we might predict using the following standard prices and standard quantities:

	Price		Quantity
Direct labour	£5 per hour	for	2 hours
Direct materials	£1 per metre	for	5 metres of wood
Variable overheads (incurred on basis of direct labour hours)	£2.0 per hour	for	2 hours

When our actual price and actual quantity vary from standard, we will have price and quantity variances. In other words, the overall cost variances for direct labour, direct materials and variable overheads can be divided into a quantity and a price variance. **Price variances** are caused when the **standard price** of a product *differs* from the **actual price. Quantity variances** are caused when the **standard quantity** *differs* from the **actual quantity.** These differences between the standard and the actual quantity when multiplied by standard price will give us the overall quantity variance. Favourable variances are where we have done better than expected; unfavourable variances are where we have done worse than expected. For fixed overheads, which do not vary with production, we compare the actual fixed overheads incurred with the standard. We call this difference, the fixed overheads quantity variance.

An overview of all these variances is given in Figure 5.3 and in Figure 5.4 the main elements of all the variances are summarised. For simplification, this book uses the terms price and quantity variances throughout. Often, however, more technical terminology is used (these alternative technical terms are shown in the second column of Figure 5.4).

Figure 5.3   Diagram of Main Variances

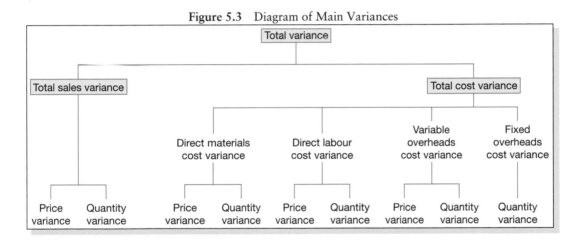

Figure 5.4   Calculation of the Main Variances

Variances	Technical Name	Calculation
i. SALES *(a) Overall Variance*	Sales	Not usual to calculate an overall sales variance
(b) Price	Price	(Standard price per unit – actual price per unit) × actual quantity of units sold
(c) Quantity	Volume	(Standard quantity of units sold – actual quantity of units sold) × standard contribution per unit

Figure 5.4   Calculation of the Main Variances (*continued*)

ii. COSTS		
Direct Materials		
(a) Overall Variance	Cost	Standard cost of materials for actual production less actual cost of materials used in production
(b) Price	Price	(Standard price per unit of material – actual price per unit of material) × actual quantity of materials used.
(c) Quantity	Usage	(Standard quantity of materials for actual production – actual quantity of materials used) × standard material price per unit of materials
Direct Labour		
(a) Overall Variance	Cost	Standard cost of labour for actual production less actual cost of labour used in production
(b) Price	Rate	(Standard price per hour – actual price per hour) × actual quantity of labour hours used
(c) Quantity	Efficiency	(Standard quantity of labour hours for actual production – actual quantity of labour hours used) × standard labour price per hour
Variable Overheads		
(a) Overall Variance	Cost	Standard cost of variable overheads for actual production less actual cost of variable overheads for production
(b) Price	Efficiency	(Standard variable overhead price per hour – actual variable overheads prices per hour) × actual quantity of labour hours used
(c) Quantity	Expenditure	(Standard quantity of labour hours for actual production – actual quantity of labour hours used) × standard variable overheads price per hour
Fixed Overheads		
(a) Quantity	Spending	(Standard fixed overheads – actual fixed overheads)

Figure 5.4   Calculation of the Main Variances (*continued*)

Helpnote
At first sight this table looks daunting. However, in essence the way we calculate all the overall variances, price variances and quantity variances is remarkably similar. The key essentials are explained below. *Note that in standard costing, standard refers to the budget.*

i. Overall Variances
Here we are interested in comparing the budgeted cost of the actual items we produce **(standard cost of actual production)** with the actual cost of items we produce **(actual cost of production).** The only variation is whether we are talking about direct materials, direct labour or variable overheads. The overall variance can be split into **price and quantity variances.** There is no overall variance for sales or fixed overheads. It is important to realise that, in practice, the **overall variance is normally calculated just by flexing the budget.** The difference between the flexed budget and the actual results gives the overall variance.

ii. Price Variances
Here we are interested in comparing the **standard price for the actual quantity used or sold** with the **actual price for the actual quantity used or sold.** The only variation is whether we are relating this to sales, direct materials, direct labour, or variable overheads. For variable overheads we use the actual quantity of labour hours used, as we are recovering variable overheads using labour hours. There is no price variance for fixed overheads. The standard formula is:

(Standard price – actual price) × actual quantity used or sold

iii. Quantity Variances
In this case, we are interested in comparing the budgeted cost of the actual items produced or sold **(standard cost of actual production or standard quantity for sales)** with the actual quantity produced or sold **(actual quantity used or sold).** This gives us the quantity difference. This is then multiplied by the standard contribution per item for the sales variance and by the standard price per unit **(normally, metres or hours)** for the other variances. The only variation is whether we are considering the standard price of direct materials, direct labour or variable overheads, or the standard selling price. For variable overheads, we use the standard quantity of labour hours and the actual quantity of labour hours used as we are recovering variable overheads using labour hours. The standard formula is:

Standard quantity of actual production (or, for sales, standard quantity for sales) less actual quantity used (or, for sales, actual quantity sold) × standard price (or, for sales, standard contribution per item)

For fixed overheads, the quantity variance is simply standard fixed overheads less actual fixed overheads.

In order to see how these variances all interlock, we now expand the Alan Carpenter example (see Figure 5.5).

Figure 5.5   Worked Example: Alan Carpenter's Standard Costs for June

i. Standard Cost per Table	£	£
Selling Price		30
Direct materials: 5 metres of wood at £1 per metre	(5)	
Direct labour: 2 hours at £5 per hour	(10)	
Variable overheads (recovered on labour hours): 2 hours at £2 per hour	(4)	
Fixed overheads: £10 in total divided by 10 tables	(1)	(20)
Budgeted Profit		10

ii. Budgeted (i.e. standard) Results for June: 10 Tables	£	£
Selling Price		300
Direct materials: 50 metres of wood at £1 per metre	(50)	
Direct labour: 20 hours at £5 per hour	(100)	
Variable overheads: 20 hours at £2 per hour	(40)	
Fixed overheads	(10)	(200)
Budgeted Profit		100

iii. Actual Results for June: 9 Tables	£	£
Selling Price		290
Direct materials: 44 metres of wood at £1.20 per metre	(52.80)	
Direct labour: 16 hours at £5.50	(88.00)	
Variable overheads	(33.00)	
Fixed overheads	(12.20)	(186)
Actual Profit		104

Using Figure 5.5, we now calculate the variances in two steps: flexing the budget and calculating the individual variances.

Flexing the Budget

Note that fixed overheads are not flexed! This is because by their very nature they do not vary with production. The flexed budget is used in the calculation of variances so that the levels of activity are the same and can be used as a basis for meaningful comparisons.

	Budget (i.e., standard)		Flexed Budget (i.e., standard quantity of actual production)		Actual Results		Overall Variances	
	10 Tables		9 Tables		9 Tables			
	£	£	£	£	£	£	£	
Sales		300		270		290.00	20.00	Fav.
Direct materials	(50)		(45)		(52.80)		(7.80)	Unfav.
Direct labour	(100)		(90)		(88.00)		2.00	Fav.
Variable overheads	(40)	(190)	(36)	(171)	(33.00)	(173.80)	3.00	Fav.
Contribution*		110		99		116.20		
Fixed overheads		(10)		(10)		(12.20)	(2.20)	Unfav.
Profit		100		89		104.00		

*This is sometimes known as profit before fixed overheads.

By flexing the budget, *we have automatically calculated (1) the sales price variance, and (2) the overall cost variances* for direct materials, direct labour and variable overheads. It is important to note that the *flexed budget gives us the standard quantity of the actual production.* The cost variances will then be broken down into the individual price and quantity variances (see Figure 5.6). However, *first* we need to calculate the sales quantity variance.

Calculating Individual Variances

(a) Sales Quantity Variance

Standard quantity of units sold	−	actual quantity of units sold	×	contribution*	
10	−	9	×	£11**	= £ 11 Unfav.

Notes:

* This is budgeted profit before fixed overheads (£110) divided by the budgeted number of tables (10). Therefore, we have, £110 ÷ 10 = £11. Note that this is calculated *before* fixed overheads. This is because fixed overheads will remain the same whatever the value of sales. They must be excluded from the calculation and their variance calculated separately.
** This represents the difference between the budgeted profit (£100) less the flexed budget (£89). *In practice, this is the easiest way to calculate this variance.*

(b) Individual Price and Quantity Variances

When we calculate the price and quantity variances based on our flexed budget, we can use the standard price and quantity formulas given below (see Figure 5.6). We then need to remember that the standard price for sales is the standard selling price per unit, for direct materials it is the price per unit of direct materials used and so on. For quantity we need to remember that we are concerned with the standard quantity of materials, labour, etc. Figure 5.6 is based on Figure 5.5 and our flexed budget.

Figure 5.6   Calculation of Individual Price and Quantity Variances for Alan Carpenter

Overall Variance =	Price Variance +	Quantity Variance
	(standard price – actual price sold or used) × actual quantity sold or used	*(standard quantity of actual production – actual quantity used) × standard price*
(a) *Sales* *i. Sales price* *Note the sales price variance is automatically given by flexing the budget*	**Price calculations** **Notes** (£30 – £32.22*) × 9 tables = £20 Fav. **(1)** *£290 sold ÷ 9 tables sold = (£32.22)	**Quantity calculations** **Notes** ii. Sales quantity See calculation above (2a) for **(2)** sales quantity variance
(b) *Direct Materials* Overall **(£7.80) Unfav.**	(£1– £1.20 × 44 metres = (£8.80) *Unfav.* **(3)** = **(£8.80) Unfav.** **+**	 (45 metres – 44 metres) × £1 = £1 Fav. **(4)** **£1 Fav.**
(c) *Direct Labour* Overall **£18 Fav**	(£5 – £5.50) × 16 hours = **£8 Unfav.** **(5)** = **£8 Unfav.** **+**	 (18 hours – 16 hours) × £5 = £10 Fav. **(6)** **£10 Fav.**
(d) *Variable Overheads* Overall **£3 Fav.**	(£2.00 – £2.06*) × 16 hours = (£1) *Unfav.* **(7)** *£33 actual at 16 hours = £2.06 per hour = **(£1) Unfav.** **+**	 (18 hours – 16 hours) × £2 = £4 Fav. **(8)** **£4 Fav.**
(e) *Fixed Overheads* Overall **(£2.20) Unfav.**	 **=**	Standard less actual £10 – £12.20 = (£2.20) *Unfav.* **(9)** **(£2.20) Unfav.**

Notes:
1. **Sales Price Variance:** The standard selling price is £30 per unit. However, we sell at £32.22 per table (£290 ÷ 9). Therefore, overall, across the nine tables, we make £20 (9 × £2.22) more than we expected.
2. **Sales Quantity Variance:** The standard quantity expected to be sold was ten tables. We actually sold nine tables. Therefore, we lose the contribution on one table of £11. This was the overall contribution expected of £110 divided by the standard quantity of ten tables.
3. **Direct Materials Price Variance:** The standard price (£1.00) per metre is less than the actual price (£1.20) paid per metre by £0.20 pence per metre. As 44 metres were used this results in an unfavourable variance of £8.80.
4. **Direct Materials Quantity Variance:** The standard quantity to make nine tables is 45 metres. However, only 44 were actually used. As the standard price was £1 per metre, Alan Carpenter gains £1, which is a favourable variance.
5. **Direct Labour Price Variance:** The standard price (£5.00) per labour hour is less than the actual price paid (£5.50). As 16 labour hours were used, the result is an £8 unfavourable variance.
6. **Direct Labour Quantity Variance:** The standard quantity to make nine tables is 18 hours. Alan Carpenter has taken 16 hours. As the standard price per labour hour is £5, there is a £10 favourable variance.
7. **Variable Overhead Price Variance:** The standard recovery rate is £2.00 per hour. However, Alan Carpenter has recovered £33 in the 16 hours actually worked (i.e., £2.0625 per hour). Given the 16 hours worked, this results in an overall over-recovery of £1 (i.e. 16 × £0.0625). In other words, we expected to recover £32, but we actually recovered £33 (16 hours × £2.06). We thus recovered £1 more than expected, which is unfavourable.
8. **Variable Overheads Quantity Variance:** It was anticipated that 18 hours would be used to recover variable overheads. In actual fact, 16 hours were used. Since £2 per hour is recovered, there is an under-recovery of £4. This is favourable.
9. **Fixed Overhead Volume Variance:** The fixed overhead was expected to be £10. In fact, it was £12.20. This is £2.20 more than expected. Therefore, we have a £2.20 unfavourable variance.

We can now draw up a standard cost reconciliation statement. This statement reconciles the budgeted profit of £100 to the actual profit of £104.

Alan Carpenter: Standard Cost Reconciliation Statement for June			
	£	£	£
Budgeted Profit			100
Sales quantity variance			(11) Unfav.
Budgeted Profit at Actual Sales			89
	Fav.	Unfav.	
Variances	£	£	
Sales price	20		
Direct materials price		8.80	
Direct materials quantity	1		
Direct labour price		8	
Direct labour quantity	10		
Variable overhead price		1.00	
Variable overhead quantity	4		
Fixed overhead variance	—	2.20	
	35	20.00	15 Fav.
Actual Profit			104

Interpretation of Variances

A key aspect of both budgeting and standard costing is the investigation of variances. In Figure 5.7 we look at some possible reasons for variances.

Figure 5.7   Possible Causes of Variances

Variance	Favourable	Unfavourable
1. Sales Quantity	We sell more than we expect because of • good market conditions • good marketing.	We sell less than we expect because of • poor market conditions • bad marketing.
2. Sales Price	We sell at a higher price than expected because of • unexpected market demand • good economy.	We sell at a lower price than expected because of • tough competition • poor economy.
3. Direct Materials Quantity	We use more material than expected because of • poor-quality material • sloppy production.	We use less material than expected because of • high-quality material • efficient production.
4. Direct Materials Price	Our material costs are more than expected because of • a price rise.	Our material costs are less than we expect because • we find an alternative cheaper supplier.
5. Direct Labour Quantity	We use more labour than we expected because of • inefficient cheaper workers who take longer • labour problems.	We use less labour than expected because of • efficient workers who are quicker.
6. Fixed Overheads	The overall costs are more than expected because of • inflation.	The overhead costs are less than expected because • we change to a cheaper source.

These variances represent differences in what actually happened to what we expected to happen. It must be remembered that variances are only as good as the original budgets or standards that are set. Therefore, if unrealistic, incorrect or unattainable standards are set, this will create misleading variances. As we saw earlier, setting the original standards can often cause severe tensions between the standard setters and the employees. In standard costing a more sophisticated, systematic approach is taken to the investigation of variances than in budgeting.

The nature of variable overheads means that these variances are tied into the basis of absorption (for example, direct labour hours). The causes for the variable overhead variances will, therefore, tend to reflect those for the direct labour hours. It is not, therefore, particularly meaningful to investigate the reasons for these variances separately. Variable overheads have, therefore, been excluded from Figure 5.7.

SOUNDBITE 5.1

Behavioural Aspects of Standards

'All persons concerned with setting standards are striving to gain some measure of personal control over factors which are important in their organisational lives.'

Source: A. Hopwood, *Accounting and Human Behaviour* (1974), pp. 6–7

PAUSE FOR THOUGHT 5.2

Compensating Variances

Why might there be compensating variances? For example, an unfavourable material quantity variance, but a favourable material price variance.

Sometimes the quantity and price variances are interconnected. For example, we plan to make a product and we budget for a high quality material. If we then substitute a low quality material, it will be likely to cost less. However, we will need to use more. Therefore, we would have an unfavourable material quantity variance, but a favourable price variance.

Conclusion

Standard costing is a sophisticated form of budgeting. It was originally used in manufacturing industries, but is now much more widespread. Standard costing involves predetermining the cost of the various elements of a product or service (such as selling price, direct materials, direct labour and variable overheads). These standard costs are then compared with the actual costs and any differences, called variances, investigated. These variances are split into price and quantity variances. Standard costing allows costs to be monitored very closely. In many businesses, it is thus a very useful form of planning, control and performance.

Q&A   Discussion Questions

Questions with numbers in blue have answers at the back of the book.

Q1 'Setting the standards is the most difficult part of standard costing.'
What considerations should be taken into account when setting standards?

Q2 'Standard costing is good for planning and control, but unless great care is taken can often be very demotivational.' Discuss.

Q3 Standard costing is more about control than motivation. Do you agree with this statement?

Q4 'The key to standard setting is providing a good, fair initial set of standards.' Discuss.

Q5 State whether the following statements are true or false. If false, explain why.
(a) Favourable cost variances are where actual costs are less than standard costs.
(b) Flexing the budget means adjusting the budget to take into account the actual prices incurred.
(c) Price and quantity variances are the main constituents of the overall cost variances.
(d) The direct materials price variance is: (standard price per unit of material – actual price per unit of material) × actual quantity of materials used.
(e) The direct labour quantity variance is: (standard price of labour hours for actual production – actual price of labour hours used) × standard labour price per hour.

Q&A   Numerical Questions

Questions with numbers in blue have answers at the back of the book.

Q1 Stuffed restaurant has the following results for May 2006

	Budget	Actual
Number of meals	10,000	12,000
	£	£
Price per meal	10.00	10.60
Food cost	30,000	37,200
Labour cost	35,000	36,000
Variable overheads	5,000	6,000
Fixed overheads	3,000	3,100

Required:

(a) Calculate the flexed budget.

(b) Calculate the sales price variance.

(c) Calculate the overall cost variances for materials, labour, variable overheads and fixed overheads (note: you do not have enough information to calculate the more detailed price and quantity variances).

(d) Calculate the sales quantity variance.

(e) Discuss the variances. In particular, highlight what extra information might be needed.

Q2   Engines Incorporated, a small engineering company, has the following results for April 2006 for its product, the Widget. It budgeted to sell 12,500 widgets at £9.00 each. However, 16,000 widgets were actually sold at £8.80 each. The budgeted and actual costs are given below.

	Budget	Actual
Number of widgets	12,500	16,000
	£	£
Price per widget	9.00	8.80
Direct materials	40,000	42,000
Labour cost	32,000	29,000
Variable overheads	6,000	8,000
Fixed overheads	8,000	10,000

Required:

(i) Calculate the flexed budget.

(ii) Calculate the sales price and sales quantity variances.

(iii) Calculate the overall cost variances for materials, labour, variable overheads and fixed overheads (note: you do not have enough information to calculate the more detailed price and quantity variances).

(iv) Discuss the variances. In particular, highlight what extra information might be needed.

Q3   Birch Manufacturing makes bookcases. The company has the following details of its June production.

	Estimated	Actual
Number of bookcases	10,000	11,000
Metres of wood	100,000	120,000
Price per metre	0.50p	0.49p

Required: Calculate the:

(i) overall direct materials cost variance

(ii) direct materials price variance

(iii) direct materials quantity variance.

Q4 Sweatshop has the following details of direct labour used to make tracksuits for July.
(a) Standard: 550 sweatshirts at 2 hours at £5.50 per hour.
(b) Actual production: 500 sweatshirts at 1,050 hours for £5,880.

Required: Calculate the:
(i) overall direct labour cost variance
(ii) direct labour price variance
(iii) direct labour quantity variance.

Q5 Toycare manufactures puzzlegames. It has the following details of its March production.

	Estimated	Actual
Number of puzzlegames	11,000	12,000
Kilos of raw materials	5,500	4,800
Price per kilo	0.45p	0.46p
Direct labour (hours)	6,600	4,800
Direct labour price per hour	£5.50	£5.30

Required: Calculate the:
(i) overall direct materials cost variance
(ii) direct materials price variance
(iii) direct materials quantity variance
(iv) overall direct labour cost variance
(v) direct labour price variance
(vi) direct labour quantity variance.

Q6 Wonderworld has the following details for its variable overheads for August for its Teleporter. Each Teleporter is expected to take two labour hours and variable overheads are expected to be £2.50 per labour hour. Wonderworld expects to make 100,000 teleporters. In actual fact, it makes 110,000 teleporters using 230,000 labour hours. Its budgeted fixed overheads were £10,000. However, it actually spends £9,800 on fixed overheads. Actual variable overheads are £517,500.

Required: Calculate the:
(i) overall variable overheads cost variance
(ii) variable overheads price variance
(iii) variable overheads quantity variance
(iv) fixed overheads variance.

Q7   Special Manufacturers has the following details for its variable overheads for July on its Startrek product. Each Startrek is expected to take three labour hours and variable overheads are expected to be £4.25 per labour hour. The firm expects to make 200,000 Startreks. In actual fact, it makes 180,000 Startreks using 630,000 labour hours. Its budgeted fixed overheads were £25,000. However, it actually spends £23,000 on fixed overheads. Actual variable overheads are £2,800,000.

Required: Calculate the:
  (i) overall variable overheads cost variance
 (ii) variable overheads price variance
(iii) variable overheads quantity variance
(iv) fixed overheads variance.

Q8   Peter Peacock plc manufactures a subcomponent for the car industry. There are the following details for August.
(a) *Budgeted data*
    Sales: 200,000 subcomponents at £2.80 each
    Direct labour: 40,000 hours at £7.25 per hour
    Direct materials: 100,000 sheets of metal at £1.25 each
    Variable overheads: £40,000 recovered at £1.00 per direct labour hour
    Fixed overheads: £68,000
(b) *Actual data*
    220,000 subcomponents were actually sold and produced
    Sales: 220,000 subcomponents at £2.78 each
    Direct labour: 43,500 hours at £7.30 per hour
    Direct material: 125,000 sheets of metal at £1.20
    Variable overheads: £42,500
    Fixed overheads: £67,000

Required:
  (i) Calculate the flexed budget and overall variances.
 (ii) Calculate the individual price and quantity variances.
(iii) Calculate a standard cost reconciliation statement for August.
(iv) Comment on the results.

Q9 Supersonic plc manufactures an assembly mounting for the aircraft industry. In July, it was expected that 80,000 assembly mountings would be sold at £18.80 each. In actual fact, 76,000 assembly mountings were sold for £20.00 each. The cost data are provided below.

	Budgeted data	Actual data
Direct materials	200,000 sheets of metal at £2.10 each	150,000 sheets of metal at £2.20 each
Direct labour	50,000 hours at £8.00 per hour	51,000 hours at £7.50 per hour
Variable overheads	£45,000 recovered at £0.90 per direct labour hour	£41,000
Fixed overheads	£78,000	£80,000

Required:

(i) Calculate the flexed budget and overall variances.

(ii) Calculate the individual price and quantity variances.

(iii) Calculate a standard cost reconciliation statement for July.

(iv) Comment on the results.

Chapter 6

"So there I was, fresh from the annual meeting of the Society for Judgement and Decision Making, and behaving like Buridan's Ass – the imaginary creature which starved midway between two troughs of hay because it couldn't decide which to go for."

Ditherer's Dilemma, Peter Aytan, *New Scientist*, **12 February 2000, p. 47**

Learning Outcomes

After completing this chapter you should be able to:

✔ **Explain the nature of short-term business decisions.**

✔ **Understand the concept of contribution analysis.**

✔ **Investigate some of the decisions for which contribution analysis is useful.**

✔ **Draw up break-even charts and contribution graphs.**

Short-Term Decision Making

In a Nutshell

- *In business, decision making involves choosing between alternatives and involves looking forward, using relevant information and financial evaluation.*

- *Businesses face a range of short-term decisions such as how to maximise limited resources.*

- *It is useful to distinguish between costs that vary with production or sales (variable costs) and costs that do not (fixed costs).*

- *Sales less variable costs equals contribution.*

- *Contribution less fixed costs equals net profit.*

- *Contribution and contribution per unit are useful when making short-term business decisions.*

- *Contribution analysis can help determine which products or services are most profitable, which are making losses, whether to buy externally rather than make internally and how to maximise the use of a limited resource.*

- *Throughput accounting attempts to remove bottlenecks from a production system; it treats direct labour and variable overheads as fixed.*

- *Break-even analysis shows the point at which a product makes neither a profit nor a loss.*

- *Both break-even charts and contribution graphs are useful ways of portraying business information.*

Introduction

Businesses, like individuals, are continually involved in decision making. A decision is simply a choice between alternatives. It is forward looking. Business decisions may be long-term strategic ones about raising long-term finance or capital expenditure. Alternatively, the decisions may be short-term, day-to-day, operational ones, such as whether to continue making a particular product. This particular chapter looks at short-term decisions. When making short-term decisions, it is important to consider only factors relevant to the decision. Depreciation, for example, will not generally change whatever the short-term decision. It is not, therefore, included in the short-term decision-making calculations.

Decision Making

Individuals make decisions all the time. These may be short-term decisions: Shall we go out or stay in? If we go out, do we go for a meal, to the cinema or to a pub? Or long-term decisions: Shall we get married? Shall we buy a house? These decisions involve choosing between various competing alternatives.

Managers also make continual decisions about the short-term and long-term future. Shall we make a new product or not? Which product shall we make: A or B? Figure 6.1 gives some examples of short-term business decisions.

Figure 6.1   Some Short-Term Managerial Decisions

- Which products should the business continue to make this year?
- Which departments should the business close down this year?
- How should the business maximise limited resources this year?
- At what level of production does the business currently break even?
- How can the business maximise current profits?

Whatever the nature of the decision, informed business decision making will share certain characteristics, such as being forward-looking, using relevant information and involving financial evaluation.

(a) Forward-looking

Decisions look to the future and, therefore, require forward-looking information. Past costs that have no ongoing implications for the future are irrelevant. These costs are sometimes known as **sunk costs** and should be *excluded from decision making*.

(b) Relevant Information

When choosing between alternatives, we are concerned only with information which is relevant to the particular decision. For example, after arriving in the centre of town by taxi, you are trying to choose between going to the cinema or pub. The taxi fare is a sunk cost which is not relevant to your decision. You cannot alter the past. *Relevant costs and revenues are, therefore, those costs and revenues that will affect a decision. Sunk costs are non-relevant costs.*

To make an informed decision only relevant information is needed. This information may be financial or non-financial. The non-financial information will normally, however, have indirect financial consequences. For example, a drop in the birthrate may have financial consequences for suppliers of baby products.

(c) Financial Evaluation

In business, effective decision making will involve financial evaluation. This means gathering the relevant facts and then working out the financial benefits and costs of the various alternatives. There are a variety of techniques available to do this, which we will be discussing in subsequent chapters.

Decisions may have **opportunity costs**. *Opportunity costs are the potential benefit lost by rejecting the best alternative course of action.* If you work in the union bar at £7 per hour and the next best alternative is the university bookshop at £6 per hour, then the opportunity cost is £6 per hour. This is because you forgo the chance of working in the bookshop at £6 per hour.

However, from the above, it should not be assumed that business decision making is always wholly rational. As we all know, many factors, not all of them rational, enter into real-life decision making (see Real-Life Nugget 6.1).

REAL-LIFE NUGGET 6.1

Decision Making

The upshot? Although you might think that asking what you want should be the flip-side of asking what you don't want, it isn't. When you reject something you focus more on the negative features; when you select something you're focusing on the positive. So whether it's an ice cream or a prospective employee, deciding what (or who) you want by a process of rational elimination may not actually give you what you want. There is no simple panacea to ease the pain of choice other than passing the buck, of course (hence the irksome cliché: 'No, you decide').

As for you sadistic purveyors of all this choice, don't get too smug. When Sheena Sethi-Iyengar, from the Massachusetts Institute of Technology, set up a tasting counter for exotic jams in a grocery, she found that too much choice can be bad for business. More customers stopped to sample from a 24-jam counter than from a 6-jam counter. But only 3 per cent bought any jam when 24 were on offer, compared with 30 per cent when there were 6 to choose from.

Source: Ditherer's Dilemma, Peter Aytan, *New Scientist*, 12 February 2000, p. 471

Contribution Analysis

When making short-term decisions, a technique called contribution analysis has evolved. This technique has several distinctive features (see Figure 6.2).

Figure 6.2   Key Features of Contribution Analysis

- Distinction between those costs that are the same whatever the level of production or service (*fixed costs*) and those that vary with the level of production or service (*variable costs*).
- Profit is no longer the main criterion by which decisions are judged. The key criterion becomes *contribution to fixed costs.*
- Calculations are often performed on the basis of *unit costs* rather than in total.
- Contribution analysis focuses on the *extra cost of making an extra product* or providing an extra unit of service.

It is now important to look more closely at the key elements of contribution analysis: fixed costs, variable costs and contribution. The analysis and interaction of these elements is sometimes called cost-profit-volume analysis. In this book, the term contribution analysis is used because it is considered easier to understand and more informative.

PAUSE FOR THOUGHT 6.1

Fixed Costs

In the long run all fixed costs are variable. Why do you think this is so?

....

This is because at some stage the underlying conditions will change. For example, at a certain production level it will be necessary to buy extra machines, this will necessitate extra depreciation and insurance both normally fixed costs. Alternatively, if a factory closes then even the fixed costs will no longer be incurred.

(i) Fixed Costs

Fixed costs *do not change* if we sell more or less products or services. **They are thus irrelevant for short-term decisions.** For a business, fixed costs might be business rates, depreciation, insurance or rent. On a normal household telephone bill, for example, the fixed cost is the amount of the rental. It should be stressed that fixed costs will not change over the short term, but over the long term all costs will change (see Pause for Thought 6.1).

(ii) Variable Costs

These costs *do vary* with the level of production or service provided. **They are thus relevant for short-term decisions.** If we take a business, variable costs might be direct labour, direct materials, or overheads directly linked to service or production.

In practice, it may be difficult to ascertain which costs are fixed and which are variable. In addition, some costs will have elements of both a fixed and variable nature. For example, an electricity bill has a fixed standing charge and then an amount per unit of electricity used. However, to simplify matters, we shall treat costs as either fixed or variable.

(iii) Contribution

Contribution to fixed overheads, or contribution in short, is simply sales less variable costs. If sales are greater than variable costs, it means that for each product made or service provided the business contributes to its fixed overheads. Once a business's fixed overheads are covered, a profit will be made.

Contribution, as we shall see, is a very useful technique which enables businesses to choose the most profitable goods and services. Contribution analysis is sometimes called **marginal costing**. This comes from economics where a marginal cost is the *extra cost or 'incremental' cost needed to produce one more good or service*. Figure 6.3 demonstrates how contribution analysis works.

Figure 6.3   Demonstration of Contribution Analysis

Clueless has two products (X and Y) and the following abridged trading and profit and loss account.

	£	£
Sales		100,000
Less: *Costs*		
Direct materials	25,000	
Direct labour	35,000	
Overheads	20,000	80,000
Net Profit		20,000

Which of the two products is the most profitable?

To answer this question, we need additional information about X and Y and about which costs are fixed and which are variable. We can then use contribution analysis.

Additional information	**X**	**Y**
Sales units	1,000	2,000
	£	£
Sales	50,000	50,000
Direct materials	15,000	10,000
Direct labour	20,000	15,000
Variable overheads	7,000	3,000
Fixed overheads	10,000	

Contribution Analysis

	X (1,000 units)				Y (2,000 units)			
	Per unit		Total		Per unit		Total	
	£	£	£	£	£	£	£	£
Sales		50		50,000		25		50,000
Less: *Costs*								
Direct materials	15		15,000		5.0		10,000	
Direct labour	20		20,000		7.5		15,000	
Variable overheads	7	42	7,000	42,000	1.5	14	3,000	28,000
Contribution		8		8,000		11		22,000
X's contribution								8,000
Total Contribution								30,000
Fixed overheads								(10,000)
Net Profit								20,000

We can thus see that:
1. X make a contribution of £8 per unit, while Y makes a contribution of £11 per unit.
2. X contributes £8,000 to fixed overheads, while Y contributes £22,000 to fixed overheads.

The contribution data in Figure 6.3 can be used to answer a series of 'what if' questions, varying the levels of sales for X and Y. Contribution analysis is thus very versatile (as Figure 6.4 shows).

Figure 6.4   'What if' Questions for Products X and Y

	£
(i) What if sales of X and Y double?	
(ii) What if sales of X and Y halve?	
(i) If sales of X and Y double, the contribution would double. Thus,	
	£
X (Existing contribution £8,000)	16,000
Y (Existing contribution £22,000)	44,000
	60,000
Fixed overheads	(10,000)
Net Profit	50,000
(ii) If sales of X and Y halve the contribution will halve. Thus	
	£
X (Existing contribution £8,000)	4,000
Y (Existing contribution £22,000)	11,000
	15,000
Fixed overheads	(10,000)
Net Profit	5,000

Helpnote:
The net profit (originally £20,000) increases and decreases by more than the direct increase or decrease in sales units. The contribution varies in line with sales, but fixed overheads do not vary. The overall net profit, in turn, therefore does not alter in direct proportion to the change in sales or contribution.

Decisions, Decisions

Contribution analysis can be used in a range of possible situations. All these involve the basic business questions:

- Are we maximising the firm's contribution by producing the most profitable products?
- Is the product making a positive contribution to the firm? If not, cease production.
- Should we make the products in house?
- Are we making the most of limited resources?

Although the decisions are different, the basic approach is the same (see Helpnote 6.1).

HELPNOTE 6.1

Basic Contribution Approach to Decision Making

1. **Separate the costs into fixed and variable.**
2. **Allocate sales and costs to different products.**
3. **Calculate contribution (sales less variable cost) for each product:**
   (a) **in total**
   (b) **where appropriate, per unit or per unit of limiting factor.**

It is important to realise that contribution analysis provides a rational approach to decision making. However, it should not be seen as providing a definitive answer. In the end, making the right decision will also involve an element of judgement. This is the sentiment expressed in Soundbite 6.1.

SOUNDBITE 6.1

Decision Making as an Art

'Management is more art than science. No one can say with certainty which decisions will bring the most profit, any more than they can create instructions over how to sculpt a masterpiece. You just have to feel it as it goes.'

Richard D'Aveni, *Financial Times* (September 1, 1992)

Source: *The Wiley Book of Business Quotations* (1998), p. 311

(i) Determining the Most Profitable Products

If a company makes a range of products or services, we can use contribution analysis to see which are the most profitable (see Figure 6.5).

Figure 6.5　Determining the Most Profitable Products or Services

A garage provides its customers with three services: the basic service, the deluxe service and the superdeluxe service. It has the following details.

	Selling price £	Direct labour £	Direct materials £
Basic	75	35	10
Deluxe	95	45	12
Superdeluxe	120	65	14

Variable overheads are 50% direct labour. Fixed overheads are £1,000 per month. Which services are the most profitable?

We need to calculate *per unit*	£	Basic £	£	Deluxe £	£	Superdeluxe £
Sales Price		75.00		95.00		120.00
Less: *Variable costs*						
Direct materials	10.00		12.00		14.00	
Direct labour	35.00		45.00		65.00	
Variable overheads	17.50		22.50		32.50	
Total variable costs		62.50		79.50		111.50
Contribution		12.50		15.50		8.50
Ranked by profitability		2		1		3

The deluxe service is the most profitable (£15.50 contribution per unit), followed by the basic service (£12.50 contribution per unit) and the superdeluxe (£8.50 contribution per unit). Note that we do not take fixed costs into account. This is because they are irrelevant to the decision.

(ii) Should We Cease Production of Any Products?

The key here is to see whether or not any products or services are making a negative contribution.

PAUSE FOR THOUGHT 6.2

Negative Contribution

Why should we discontinue any product or service with a negative contribution?

....

Products and services with negative contribution are bad news. This means that every extra product or service makes no contribution to our fixed costs. In actual fact, the more products or services we provide the greater our loss. This is because our variable costs per unit are greater than the selling price per unit.

Let us take the example in Figure 6.6.

Figure 6.6   Dropping Loss-Making Products

We have the following information for Dolly, which makes three sweets: the mixtures, the sweeteners and the gobsuckers.

Current Sales	£	£
Mixtures (100,000 at 50p)		50,000
Sweeteners (200,000 at 20p)		40,000
Gobsuckers (400,000 at 10p)		40,000
		130,000
Less: *Costs*		
Direct materials	50,000	
Direct labour	40,000	
Variable overheads	20,000	
Fixed overheads	10,000	
Total costs		120,000
Net Profit		10,000

The variable costs are split between the products: 50% to mixtures, 25% to sweeteners and 25% to gobsuckers.
Are all these products profitable? If not, what is the effect on profit of dropping the unprofitable one?

We need to rearrange our information to identify contribution per sweet.

	Mixtures		Sweeteners		Gobsuckers	
	£	£	£	£	£	£
Sales		50,000		40,000		40,000
Less: *Variable costs*:						
Direct materials	25,000		12,500		12,500	
Direct labour	20,000		10,000		10,000	
Variable overheads	10,000	55,000	5,000	27,500	5,000	27,500
Contribution		(5,000)		12,500		12,500
Total Contribution ((£5,000) + £12,500 + £12,500)						20,000
Fixed overheads						(10,000)
Net Profit						10,000

Sweeteners and gobsuckers thus make positive contributions of £12,500 each and are therefore profitable. By contrast, mixtures makes a negative contribution of £5,000. If we drop mixtures, profit increases by £5,000, we can see this below.

	£
Sweeteners	12,500
Gobsuckers	12,500
Total Contribution	25,000
Less: Fixed overheads	(10,000)
Net Profit	15,000

(iii) The Make or Buy Decision

Here we need to compare the cost of providing goods or services internally with the cost of buying in the goods or services. We compare the variable costs of making them internally with the external costs. Businesses often outsource (i.e., buy in) their non-essential activities. In Real-Life Nugget 6.2 British Airways has outsourced its engineering and IT services.

REAL-LIFE NUGGET 6.2

British Airways and Outsourcing

At the height of its prosperity in the mid-1990s, BA brought in an ambitious plan to cut £1 billion off its £8 billion annual costs. So far it has found savings of about £700m; it hopes to hack out the other £300 m by March. A cull of 1,000 middle managers should lop a further £225 m off costs. This was proclaimed as a precautionary measure to prepare BA for the next downturn, when price competition was bound to intensify. BA also started to outsource as much as it could, getting rid of such services as engineering, IT and catering. Its bosses talked of 'a virtual airline', one that concentrated only on selling seats and operating flights. Analysts noted approvingly that BA had been the first international airline to emerge smiling from the 1990–91 slump, thanks to similar prompt action.

Source: Diving for Cover, *The Economist*, 16 October 1999

This sort of decision is also often faced by local governments in tendering or contracting out services such as cleaning (see Figure 6.7).

Figure 6.7   The Make or Buy Decision

A local government is looking at a particular cleaning contract. One of the existing local government departments has bid for a particular contract, with the following costs.

	£
Direct materials	28
Direct labour, 25 hours at £5.10	
Variable overheads	12

Speedyclean, a private company, has offered to do the contract for £165, should we accept?

Internally	£
Direct materials	28.00
Direct labour (25 hours at £5.10)	127.50
Variable overheads	12.00
	167.50
Externally	165.00

Yes, on pure cost grounds it should be awarded externally to Speedyclean.

PAUSE FOR THOUGHT 6.3

Other Factors in Make or Buy Decisions

What other factors, apart from the costs, should you take into account in make and buy decisions?

....

In practice, make or buy decisions can involve many other factors. For example:

- Have the internal employees other work?
- Is the external price sustainable over time?
- Do we want to be dependent on an external provider?
- Will we be able to take action against the external provider if there is a deficient service?
- What consequences will awarding the contract externally have for morale, staff turnover?

(iv) Maximising a Limiting Factor

Businesses often face a situation where one of the key resource inputs is a limiting factor on production. For example, the quantity of direct materials may be limited or labour hours may be restricted. The basic idea, in this case, is to **maximise the contribution of the limiting factor**. Figure 6.8 demonstrates this concept for a hotel which has three restaurants, but a limited amount of direct labour hours.

Figure 6.8   Maximising Contribution per Limiting Factor

A hotel has three restaurants (Snack, Bistro and Formal). There are only 1,150 labour hours available at £10 per hour. If the restaurants opened normally for the coming week then 1,300 hours would be used: 400 hours for Snack, 500 hours for Bistro and 400 hours for Formal. Under normal opening you expect the following:

	Snack		Bistro		Formal	
Customers	2,000		3,000		2,000	
	£	£	£	£	£	£
Sales		10,000		12,000		16,000
Less: *Costs*						
Direct materials	2,000		2,500		7,500	
Direct labour	4,000		5,000		4,000	
Variable overheads	1,000		1,250		2,000	
Fixed overheads*	2,000	9,000	3,000	11,750	2,000	15,500
Net Profit		1,000		250		500

*Allocated by number of customers

You are required to maximise profit.

Figure 6.8   Maximising Contribution per Limiting Factor (*continued*)

To maximise profit, we need to **maximise our contribution per unit of limiting resource,** i.e., labour hours. We need to maximise this as *labour is limited to 1,150 hours.* We must, therefore, first determine our overall contribution and the contribution per labour hour.

Labour hours	Snack 400		Bistro 500		Formal 400	
	£	£	£	£	£	£
Sales		10,000		12,000		16,000
Less: *Variable costs*						
Direct materials	2,000		2,500		7,500	
Direct labour	4,000		5,000		4,000	
Variable overheads	1,000	7,000	1,250	8,750	2,000	13,500
		3,000		3,250		2,500
Contribution						

Contribution per labour hour:

Contribution	£3,000		£3,250		£2,500	
Hours	400 hours	= £7.50	500 hours	= £6.50	400 hours	= £6.25

Above, we have divided the coming week's contribution by the number of labour hours available. We ought, therefore, to use our labour first in the Snack, then in the Bistro, and only, lastly, on the Formal restaurant. This is because our contribution is greatest for the Snack at £7.50 per hour, next for the Bistro at £6.50 per hour and least for the Formal at £6.25 per hour. Our maximum profit (to the nearest £) is therefore:

			£
Snack 400 hours (i.e. the Snack's capacity)	× £7.50		3,000
Bistro 500 hours (i.e. the Bistro's capacity)	× £6.50		3,250
Formal 250 hours (i.e. the balance)	× £6.25		1,563
1150 hours			7,813
Less: Fixed costs			(7,000)
Net Profit			813

Any other allocation would result in less profit. For example, if we allocated the hours according to *maximum contribution per customer* (i.e., in the order Snack, Formal, Bistro).

			£
Snack	400 hours (i.e. Snack's capacity)	× £7.50	3,000
Formal	400 hours (i.e. Formal's capacity)	× £6.25	2,500
Bistro	350 hours (i.e. Balance)	× £6.50	2,275
	1150 hours		7,775
Less: Fixed costs			(7,000)
Net Profit			775

Throughput Accounting

Throughput accounting is a relatively new approach to production management, and uses a variant of contribution per limiting factor. This approach looks at a production system from the perspective of bottlenecks. It essentially asks what are a system's main bottlenecks? For instance, is it shortage of machine hours in a certain department? Every effort is then made to eliminate the bottlenecks. Goldratt and Cox in *The Goal* (1992) look at throughput contribution (defined as sales less direct materials) as a key measure. Interestingly, therefore, all other costs are treated as fixed. Thus, direct labour and variable overheads are seen as fixed overheads in this system. Figure 6.9 provides an example of a throughput operating statement. The throughput contribution is £40,000 (i.e., sales of £105,000 less direct materials at £65,000).

Figure 6.9   Throughput Accounting

Sanderson Engineering has the following details from its accounting records for May 2006.

	£000		£000
Sales	105,000	Production overheads	10,000
Direct materials	65,000	Administrative expenses	6,000
Direct labour	18,000	Selling and distribution expenses	5,000

Prepare a throughput accounting statement.

Sanderson Engineering Throughput Accounting Statement for May 2006

	£000	£000
Sales		105,000
Direct materials		(65,000)
Throughput Contribution		40,000
Direct labour	(18,000)	
Production overheads	(10,000)	
Administrative expenses	(6,000)	
Selling and distribution expenses	(5,000)	(39,000)
Net Profit		1,000

Break-Even Analysis

The contribution concept is particularly useful when determining the break-even point of a firm. The break-even point is simply that point at which a firm makes neither a profit nor a loss. A firm's break-even point can be expressed as follows:

$$Sales - Variable\ costs - Fixed\ costs = 0$$

Figure 6.10   The Essentials of Break-Even Analysis

Break-Even Point	Contribution	Break-Even Point in Units
The point at which a business makes neither a profit or a loss	Sales – Variable costs	$\dfrac{Fixed\ costs}{Contribution\ per\ unit}$

In other words, the break-even point is the point where contribution equals fixed costs. We can find the break-even point in units by dividing fixed costs by contribution per unit. Figure 6.11 shows how the break-even point works.

Figure 6.11   An Example of Break-Even Analysis

A restaurateur, William Bunter, has expected sales of 15,000 meals at £20 each. His variable costs are £8 per meal. If the fixed costs are £120,000, what is the break-even point? What is sales revenue at break-even profit?

We, therefore, have

$$\frac{\text{Fixed costs}}{\substack{\text{Contribution per unit (i.e. meal)} \\ \text{(sales – variable cost per unit (i.e. meal))}}} = \frac{£120,000}{£20 - £8} = \frac{£120,000}{£12} = 10,000 \text{ meals}$$

Sales revenue at break-even is thus $10,000 \times £20 = £200,000$.

Assumptions of Break-Even Analysis

The beauty of break-even analysis is that it is comparatively straightforward. However, break-even analysis is underpinned by several key assumptions. Perhaps the main one is **linearity**. Linearity assumes that the behaviour of the sales and costs will remain constant despite increases in the level of sales. Sales and variable costs are assumed always to be strictly variable and fixed costs are assumed to be strictly fixed. For instance, in Figure 6.11 it is assumed that sales will remain at £20 per meal, variable costs will remain at £8 per meal and fixed costs will remain at £120,000, whether we sell 1,000 meals, 10,000 meals or 100,000 meals. In practice, it is more likely that these costs will be fixed or variable within a particular range of activity (often called the **relevant range**). The break-even point also implies a precision which is perhaps unwarranted. A better description might be the break-even area.

Other Uses of Break-Even Analysis

Break-even analysis can also form the basis of more sophisticated analyses such as (i) calculating the margin of safety, (ii) the basis for 'what-if' analysis, or (iii) the basis for graphical analysis.

(i) Margin of Safety

Bunter may wish to calculate how much he has sold over and above the break-even point. This is called the margin of safety. Bunter's margin of safety is calculated using a general formula:

$$\frac{\text{Actual units sold} - \text{units at break-even point}}{\text{Actual units}}$$

The break-even point can be calculated in either (a) units (i.e., in this case, meals) or (b) in money. Therefore,

(a) Bunter's margin of safety (units) $= \dfrac{15,000 - 10,000}{10,000} = 50\,\%$

(b) Bunter's margin of safety (£s) $= \dfrac{£300,000 - £200,000}{£200,000} = 50\,\%$

(ii) What-if Analysis

The break-even point can also be used as a basis for 'what-if' analysis. For instance, we know that each unit sold in excess of the break-even point adds one unit's contribution to profit. Similarly, each unit less than the break-even point creates a loss of one unit's contribution. So, we can easily answer questions such as 'what is the profit or loss if Bunter sells (a) 8,000 meals or (b) 13,000 meals?'

(a) **8,000 meals**. This is 2,000 meals less than the break-even point of 10,000 meals. The loss is, therefore, 2,000 meals × contribution per meal. Thus,

2,000 meals × £12 contribution per meal = £24,000 loss

(b) **13,000 meals**. This is 3,000 meals more than the break-even point of 10,000 meals. The profit is thus.

3,000 meals × £12 contribution per meal = £36,000 profit

The break-even point is a very flexible concept and provides potentially rewarding insights into business.

(iii) Graphical Break-Even Point

Another benefit of break-even analysis is that it can be shown on a graph (see Figure 6.12).

Figure 6.12   Graphical Break-Even Point

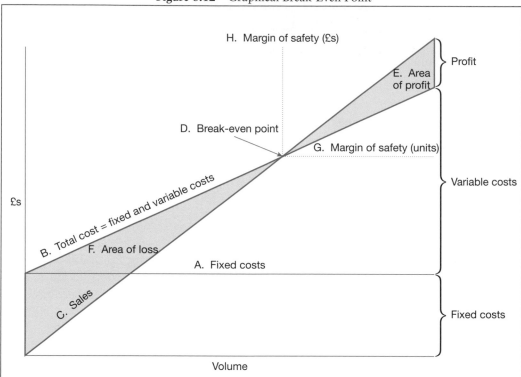

On the graph, it is important to note the following points:

A. **Fixed costs.** This is a straight horizontal line.

B. **Variable costs (total cost).** This is a straight line which starts on the vertical Y axis and 'piggybacks' the fixed cost line.
   Effectively, the variable cost line also represents the **total cost (fixed cost plus variable costs).**

C. **Sales.** The sales line starts at the origin and then climbs steadily.

D. **Break-even point.** This is the point where the sales line (C) and the total cost line (B) (i.e., variable costs line) cross.

E. **Area of profit.** This is where the sales line (C) is higher than the total cost line (B). A profit is thus being made.

F. **Area of loss.** This is where the sales line (C) is lower than the total cost line (B). There is thus a loss.

G. **Margin of safety (units).** This is the difference between current sales and the sales needed to break even in units.

H. **Margin of safety (£s).** This is the difference between current sales and the sales needed to break even in £s.

Figure 6.13 is the graph for William Bunter. Sales are set at four levels: 0 meals; 5,000 meals; 10,000 meals; and 15,000 meals. Break-even point is 10,000 meals.

Figure 6.13   Bunter's Break-Even Chart

First, we need to work out the figures to graph.
Remember: each sale is £20, variable costs are £8 and fixed costs are £120,000.

Number of Meals	Fixed Costs	Variable Costs	Total Costs	Sales	Profit (Loss)
£	£	£	£	£	£
–	120,000	–	120,000	–	(120,000)
5,000	120,000	40,000	160,000	100,000	(60,000)
10,000	120,000	80,000	200,000	200,000	–
15,000	120,000	120,000	240,000	300,000	60,000

Now, we can draw the break-even chart.

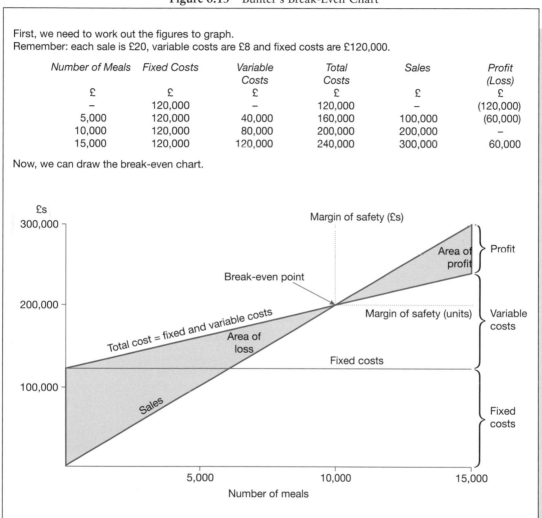

Contribution Graph

A further limitation of the break-even chart is that it can be used for only one product. This disadvantage is overcome by using a contribution graph (see Figure 6.14). This is sometimes called a *profit/volume chart*. However, in this book we use the term contribution graph as it is easier to understand. A contribution graph looks a bit like a set of rugby posts! It is based on the idea that each unit sold generates one unit's contribution. Initially, this contribution covers fixed costs and then generates a profit. The horizontal line represents level of sales (either in units or £s). Above the horizontal line is profit, while below the line is loss. The diagonal line represents contribution. In effect, it is the cumulative profit or loss plotted against cumulative sales. So when sales are zero there is a loss (point A). This loss is, in effect, the total fixed costs. The company then breaks even at point B. At this point contribution equals fixed costs. Above point B each unit sold adds one unit of contribution to the company's profit. Finally, point C represents maximum cumulative sales and maximum contribution.

Figure 6.14   Contribution Graph

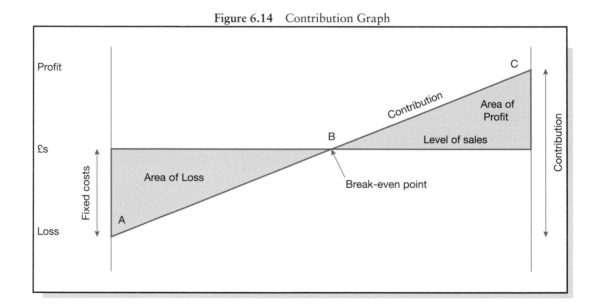

The relationship between contribution and sales is defined as $\frac{\text{Contribution}}{\text{Sales}}$. Sometimes this is known as the profit/volume ratio.

This ratio provides an easy way of comparing the contributions of different products. We take, as an example, a department store which has three departments: toys, clothes and records (see Figure 6.15).

Figure 6.15   Contribution Graph for a Department Store

Department	Sales	Variable Costs	Contribution	Contribution/Sales Ratio		Ranking
	£	£	£	%		
Toys	20,000	10,000	10,000	50	(£10,000/£20,000)	1
Clothes	40,000	30,000	10,000	25	(£10,000/£40,000)	3
Records	60,000	40,000	20,000	33⅓	(£20,000/£60,000)	2
Total	120,000	80,000	40,000	33⅓	(£40,000/£120,000)	
Fixed costs			(20,000)	33⅓		
Net Profit			20,000	33⅓		

Using this information draw a contribution graph.

First we draw up a cumulative profit/loss table ranked by the highest contribution/sales ratio. The cumulative profit/loss is simply cumulative contribution less fixed costs.

	Cumulative Sales	Cumulative Contribution	Cumulative Profit/(Loss)
	£	£	£
Fixed costs			(20,000)
Toys	20,000	10,000	(10,000)
Records	80,000	30,000	10,000
Clothes	120,000	40,000	20,000

We are now in a position to draw up a graph.

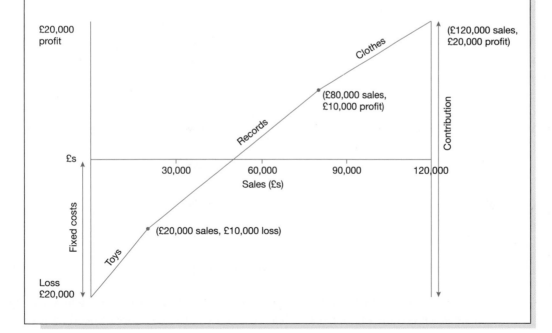

In many industries, there are substantial fixed costs. In the retail industry, for example, as Real-Life Nugget 6.3 shows, the concept of break-even becomes very important.

REAL-LIFE NUGGET 6.3

Fixed Costs and Supermarkets

The question is of particular interest in Britain, where the competition authorities are investigating newspaper claims that the big four supermarket chains Tesco, J. Sainsbury, Asda and Safeway are making excessive profits.

In recent years these four chains have tried to avoid price wars because price-slashing makes little sense in markets where a few big operators with similar cost structures operate.

The reason is that each has substantial fixed costs, making a profit by driving more than enough volume through its stores to cover its overheads. If one operator cuts prices, the others are compelled to follow for fear of seeing their own volumes fall below the break-even point. So nobody gains market share, and everybody's profits fall.

Source: Marketing Value for Money, Richard Tomkins, *Financial Times*, 14 May 1999

Conclusion

Businesses constantly face short-term decisions such as how to maximise a limited resource. When making these decisions it is useful to distinguish between fixed and variable costs. Fixed costs do not, in the short run, change with either production or sales (for example, insurance or depreciation). Variable costs, by contrast, do change when the production volume or sales volume changes (examples are direct materials and direct labour). Sales less variable costs gives contribution. Contribution is a useful accounting concept. By calculating contribution we can, for example, determine which products are the most profitable. Break-even analysis is another useful concept that builds on contribution analysis. The break-even point is the point at which a business makes neither a profit or a loss. It is determined by dividing fixed costs by the contribution per unit. The break-even chart shows the break-even point graphically. The contribution graph is a useful way of graphing the profit or loss of one or more products.

Discussion Questions

Questions with numbers in blue have answers at the back of the book.

Q1 Distinguish between fixed and variable costs. Why are fixed costs irrelevant when making a choice between certain alternatives such as whether to produce more of product A or of product B?

Q2   What is contribution per unit and why is it so useful in short-term decision making?

Q3   What are the strengths and weaknesses of break-even analysis?

Q4   State whether the following statements are true or false? If false, explain why.
  (a) Fixed costs are those that do not vary with long-term changes in the level of sales or production.
  (b) Contribution is sales less variable costs.
  (c) Break-even point is $\dfrac{\text{Variable costs}}{\text{Contribution per unit}}$
  (d) Contribution/sales ratio is $\dfrac{\text{Profit}}{\text{Sales}}$
  (e) Non-financial items are not important in decision making.

Numerical Questions

Questions with numbers in blue have answers at the back of the book.

Q1   Jungle Animals makes 10 model animals with the following cost structure.

	Selling Price £	Direct Labour £	Direct Materials £	Variable Overheads £
Alligators	1.00	0.50	0.20	0.35
Bears	1.20	0.60	0.10	0.30
Cougars	1.10	0.66	0.15	0.33
Donkeys	1.15	0.60	0.18	0.30
Eagles	1.20	0.56	0.12	0.28
Foxes	0.90	0.50	0.10	0.25
Giraffes	1.05	0.40	0.25	0.20
Hyenas	1.25	0.56	0.10	0.28
Iguanas	0.95	0.40	0.12	0.20
Jackals	0.80	0.40	0.13	0.20

Required:
  (i) Calculate the contribution per toy.
  (ii) Calculate the contribution/sales ratio per toy.
  (iii) Which two toys bring in the greatest contribution?
  (iv) Which three toys have the highest contribution/sales ratio?
  (v) Which two toys would you not manufacture at all?

Q2   An insurance company, Riskmore, has four divisions: car, home, personal and miscel-
laneous. These four divisions account, respectively, for 40 %, 30 %, 20 % and 10 % of
sales and 25 % each of the variable costs. Riskmore has the following summary profit
and loss account.

	£
Sales	200,000
Less: *Costs*	
Variable costs	100,000
Fixed costs	50,000
Net Profit	50,000

Required: Calculate the profitability of the divisions.

Q3   Scrooge Ltd is looking to outsource its accounts department. Ghost Ltd, has approached
Scrooge and offered to provide the service for £160,000. Scrooge Ltd ascertains the
following costs are involved internally.

Clerical labour	10,000 hours at £6
Supervisory labour	6,000 hours at £10
Direct materials	£15,000
Variable overheads	£3 per clerical labour hour
Fixed overheads	£8,000

Required: Calculate whether or not Scrooge Ltd should accept Ghost's bid. State any
assumptions you have made and other factors you might take into account.

Q4   A large hotel, The Open Umbrella, has two kiosks. One sells sweets and is open 35 hours
per week. The second sells newspapers and magazines and is open 55 hours per week.
Unfortunately, next week labour is restricted to 70 hours. Labour is £5 per hour. Last
week's results when both were fully open and 90 labour hours were available are set out
below.

	Kiosk 1 (Sweets)		Kiosk 2 (Newspapers)	
	£	£	£	£
Sales		900		1,200
Less: *Costs*				
Direct labour	175		275	
Direct materials	600		700	
Variable overheads	70	845	110	1,085
Contribution		55		115

Required: How would you maximise the profits using the 70 labour hours available?

Q5 Globeco makes four geographical board quiz games: France, Germany, UK and US. Globeco has the following recent results.

	France		Germany		UK		US	
Units sold	1,000		1,500		4,000		6,000	
	£	£	£	£	£	£	£	£
Sales		2,000		3,000		12,000		24,000
Less: *Variable Costs*								
Direct labour	800		1,350		6,000		15,600	
Direct materials	200		300		1,300		1,400	
Variable overheads	80		135		600		1,560	
Fixed overheads (equal allocation)	1,000		1,000		1,000		1,000	
		2,080		2,785		8,900		19,560
Net Profit (loss)		(80)		215		3,100		4,440

For next year, there are only 3,000 direct labour hours available. Last year's results used 4,750 direct labour hours. Direct labour is paid at £5 per hour. The maximum sales (in units) are predicted to be 2,000 France, 3,500 Germany, 6,000 UK and 8,000 US.

Required: Calculate the most profitable production schedule, given that direct labour hours, the limiting factor, are restricted to 3,000 hours.

Q6 Freya manufactures heavy-duty hammers. They each cost £4 in direct materials and £3 in variable expenses. They sell for £10 each. Fixed costs are £30,000. Currently 20,000 hammers are sold.

Required:
  (i) What is the break-even point?
 (ii) What is the profit if the number of hammers sold is:
      (a) 4,000   (b) 14,000?
(iii) What is the current margin of safety in (a) units and (b) £s?
 (iv) Draw a break-even chart.

Q7 Colin Xiao runs a restaurant which serves 10,000 customers a month. Each customer spends £20, variable costs per customer are £15. Fixed costs are £10,000.

Required:
  (i) What are the current break-even point and margin of safety in £s?
 (ii) Calculate the new break-even point and margin of safety in £s if the average spend per customer is:
      (a) £17   (b) £19   (c) £25
      Assume all other factors remain the same.

Q8   A computer hardware distributor, Modem, has three branches in Cardiff, Edinburgh and London. It has the following financial details.

	Sales	Direct Labour	Other Variable Overheads
	£	£	£
Cardiff	200,000	60,000	105,000
Edinburgh	300,000	80,000	150,000
London	1,000,000	350,000	520,000

Head office fixed overheads are £150,000.

Required:
 (i) Calculate the contribution/sales ratios.
(ii) Draw the contribution graph.

Chapter 7

"Today's management accounting information, driven by the procedures and cycle of the organisation's financial reporting system, is too late, too aggregated, and too distorted to be relevant for managers' planning and control decisions."

H.T. Johnson and R.S. Kaplan (1987), *Relevance Lost: The Rise and Fall of Management Accounting*, p. 1

Learning Outcomes

After completing this chapter you should be able to:

✔ Explain the nature and importance of strategic management accounting.

✔ Understand and explain techniques used to assess the current position of the business.

✔ Appreciate the techniques of SWOT analysis, balanced scorecard and benchmarking.

✔ Discuss the strategic choices facing companies.

Strategic Management Accounting

In a Nutshell

■ *Strategic management accounting is externally orientated and concerns a business's future long-term strategy.*

■ *Strategic management accounting is a relatively new topic.*

■ *The three stages of strategic management accounting are (i) assessment of the current position of the business, (ii) appraisal of the current position of the business, and (iii) strategic choice of future direction of the business.*

■ *The assessment of the current position of the business is concerned with both the external and internal environment and may use techniques such as value chain analysis, life cycle analysis and the product portfolio matrix.*

■ *The appraisal of the current position of the business may use SWOT (strengths, weaknesses, opportunities and threats) analysis, the balanced scorecard and benchmarking.*

■ *Strategic choice may involve exploiting inherent strengths such as the business's products or customer base and/or external diversification through acquisition or merger.*

Introduction

Strategic management accounting attempts to involve management accountants in wider business strategy. It concerns a business's future, long-term direction. As Soundbite 7.1 shows, essentially strategy is concerned with where a business is now and where it wants to be in the future. Strategic management accounting is thus an attempt by management accountants to move away from a narrow, functional specialism towards full participation in the long-term strategic planning of businesses. In a sense, this continues a long historical process whereby management accountants have consistently widened the scope of their activities, for example, from costing to management accounting. It also meets the criticism that management accounting has failed to respond to changing environmental circumstances and focuses too much on a business's internal activities and too little on a business's external environment. In short, traditional management accounting is criticised for being too narrow. Strategic management accounting is a very contentious topic. For some, it represents the next stage in the evolution of the management accounting profession. For others, it is seen as a step too far, an unsuitable activity for management accountants.

SOUNDBITE 7.1

Strategy

'There's no rocket science to strategy... you're supposed to know where you are, where your competition is, what your cost position is, and where you want to go. Strategies are intellectually simple, their execution is not.'

Lawrence A. Bossidy, *Harvard Business Review*, March–April, 1995

Source: *The Wiley Book of Business Quotations* (1998), p. 88

Nature of Strategic Management Accounting

Strategic management accounting is relatively new. It dates from the 1980s. At this time, considerable concern was expressed that management accounting had lost its way. Johnson and Kaplan capture this concern in a book entitled *Relevance Lost: The Rise and Fall of Management Accounting*. They argue that conventional management accounting has failed to adapt to a changing industrial environment, that traditional product costing systems are increasingly inappropriate, that financial accounting dominates management accounting and that management accounting needs to reflect the external environment (see Real-Life Nugget 7.1).

REAL-LIFE NUGGET 7.1

Criticisms of Traditional Management Accounting

'Most [of today's] accounting and control systems have major problems: they distort product costs; they do not produce the key financial data required for effective and efficient operations; and the data they do produce reflect external reporting requirements far more than they do the reality of the new manufacturing environment.'

Source: Yesterday's Accounting Undermines Production', R.S. Kaplan, *Harvard Business Review*, 1984, p. 95

Strategic management accounting is one response to these criticisms. It attempts to involve management accountants in strategic business decisions and in the planning of a business's future long-term direction. The exact nature and extent of strategic management accounting is still, however, somewhat vague. In Definition 7.1, we provide a working definition and the Chartered Institute of Management Accountants' formal definition.

DEFINITION 7.1

Strategic Management Accounting

Working definition
A form of management accounting which considers both an organisation's internal and external environments.

Formal definition
'A form of management accounting in which emphasis is placed on information which relates to factors external to the firm as well as non-financial information and internally-generated information.'

Source: Chartered Institute of Management Accountants (2000), *Official Terminology*

This book takes strategic accounting to be a form of management accounting, which emphasises the external and future environment of the business, but also takes into account

Figure 7.1 Overview of Strategic Management Accounting

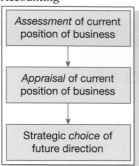

the internal environment of a business. In essence, it is the way in which a business seeks to implement its long-term strategic objectives, such as to be the world's leading supplier of a particular good or service. Figure 7.1 shows the three main stages of strategic management accounting. These stages are outlined briefly here and then discussed in more detail in the following section.

(i) Assessment of current position of the business

This is essentially an information gathering stage. Information is gathered on the current internal and external environment of the business.

(ii) Appraisal of current position of the business

This involves a hard look at the current position of the business investigating its strengths, weaknesses and competitiveness.

(iii) Strategic choice of future direction of the business

Once the current position of the business has been identified and appraised, it is time to choose the future direction of the business. This may involve diversification into new areas or the fuller exploitation of old areas.

It is important to appreciate that these strategic management activities are ongoing, not one-off. A well-run business will continually be assessing and appraising its current position and looking at its strategic choices. Assessment and appraisal are not distinct activities, but overlap. However, it is useful here to deal with them separately. As Soundbite 7.2 shows, it is harder to implement than plan business strategy.

SOUNDBITE 7.2

Implementation of Strategy

'Strategy is easy, implementation is hard ... [O]nly the superb companies actually find a way to do what they say they're going to do.'

Raymond Smith, Speech (1 November 1995)

Source: The Wiley Book of Business Quotations (1998) p. 88

Assessment of Current Position of the Business

The first step in strategic management accounting is an assessment of the current position of the business. In essence, this is an information-gathering exercise. Information is gathered about the national and international external environment and the business's internal environment. Figure 7.2 outlines some of the issues that might be covered.

Figure 7.2   Information Useful in Assessment of Current Position

External Environment	Internal Environment
Political and legal environment	Resources
Economic environment	Current products
Social and cultural environment	Operating systems
Technological change	Internal organisation
Interest and pressure groups	Customers
Environmental issues	Sources of finance
Competitors	

External Environment

The seven factors listed in Figure 7.2, and discussed briefly below, serve as a basis for assessing both the current national and international environment. The importance of each factor varies from business to business.

Political and Legal Environment

This may involve the legal framework, national and international laws, and government policy. For example, privatised utilities in the UK, such as the water companies, are subject to a complex regulatory system.

Economic Environment

The economy is a key consideration for any business. Indeed, correctly assessing the current and future state of the economy is probably the most important external factor in business success.

PAUSE FOR THOUGHT 7.1

Economic Environment

What are some of the considerations which a business might take into account when assessing the economy?

. . . .

These are varied, but they include:

- current economic indicators (such as economic growth, inflation, interest rates, taxation and unemployment) at the regional, national and international level
- stage in economic cycle (boom or slump)
- long-term trends (such as towards a knowledge-based economy)
- government economic policy (such as spending, subsidy, privatisation)
- international trade (different economic conditions in different countries, exchange rates).

Social and Cultural Environment

Society continually evolves. For example, in developed countries there are increasing numbers of retired people and single-person households. These long-term demographic trends need to be matched to a company's products and services.

Technological Change

A business needs to look closely at technological change. Well-positioned businesses are best-placed to exploit social trends such as the use of mobile phones or laptop computers.

Interest and Pressure Groups

It is important to realise that a business operates within society not outside society. Businesses must, therefore, keep an eye on public opinion, which is often manifested in pressure groups. For example, mutual building societies often face pressure from groups wishing to abolish their mutual status and turn them into publicly listed companies.

Environmental Issues

Nowadays, environmental issues are critically important for businesses. Companies must increasingly take on board environmental concerns. Indeed, many businesses have separate environmental departments. Some companies, such as Body Shop, have built their businesses upon a strong environmental ethic.

Competitors

A business needs to be aware of its competitors and the competitive environment in which it operates. Both customers and suppliers have potential power over a business. Businesses must also be aware of potential entrants to an industry as well as potential substitute products. For example, the entry of the US supermarket chain Wal-Mart into the UK caused repercussions for UK companies such as Sainsbury and Tesco.

Internal Environment

A business's internal environment, like its external environment, varies from business to business. The six factors listed in Figure 7.2 (resources, current products, operating systems, internal organisation, customers and sources of finance) are reviewed below. We will then look at three techniques useful in assessing the internal environment: value chain analysis, product life cycle and the product portfolio matrix.

Resources

The resources potentially important in an internal assessment include materials, management, fixed assets, working capital, human resources, brands and other intangibles, and intellectual capital. Nowadays, in an increasingly knowledge-driven society, the last three resources are becoming ever more important. An important element of the resource assessment is the determination of any limiting factors or bottlenecks which will stop a business fulfilling its plans.

Current Products

It is important for a company to review its current product mix. This may include its current competitiveness, a product life cycle analysis, a product profitability review and an analysis of its customers.

Operating Systems

Operating systems are those information systems that form the backbone of a company, such as the sales invoicing system or the payroll system. Their effectiveness needs to be carefully assessed.

Internal Organisation

The effectiveness of the organisational structure of a business, such as the relationship between the head office and the department, needs to be carefully examined.

Customers

A key element of any internal assessment is the customer base. There is a need to gather data and profile customers, for example, by age, ethnicity, sex and social class.

Sources of Finance

It is useful to assess the sources of short-term and long-term capital and the mix between debt and equity. This important topic will be covered in more detail in Chapter 9.

Three techniques potentially useful in the internal assessment are now discussed: the value chain, the product life cycle and the product portfolio matrix.

(i) Value chain analysis

Value chain analysis was devised by Porter (1985). It represents a systematic way of looking at a business. Porter's idea is that each business has a value chain consisting of primary activities and support activities. The primary activities represent a set of value-creating activities from the handling of the raw materials (receiving goods) to after-sales service (service). These primary activities are supported by a set of support activities such as the personnel department (human resource management) or computer department (technology department) (see Figure 7.3).

Figure 7.3   Value Chain Analysis

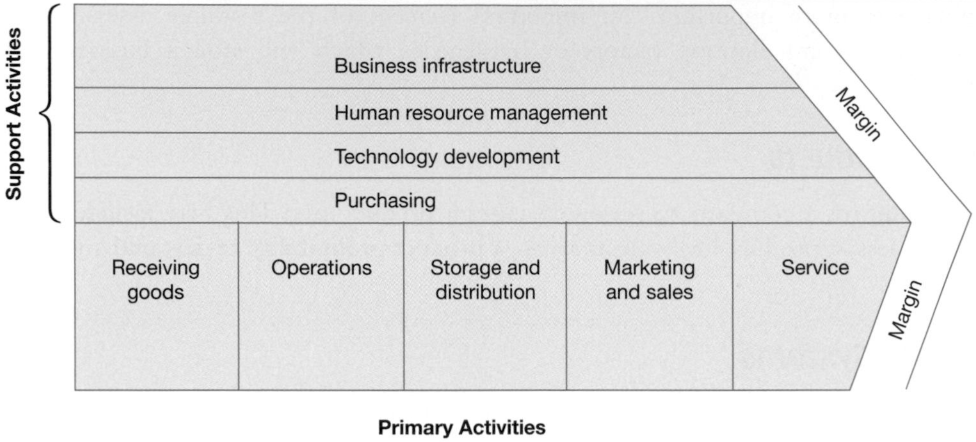

Source: Adapted from M.E. Porter (1985), *Competitive Advantage: Creating and Sustaining Superior Performance*, p. 37. Some of the terminology has been changed to aid understanding.

In Figure 7.4 we set out a value chain for a retail computer superstore.

Figure 7.4   Value Chain for a Retail Computer Superstore

Activity	Definition	Example
A. Primary Activities		
1. Receiving goods	Activities of receiving, handling inputs	Warehousing, transport, stock control
2. Operations	Conversion of inputs to outputs	Preparing computers for sale, service staff
3. Storage and distribution	Activities concerned with storing and distributing the product	Packaging, warehousing, delivery
4. Marketing and sales	Activities which inform and persuade customers	T.V. advertising campaigns
5. Service	After sales	Computer helplines
B. Support Activities		
1. Purchasing	Acquisition of resources	Computers for resale
2. Technology development	Techniques and work organisation	New computer system
3. Human resources management	Recruiting, training, developing and rewarding people	Induction course, computer training course
4. Business infrastructure	Information and planning systems	Sales invoicing system, budgetary system

The cost of these activities is determined by certain cost drivers (i.e., factors which determine the cost of each activity) such as location. Once these cost drivers have been established, then the management accountant can work out the organisation's sustainable competitive advantage. This involves reducing the costs of each activity while increasing the final sales.

PAUSE FOR THOUGHT 7.2

Value Chain Cost Drivers

Porter identified 10 possible cost drivers. How many can you identify?

- **Location**. Is the business in the correct geographical location?
- **Economies of scale**. For example, often the greater the amount purchased, the cheaper the cost per unit.
- **Learning curve**. How experienced is the company at delivering its product or service?
- **Capacity utilisation**. Is the company fully utilising its production capacity?
- **Linkages**. How well are business linkages utilised, such as relationships with suppliers?
- **Interrelationships**. How good are the relations with other units within the group?
- **Timing**. Does the business buy and sell (assets, for example) at the right time?
- **Integration**. How well are the business's individual departments integrated?
- **Discretionary policies**. For example, has the business chosen the optimal computer operating systems?
- **Institutional factors**. Are the business's organisational structures (for example, its management structures) optimal?

(ii) Product life cycle analysis

Most products have a life cycle. Just as with human beings, this involves birth (known as introduction), growth, maturity, decline and senility (known as withdrawal). The key point is that each of these stages is associated with a certain level of sales and profit. Essentially, a product will make a profit once it becomes established. A period of growth will follow in both sales and profits. A period of maturity will then exist and, in this period, profitability will be maximised. The product's sales and profits will then decline and, finally, the product will be withdrawn.

A life cycle analysis graph is shown in Figure 7.5. It is important to realise that for some products, such as the latest children's toy, the product life cycle is short. On the other hand, for certain products, such as a prestige car, the life cycle is very long.

Figure 7.5   Life Cycle Analysis

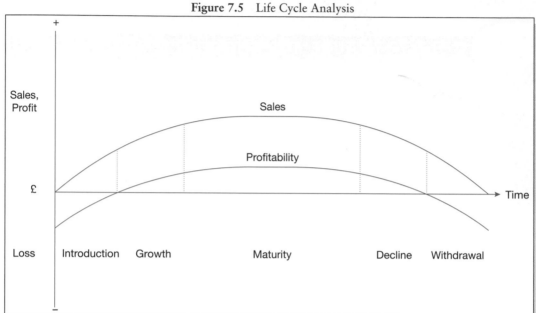

PAUSE FOR THOUGHT 7.3

Product Life Cycles

Are product life cycles today longer or shorter than in the past? If so, what are the consequences for a business?

It is difficult to give a definitive answer. However, the expectation would be shorter. Technology and society are changing at an ever-faster pace, with new technology flourishing. Consumers also, in general, become rich with greater spending power. You would, therefore, expect fashion, styles and products to change more rapidly. Most products thus have shorter life cycles.

The consequences are that businesses need to invest more resources into product development and associated activities such as research and development. If they don't they will not keep pace with the changing market. In addition, it is likely that they will have to relaunch existing products and spend more on advertising and marketing.

Businesses will obviously try, through advertising and other means, to prolong the length of their product life cycle, especially in its mature phase. However, whatever the length of the product's life cycle, a business needs to develop new products for the eventual replacement of the existing product. Just as products have life cycles, it is also true that industries have life cycles (see, for example, Real-Life Nugget 7.2).

REAL-LIFE NUGGET 7.2

Industry Life Cycle

Industries are born, grow, mature and die, and for investors the most spectacular gains are to be had when an industry breaks through from immaturity to growth. This may seem a simple-minded truism to rank alongside "buy low, sell high" but, according to research by the investment bank Schroder Salomon Smith Barney, plotting the position of each sector on the growth/decline curve is fiendishly tricky.

The reason? Industries simply do not behave as they should.

On paper it looks straightforward, with the life-cycle of an industry resembling a motorway flyover. There is an up ramp (immaturity and growth), a flat stretch (maturity) and a down ramp (decline). Salomon is too delicate to include the final stage, but, as Edward G Robinson said in Double Indemnity: "The last stop's the cemetery."

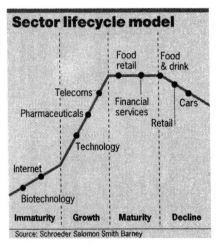

Source: Dead but Refusing to Lie Down, Don Atkinson, *The Guardian*, 7 June 2000, p. 27.
© Guardian Newspapers Limited 2000

(iii) The product portfolio matrix

The Boston Consulting Group (BCG) developed a product portfolio matrix based partially on the ideas behind the product life cycle. There are four major categories of products: stars, cash cows, question marks and dogs.

(a) **Stars.** Stars are characterised by high market growth and high market share. Perhaps the mobile phone in its developmental stage. Stars may be cash earners or cash drains, requiring heavy capital expenditure.

(b) **Cash cows.** Cash cows are a company's dream product. They are well-established products which require little capital expenditure, but generate high returns.

(c) **Question marks**. They have low market share, but are in high market growth industries. So the potentially difficult problem for businesses is should they invest in marketing, advertising or capital expenditure in order to gain market share? Alternatively, should they completely withdraw from the market?

(d) **Dogs**. Dogs are cash traps with low market growth and low market share. Dogs tie up capital and often should be 'withdrawn'.

The product portfolio matrix is set out in Figure 7.6.

Figure 7.6   Boston Consulting Group's Product Portfolio Matrix

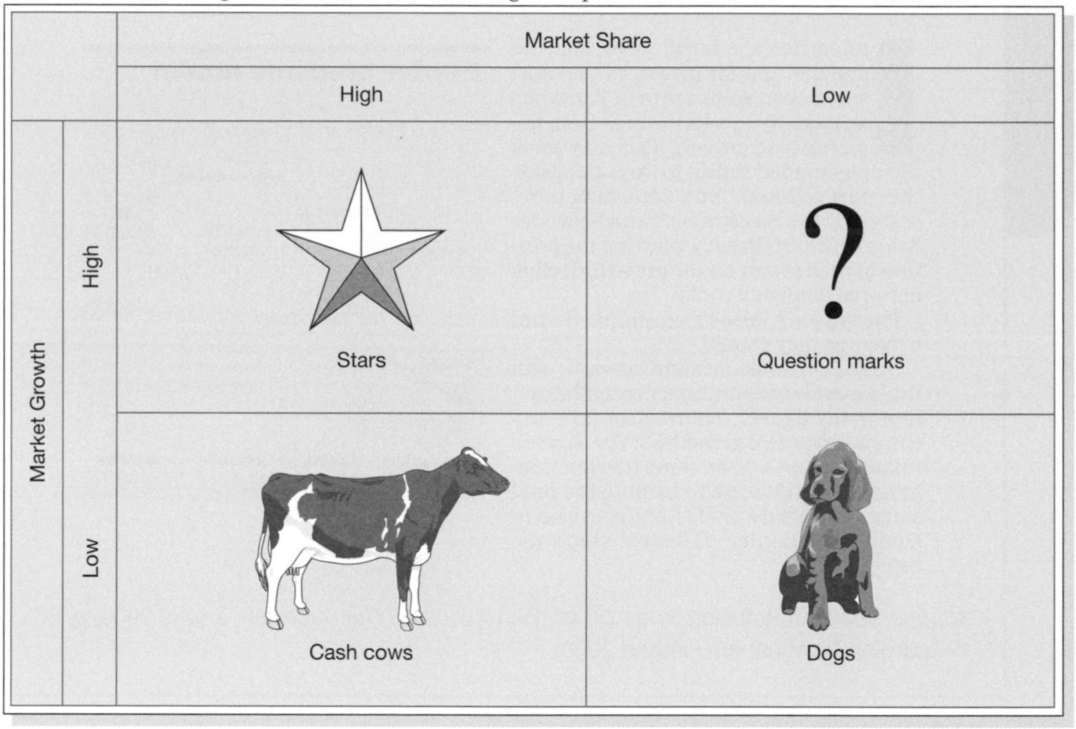

Appraisal of Current Position of the Business

Once the current position of the business has been assessed, it needs to be appraised. We focus here on three major appraisal methods: SWOT analysis; the balanced scorecard; and benchmarking. These appraisal methods take both financial and non-financial factors into account. The appraisal of a business also includes ratio analysis.

(i) SWOT Analysis

SWOT analysis is a way of critically assessing a business's strengths and weaknesses, opportunities and threats. SWOT analysis is thus wide-ranging and looks at internal and external factors. As Figure 7.7 shows, SWOT analysis embraces the whole business and might include marketing, products, finance, infrastructure, management, organisational structure and resources. This list is illustrative rather than exhaustive. SWOT analysis involves the management accountant in detailed financial analysis using quantitative and qualitative data.

Figure 7.7   Typical Factors included in SWOT Analysis

(i) Marketing
- What is our market share?
- Are advertising campaigns effective?
- Are customers happy?

(ii) Products
- Is the branding strong?
- Do we have cash cows or dogs?
- Where are the products in their life cycle?

(iii) Finance
- Are the accounting ratios healthy?
- What is the contribution per product?
- Are the sources of finance secure?
- What is the product cost structure?
- Are we profitable and liquid?
- Do we have optimal gearing?

(iv) Infrastructure
- What is the age of our fixed assets?
- What is the market value of the assets?
- Have we sufficient space for expansion?

(v) Management
- What is the age spread?
- Have we training programmes in place?
- Do we have an appropriate skills base?

(vi) Organisational Structure
- Is our organisational structure appropriate?
- Is there a clear command structure?
- Is the management style appropriate?

(vii) Resources
- Are our sources of supply secure?
- Have we any resource bottlenecks?
- Have we good stock control?

Once the strengths and weaknesses of the business are identified, we can investigate the potential opportunities and threats. Major strengths are matched with profitable opportunities and major weaknesses with potential threats. For example, if a particular product is selling well in Italy [strength], we may decide to market it in Spain [opportunity]. Or if an advertising campaign has gone wrong [weakness], a potential competitor might see a chance to launch a new competing product [threat].

So how does this analysis work in practice? Figure 7.8 attempts to answer this question. A SWOT analysis is conducted for a sweet manufacturer.

Figure 7.8   Illustration of SWOT Analysis

A major national company, Sweetco, has conducted an internal and external assessment of its products. It establishes the following:

- two products the Guzzler and the Geezer are only marketed in the UK
- the Guzzler is selling very well; the Geezer is struggling for sales, with many complaints, and is at the end of its product life
- long-term loan: repayment date is approaching
- computer system needs replacing
- management training is poor
- supplies of basic materials for products are running out.

Prepare a SWOT analysis

SWOT Analysis

Strengths	Weaknesses
Guzzler is a cash cow	Geezer is a dog Long-term loan Poor management training Lack of raw materials
Opportunities	**Threats**
Expand Guzzler into Europe Bring out a similar product to Guzzler Renegotiate a cheaper long- term finance package Introduce effective training programmes	Supplies of raw materials will run out Without loan, cash flow position is unhealthy. Geezer will tie up resources.

In this case, therefore, the Guzzler is clearly a strength, but the Geezer is a weakness. Sweetco, therefore, needs to focus on exploiting the Guzzler and minimising the problems caused by the Geezer.

(ii) Balanced Scorecard

The balanced scorecard attempts to look at a business from multiple perspectives. Definition 7.2 shows a working definition and the formal CIMA definition.

DEFINITION 7.2

The Balanced Scorecard

Working definition
A system of corporate appraisal which looks at financial and non-financial elements from a financial, customer, internal business and innovation perspective.

Formal definition
'An approach to the provision of information to management to assist strategic policy formulation and achievement. It emphasises the need to provide the user with a set of information which addresses all relevant areas of performance in an objective and unbiased fashion. The information provided may include both financial and non-financial elements, and cover areas such as profitability, customer satisfaction, internal efficiency and innovation.'

Source: Chartered Institute of Management Accountants (2000), *Official Terminology*

The balanced scorecard takes a strategic, holistic view of an organisation. It combines both financial and non-financial information to provide a multi-perspective view of the organisation's activities. The balanced scorecard was adapted by Norton and Kaplan (1992) from the practice of some US companies. To Kaplan's credit, it seeks to address Kaplan's earlier criticisms of management accounting (such as lack of external focus) which were expressed in Real-Life Nugget 7.1. The balanced scorecard is a way of appraising a business's performance from four perspectives: *a financial perspective* (e.g., how profitable is it?), *a customer perspective* (e.g., how good is the after-sales service?), *an internal business perspective* (e.g., how efficient is our manufacturing process?), and *an innovation and learning perspective* (e.g., how many new products do we produce?). In essence, each perspective is set goals and then a set of performance measures devised. Thus, from the financial perspective the goals may be survival and profitability. These might be measured using cash flow and return on capital employed. As Soundbite 7.3 shows, a balanced scorecard is concerned with implementing rather than formulating strategy.

SOUNDBITE 7.3

The Balanced Scorecard

'The [balanced] scorecard is not a way of formulating strategy. It's a way of understanding and checking what you have to do throughout the organization to make your strategy work.'

David Norton and Robert Kaplan, quoted in *Financial Times* (1 April 1997)

Source: The Wiley Book of Business *Quotations* (1998), p. 295

Businesses such as Apple Computers have successfully used the balance scorecard. Figure 7.9 gives an example of a balanced scorecard.

Figure 7.9   Illustration of the Balanced Scorecard

Financial Perspective		Customer Perspective	
Goals	*Measures*	*Goals*	*Measures*
Survival	Cash flow	Quality product	Defect rate
Profitability	Return on capital employed	Good after-sales service	Response time

Internal Business Perspective		Innovation and Learning Perspective	
Goals	*Measures*	*Goals*	*Measures*
Managerial efficiency	Throughput of products	Continual improvement	Number of employee suggestions
Advertising success	Increase in customer spend	Develop new products	Number of new product launches

The balanced scorecard thus looks at a business in a comprehensive way. It devises goals and then seeks to measure them. Finally, it combines financial and non-financial measures. One problem with the balanced scorecard is that by taking a multiple-perspective view, no single goal is overriding. It is, therefore, difficult to prioritise the goals. In addition, the appropriate selection of a balanced set of measures may prove difficult, in practice.

(iii) Benchmarking

Benchmarking measures a business against its competitors. The concept is easy – find the best and compare oneself against them across a series of performance indicators. These might be, for example, customer service, number of complaints, or debtors collection period.

DEFINITION 7.3

Benchmarking

Working definition
The comparison of a business with its direct competitors or industry norms.

Formal definition
'The establishment, through data gathering, of targets and comparators, through whose use relative levels of performance (and particularly areas of underperformance) can be identified. By the adoption of identified best practices it is hoped that performance will improve.'

Chartered Institute of Management Accountants (2000), *Official Terminology*

By benchmarking, companies aim to improve their own performance by comparing themselves against their competitors. The problem is that the most effective comparison is to competitors in the same industry. These competitors will be reluctant to provide the data. Benchmarking is thus more usually conducted against industry norms. A practical example of benchmarking is given in Real-Life Nugget 7.3.

REAL-LIFE NUGGET 7.3

Benchmarking in the Dairy Industry

Farmers generally supply their milk to local, regionalised dairies. These dairies may take the milk of, say, 20–30 farmers. Every month the dairy provides these farmers with a printout of how they are doing in comparison with the other farmers. This printout might contain, for example, milk yield per cow in litres, cows per hectare, yield from grazing, litres per cow. From this printout, the individual farmers can judge their relative productivity. The printouts are anonymous so that the farmers can only identify themselves. An extract from a printout is given below.

ANNUAL ROLLING RESULTS TO: August 2000

STOCK		MILK		FEED			FORAGE
Cows in herd	Cows/ hectare	Milk price pence	Yield litres/ cow	All concs tonnes/ cow	Av concs price £/tonne	All bought feed costs pence per litre	Yield from grazing litres/cow
133	2.75	16.19	7022	1.35	95	1.88	–
87	3.46	17.33	5836	1.06	108	1.97	3065
99	1.91	18.57	8005	1.35	106	2.04	2742
175	2.43	18.46	6707	1.59	95	2.24	–
99	2.49	15.42	7870	1.57	111	2.31	2181

Source: By kind permission of *Promar International*

Strategic Choice of Future Direction

Once the current position has been assessed and appraised, there is a need to plan for future strategy. In essence, there are two main directions. A business can either exploit its inherent strengths, for example, by expanding its product range or by more effectively utilising its customer base. Or alternatively, a business can diversify externally, for example, by acquiring another business. We explore these two directions briefly below.

(i) Exploit Inherent Strengths

If a particular product or service is successful, a business may consider expanding its range to similar, but as yet untapped, markets. For instance, if the product is selling well in Brazil, the company might expand its sales to other South American countries.

PAUSE FOR THOUGHT 7.4

Exploiting a Product's Strength

Can you think of any ways other than exploiting new geographical markets in which you could use an existing product's strength?

It might be possible to do the following:

....

- target existing buyers to buy more
- target a new market segment, such as a new age range (e.g., market a child's book to adults, such as the Harry Potter series) or social group
- sell other products in association with the main product (e.g., the range of Barbie products with the Barbie doll).

An alternative to expanding its geographical range is for the business to exploit its customer base more fully. In order to gain relevant information, market research may be carried out. This may seek to ascertain the size of the customer base, the contribution of each sales item, product market share, sales growth and product demand.

Another technique is customer profitability analysis. In essence, this involves a detailed analysis of revenue looking at customer profitability and customer mix. To do this the customers are analysed by characteristics such as age, sex, spending power or social class. The aim is to focus on the most profitable customers.

Various techniques are now available which facilitate customer profitability analysis. Database mining, for example, enables a sales database to be critically examined for trends and other useful information. Interestingly, the findings from using these techniques are not always obvious, as Real-Life Nugget 7.4 shows.

REAL-LIFE NUGGET 7.4

Database Mining

A telecommunications company analysed its database using database mining. The customers were rated as low, medium and high spenders. The initial reason for the investigation was to maximise sales by encouraging the low spenders to spend more. In actual fact, the company found that the way to maximise sales was quite the reverse. The big spenders could easily be encouraged to spend still more.

(ii) External Diversification

A business may grow internally, acquire or merge with another business or cooperate with other businesses through a joint venture. This section concentrates on the acquisition/merger alternative. An acquisition is where one business takes over another (i.e., acquires more than 50 % of another company's shares), whereas a merger is where two businesses combine their resources to form a new company. From an accounting perspective, mergers have the advantage that a business's profits are pooled and available for distribution to shareholders. In acquisitions not only are profits not available for distribution, but goodwill is created.

Businesses seek mergers/acquisitions because they are a quick way of growing and also there may be certain operating advantages such as economies of scale. Vodafone, for example, acquired Mannesmann, a German company, so that it could extend its mobile phones into the European and, in particular, the German market. There are also other more specific reasons. For example, a manufacturing company's SWOT analysis might indicate a shortage of raw materials. To safeguard its supplies, the company might then purchase a key supplier.

Conclusion

Strategic management accounting attempts to overcome the inward-looking nature of management accounting. It is concerned with the long-term strategy of a business. Strategic management accounting is still evolving and is an elusive concept. However, three stages are identifiable. First, an assessment of the current position of a business. This involves an audit of a company's external environment (for example, political, legal and economic environment) and internal environment (for example, resources and current products). The techniques of value chain analysis, life cycle analysis and the product portfolio matrix are sometimes used. The second stage involves an appraisal of the business's current position. This may use SWOT analysis (strengths, weaknesses, opportunities and threats), the balanced scorecard (using financial and non-financial performance measures in a multi-perspective context) and benchmarking against competitors. And, lastly, there is the strategic choice of future direction. This may involve focusing internally on finding new product markets or more fully exploiting the customer database. Alternatively, a business may choose to diversify externally through a merger or acquisition.

Selected Reading

Johnson, H.T. and R.S. Kaplan (1987), *Relevance Lost: The Rise and Fall of Management Accounting*, Harvard University Press.
A ground-breaking book which re-examined the history of management accounting and argued it was out of touch with contemporary business needs.

Kaplan, R.S. (1984), 'Yesterday's accounting undermines production', *Harvard Business Review*, July/August, pp. 95–101.
   In the same vein as *Relevance Lost*. It argues management accounting has not kept sufficiently up-to-date.
Kaplan, R.S. and D.P. Norton (1992), 'The Balanced Scorecard: measures that drive performance', *Harvard Business Review*, January–February, pp. 71–9.
   Offers an alternative to the perceived inadequacies of management accounting.
Porter, M.E. (1985), *Competitive Advantage: Creating and Sustaining Superior Performance*, New York, Free Press.
   A well-respected book which looks at how businesses can gain competitive advantage through techniques such as value chain analysis.

Q&A   Discussion Questions

Questions with numbers in blue have answers at the back of the book.

Q1   What is strategic management accounting and how does it address some of the limitations of traditional management accounting?

Q2   Management accountants and strategy do not mix very well. Management accountants should, therefore, not involve themselves in strategic management accounting. Discuss the main arguments for and against this view.

Q3   Briefly outline the nature of the following techniques and then discuss their strengths and weaknesses:
   (a) value chain analysis
   (b) life cycle analysis
   (c) the product portfolio matrix
   (d) SWOT analysis
   (e) the balanced scorecard
   (f) benchmarking

Q4   Is growth through exploiting the internal resources of a company better than growth through acquisition/merger?

Q5   State whether the following statements are true or false. If false, explain why.
   (a) Strategic management accounting looks at both the internal and external environments of a business.
   (b) The cost of activities in value chain analysis is determined by key cost drivers.
   (c) The product portfolio matrix consists of dogs, cats, cows and horses.
   (d) The balanced scorecard uses only financial information.
   (e) SWOT analysis stands for strengths, weaknesses, openings and threats.

Q&A   Numerical Questions

Questions with numbers in blue have answers at the back of the book.

Q1 You have the following details for three products (the maxi, mini and midi) for five years.

| | Maxi | | Mini | | Midi | |
Year	Sales	Profits (losses)	Sales	Profits (losses)	Sales	Profitability
	£	£	£	£	£	£
1	8,000	(3,000)	100,000	33,000	–	–
2	25,000	4,000	60,000	18,000	1,000	(3,000)
3	100,000	25,000	30,000	6,000	25,000	8,000
4	110,000	26,000	10,000	(3,000)	50,000	18,000
5	60,000	13,000	1,000	(4,000)	55,000	26,000

Required: In Year 3, state at which stage of their life cycle you would anticipate the products to be (introduction, growth, maturity, decline or withdrawal)?

Q2 Four products (the apple, orange, pear and banana) have the following financial profiles.

	Market Share	Market Growth
Apple	70 %	80 %
Orange	15 %	70 %
Pear	80 %	10 %
Banana	20 %	15 %

Required: Classify the products into either stars, cash cows, question marks or dogs. Explain if you would expect them to be profitable.

Q3 You have the following details about Computeco, a computer games manufacturer and distributor. An internal and external audit establishes the following details of two products, the Kung and the Fu.

	Market Share	Market Growth	Sales (000's)	Contribution (000's)
Kung	70 %	80 %	£10,000	£10,000
Fu	18 %	20 %	£3,000	£500

The Kung is currently marketed only in the UK; the Fu is marketed throughout the world. The product life cycles are five years. The Kung is 18 months old; the Fu is 4-years-old. The top developmental programmer has just left. Computeco has just installed a state-of-the-art computer system. The company is small, friendly and well-connected. A Japanese company has just approached Computeco asking it to market their product.

Required: Prepare a SWOT analysis stating your recommendations to management for the future.

Q4   You have gathered the following information for a regional railway company.

(a) The mission statement of the company is to survive, be profitable, be safe, give customers good service, run an efficient service, maintain a good infrastructure, and constantly improve.

(b) The main financial indicators are cash flow, return on capital employed and return on investment.

(c) The company has recently offered full-ticket refunds to customers who are unhappy with the service provided or where trains are more than 10 minutes late.

(d) The company publishes monthly details of accidents.

(e) The company aims to use staff more efficiently and maximise the train operating times.

(f) The company operates a continual improvement programme based on staff suggestions.

(g) A new capital expenditure programme has expanded considerably the rolling stock.

Required: From this information, prepare a balanced scorecard.

Q5   You sell the Feelgood, a health cushion, to 100,000 customers. Each cushion costs £25. You obtain the following breakdown of sales by customer category.

Sales Matrix

Age	Sales £	Geographical Location	Sales £	Sex	Sales £	TV Viewing	Sales £	Newspaper	Sales £
0–20	10,000	South	150,000	Male	50,000	BBC	200,000	Mail	150,000
21–40	50,000	Midland	20,000	Female	200,000	ITV	20,000	Sun	10,000
41–60	80,000	North	70,000			Sky	30,000	Telegraph	20,000
60+	110,000	Overseas	10,000					Times	10,000
								Express	60,000
	250,000		250,000		250,000		250,000		250,000

Required:

(i) Using this customer matrix, state which customers you might target.

(ii) State whether you need any further information.

(iii) State where you might target your advertising campaign.

Chapter 8

"There are no maps to the future."

A.J.P. Taylor

Learning Outcomes

After completing this chapter you should be able to:

✔ Introduce and explain the nature of capital investment.

✔ Outline the main capital investment appraisal techniques.

✔ Appreciate the time value of money.

✔ Explain the use of discounting.

Long-Term Decision Making: Capital Investment Appraisal

In a Nutshell

- *Capital investment decisions are long-term, strategic decisions, such as building a new factory.*

- *Capital investment decisions involve initial cash outflows and then subsequent cash inflows.*

- *Many assumptions underpin these cash inflows and outflows.*

- *There are four main capital investment techniques. Two (payback and accounting rate of return) do not take into account the time value of money. Two do (net present value and internal rate of return).*

- *Payback is the simplest method. It measures how long it takes for a company to recover its initial investment.*

- *The accounting rate of return uses profit not cash flow and measures the annual profit over the initial capital investment.*

- *Net present value discounts estimated future cash flows back to today's values.*

- *Internal rate of return establishes the discount rate at which the project breaks even.*

- *Sensitivity analysis is often used to model future possible alternative situations.*

Introduction

Management accounting can be divided into cost recovery and control, and decision making. In turn, decision making consists of short-term and long-term decisions. Whereas strategic management sets the overall framework within which the long-term decisions are made, capital investment appraisal involves long-term choices about specific investments in future projects. These projects may include, for example, investment in new products or new infrastructure assets. Without this investment in the future, firms would not survive in the long term. However, capital investment decisions are extremely difficult as they include a considerable amount of crystal ball gazing. This chapter looks at four techniques (the payback period, the accounting rate of return, net present value and the internal rate of return) which management accountants use to help them peer into the future.

Nature of Capital Investment

Capital investment is essential for the long-term survival of a business. Existing fixed assets, for example, will wear out and need replacing. The capital investment decision operationalises the strategic, long-term plans of a business. As Figure 8.1 shows, long-term capital expenditure decisions can be distinguished from short-term decisions by their time span, topic, nature and level of expenditure, by the external factors taken into account and by the techniques used.

Figure 8.1   Comparison of Short-Term Decisions and Long-Term Capital Investment Decisions

Characteristic	Short-Term	Long-Term
1. Time Span	Maximum 1 to 2 years, mostly present situation	Upwards from 2 years
2. Topic	Usually concerned with current operating decision, e.g., discontinue present product	Concerned with future expenditure decisions, e.g., build new factory
3. Nature	Operational	Strategic
4. Level of Expenditure	Small to medium	Medium to great
5. External Factors	Generally not so important	Very important, especially interest rate, inflation rate
6. Sample Techniques	Contribution analysis, break-even analysis	Payback, accounting rate of return, net present value, and internal rate of return

Capital investment decisions are thus usually long-term decisions, which may sometimes look 10 or 20 years into the future. They are often the biggest expenditure decisions that a business faces. Some examples of capital investment decisions might be deciding whether or not to build a new factory or whether to expand into a new product range. A football club, such as Manchester United, for example, might have to decide whether or not to build a new stadium. A common capital expenditure decision will involve choosing between alternatives. For example, which of three particular stadiums should we build? Or which products should we currently develop for the future? These decisions are particularly important given the fast-changing world (see for example, Soundbite 8.1).

SOUNDBITE 8.1

Fast-Changing Corporate World

'Fully one third of our more than $13 billion in worldwide revenues comes from products that simply did not exist five years ago.'

Ralph S. Larsen, *Johnson and Johnson* (October 22, 1992)

Source: *The Wiley Book of Business Quotations* (1998), p. 83

A key problem with any capital investment decision is taking into account all the external factors and correctly forecasting future conditions. As the quotation by A.J.P. Taylor at the start of the chapter stated: 'There are no maps to the future'. In Real-Life Nugget 8.1 Peter Aytan wonders why everything takes longer to finish and costs more than originally budgeted.

REAL-LIFE NUGGET 8.1

Forecasting the Future
Trouble ahead

WHY does everything take longer to finish and cost more than we think it will?

The Channel Tunnel was supposed to cost £2.6 billion. In fact, the final bill came to £15 billion. The Jubilee Line extension to the London Underground cost £3.5 billion, about four times the original estimate. There are many other examples: the London Eye, the Channel Tunnel rail link.

This is not an exclusively British disease. In 1957, engineers forecast that the Sydney Opera House would be finished in 1963 at a cost of A$7 million. A scaled-down version costing A$102 million finally opened in 1973. In 1969, the mayor of Montreal announced that the 1976 Olympics would cost C$120 million and 'can no more have a deficit than a man can have a baby'. Yet the stadium roof alone – which was not finished until 13 years after the games – cost C$120 million.

Source: Peter Aytan, *New Scientist*, 29 April 2000, p. 43

The basic decision is simply whether or not a particular capital investment decision is worthwhile. In business, this decision is usually made by comparing the initial cash out-flows associated with the capital investment with the later cash inflows. We can distinguish between the initial investment, net cash operating flows for succeeding years and other cash flows.

PAUSE FOR THOUGHT 8.1

A Football Club's New Stadium

A football club is contemplating building a new stadium. What external factors should it take into account?

....

There are countless factors. Below are some that might be considered.

- How much will the stadium cost?
- How many extra spectators can the new stadium hold?
- How much can be charged per spectator?
- How many years will the stadium last?
- What is the net financial effect when compared with the present stadium?
- How confident is the club about future attendance at matches?

(i) Initial Investment

This is our initial capital expenditure. It will usually involve capital outflows on infrastructure assets (for example, buildings or new plant and machinery) or on working capital. This initial expenditure is needed so that the business can expand.

(ii) Net Cash Flows

These represent the operating cash flows expected from the project once the infrastructure assets are in place. Normally, we talk about annual net cash flow. This is simply the cash inflows less the cash outflows calculated over a year. For convenience, *cash flows are usually assumed to occur at the end of the year*.

(iii) Other Flows

These involve other non-operating cash flows. For example, the taxation benefits from the initial capital expenditure or the cash inflow from scrap.

PAUSE FOR THOUGHT 8.2

Assumptions in Capital Investment Decisions

A big problem in any capital investment decision is the assumptions that underpin it. Can you think of any of these?

....

- Costs of initial outlay
- Tax effects
- Cost of capital
- Inflation
- Cash inflows and outflows over period of project. These, in turn, may depend on pricing policy, external demand, value of production etc.

Capital Investment Appraisal Techniques

The four main techniques used in capital investment decisions are payback period, accounting rate of return, net present value and internal rate of return. An overview of these four techniques is presented in Figure 8.2. These techniques are then discussed below.

Figure 8.2   Four Main Types of Investment Appraisal Techniques

Feature	Payback	Accounting Rate of Return	Net Present Value	Internal Rate of Return
Nature	Measures time period in which *cumulative cash inflows* overtake *cumulative cash outflows*	Assesses *profitability* of initial investment	*Discounts* future cash flows to present	Determines the *rate of return* at which a project *breaks even*
Ease of use	Very easy	Easy	May be difficult	Quite difficult
Takes time value of money into account	No	No	Yes	Yes
Main assumptions	Value and volume of cash flows	Reliability of annual profits	Value and volume of cash flows, cost of capital	Value and volume of cash flows, cost of capital
Focus	Cash flows	Profits	Cash flows	Cash flows

It is important to realise that the payback period and the accounting rate of return take into account only the *actual* cash inflows and outflows. However, net present value and accounting rate of return take into account the *time value of money*.

PAUSE FOR THOUGHT 8.3

Time Value of Money

Why do you think it is important to take into account the time value of money?

....

There is an old saying that time is money! In the case of long-term capital investment decisions, it certainly is. Would you prefer £100 now or £100 in 10 years time? That one is easy! But what about £100 now or £150 in five years time? There is a need to standardise money in today's terms. To do this, we need to attribute a time value to money. In practice, we take this time value to be the rate at which a company could borrow money. This is called the cost of capital. If our cost of capital is 10%, we say that £100 today equals £110 in one year's time, £121 in 2 years time and so on. If we know the cost of capital of future cash flows we can, therefore, discount them back to today's cash flows.

As Real-Life Nugget 8.2 shows, amounts spent yesterday can mean huge sums today. Compounding is the opposite of discounting! If we discounted the $136,000,000,000 dollars back from 1876 to 1607 using a 10% discount rate we should arrive at one dollar.

REAL-LIFE NUGGET 8.2

Compound Growth

Compound Interest

From a speech in Congress more than 100 years ago:

It has been supposed here that had America been purchased in 1607 for $1, and payment secured by bond, payable, with interest annually compounded, in 1876 at ten percent, the amount would be – I have not verified the calculation – the very snug little sum of $136,000,000,000; five times as much as the country will sell for today. It is very much like supposing that if Adam and Eve have continued to multiply and replenish once in two years until the present time, and all their descendants had lived and had been equally prolific, then, saying nothing about twins and triplets, there would now be actually alive upon the earth, a quantity of human beings in solid measure more than thirteen and one-fourth times the bulk of the entire planet.

Source: Peter Hay (1988), *The Book of Business Anecdotes*, Harrap Ltd, London, p. 10

Each of the four capital investment appraisal techniques is examined using the information in Figure 8.3.

Figure 8.3 Illustrative Example of a Financial Service Company Wishing to Invest in a New On-Line Banking Service

The Everfriendly Building Society is contemplating launching a new on-line banking service, called the Falcon. There are three alternative approaches, each involving £20,000 initial outlay. In this case, cash inflows can be taken to be the same as profit. Cost of capital is 10%.

	Projects		
Year	A	B	C
Cash flows	£	£	£
0 (i.e. now)	(20,000)	(20,000)	(20,000)
1	4,000	8,000	8,000
2	4,000	6,000	8,000
3	8,000	6,000	6,000
4	6,000	3,000	6,000
5	6,000	2,000	3,000

Helpnote: The cash outflow is traditionally recorded as being in year 0 (i.e., today) in brackets. The cash inflows occur from year 1 onwards and are conventionally taken at the end of the year. To simplify matters, in this example, cash inflows have been taken to be the same as net profit. Finally, cost of capital can be taken as the amount that it cost the Everfriendly Building Society to borrow money.

Payback Period

The payback period is a relatively straightforward method of investment appraisal. It simply measures the cumulative cash inflows against the cumulative cash outflows until the project recovers its initial investment. The payback method is useful for screening projects for an early return on the investment. Ideally, it should be complemented by another method such as net present value.

DEFINITION 8.1

Payback Period

The payback period simply measures the cumulative cash inflows against the cumulative cash outflows. The point at which they coincide is the payback point.

Specific advantages

1 Easy to use and understand.
2 Conservative.

Specific disadvantages

1 Fails to take into account cash flows after payback.
2 Does not take into account the time value of money.

Taking Everfriendly Building Society's Falcon project, when do we recover the £20,000? Figure 8.4 shows this is after 3.67 years for project A, 3 years for project B and 2.67 years for project C.

Figure 8.4   Payback Using Everfriendly Building Society

	Projects		
	A	**B**	**C**
Year	£	£	£
0 (i.e. now) Cash outflows	(20,000)	(20,000)	(20,000)
Cumulative cash inflows			
1	4,000	8,000	8,000
2	8,000	14,000	16,000
3	16,000	**20,000**	**22,000**
4	**22,000**	23,000	28,000
5	28,000	25,000	31,000
Payback year	3.67 years*	3 years	2.67 years*

*For these two projects, payback will be two-thirds of the way through a year. This is because (taking project A to illustrate) after three years our cumulative inflows are £16,000 and after four years they are £22,000. Assuming, and it is a big assumption, a steady cash flow, we reach payback point after two-thirds of a year (i.e., £4,000 needed for payback, divided by £6,000 cash inflows).

Payback is a relatively straightforward investment technique. It is simple to understand and apply and promotes a policy of caution in the investment decision. The business always chooses the investment, which pays off the initial investment the most quickly. However, although useful, payback has certain crucial limitations.

PAUSE FOR THOUGHT 8.4

Limitations of Payback

Can you think of any limitations of payback?

Two of the most important limitations of payback are that it ignores both cash flows after the payback and the time value of money. Thus, a project may have a slow payback period, but have substantial cash flows once it is established. These will not be taken into account. In addition, cash flows in later years are treated as being the same value as cash flows in early years. This ignores the time value of money and may distort the capital investment decision.

Accounting Rate of Return

This method, unlike the other three methods, focuses on the profitability of the project, rather than its cash flow. Thus it is distinctly different in orientation from the other methods. The basic definition of the accounting rate of return is:

$$\text{Accounting rate of return} = \frac{\text{Average annual profit}}{\text{Capital investment}}$$

However, once we look more closely we run into potential problems. What exactly do we mean by 'profit' and 'capital investment'? For profit, do we take into account interest, taxation and depreciation? For capital investment, do we take the initial capital investment or the average capital employed over its life? Different firms will use different versions of this ratio. In this book, profit before interest and taxation, and initial capital investment are preferred (see Definition 8.2). This is because it is similar to conventional accounting ratios and seems logical! The accounting rate of return is easy to understand and use. Its main disadvantages are that profit and capital investment have many possible definitions and, like payback, the accounting rate of return does not take into account the time value of money.

DEFINITION 8.2

Accounting Rate of Return

Accounting rate of return is a capital investment appraisal method which assesses the viability of a project using annual profit and initial capital invested. We can define it as:

$$\frac{\text{Average annual profit before interest and taxation}}{\text{Initial capital investment}}$$

Specific advantages

1 Takes the whole life of a project.
2 Similar to normal accounting ratios.

Specific disadvantages

1 Many definitions of profit and capital investment possible.
2 Does not consider the time value of money.

The accounting rate of return is applied to the Everfriendly Building Society in Figure 8.5.

Figure 8.5   Accounting Rate of Return Using Everfriendly Building Society

	Project Cash Flows		
	A	**B**	**C**
Year	£	£	£
0 (i.e. now) Cash outflows	(20,000)	(20,000)	(20,000)
Net cash inflows (note)			
1	4,000	8,000	8,000
2	4,000	6,000	8,000
3	8,000	6,000	6,000
4	6,000	3,000	6,000
5	6,000	2,000	3,000
Total	28,000	25,000	31,000
Average profit	£28,000	£25,000	£31,000
	5 years	5 years	5 years
	= 5,600	= 5,000	= 6,200
Our accounting rate of return is therefore:	£5,600	£5,000	£6,200
	£20,000	£20,000	£20,000
	= 28%	= 25%	= 31%

We would, therefore, choose project C because its accounting rate of return is the highest.

Note: In this case, cash inflow equals net profit. This will not always be the case.

Returns on investment are treated very seriously by businesses. In Real-Life Nugget 8.3, Vodafone has a projected rate of return of at least 15 % on its capital investment. However, it is not absolutely clear from the press extract whether it has used the accounting rate of return.

REAL-LIFE NUGGET 8.3

Rates of Return

Vodafone AirTouch yesterday gave the first indication of how much money it expects to make from third generation mobile networks during the release of better-than-expected full-year results.

Key Hydon, finance director, said that the projected rate of return on the large capital investment required for licences and infrastructure was at least 15 per cent.

Although the £6 bn cost of Vodafone's new UK licence will be spread over its 20-year lifespan, most of the estimated £4 bn network spending and handset subsidy will be required in the first four or five years.

This implies that the company is projecting potential operating profits of about £75 m above its existing performance.

Source: Telecommunications group releases internal targets to counter criticism it overpaid for licence, Dan Roberts, *Financial Times*, 31 May 2000

Net Present Value

The net present value and internal rate of return can be distinguished from the payback period and accounting rate of return because they take into account the time value of money. Essentially, time is money. If you invest £100 in a bank or building society and the interest rate is 10 %, the £100 is worth £110 in one year's time (100 × 1.10), and £121 in two year's time (100 × 1.10^2, or 110 × 1.10).

We can use the same principle to work backwards. If we have £110 in the bank in a year's time with a 10 % interest rate, it will be worth £100 today (£110 × 0.9091, i.e. 100 ÷ 110). Similarly, £121 in two years' time would be worth £100 today (£121 × 0.8264, i.e. 100 ÷ 121).

PAUSE FOR THOUGHT 8.5

Discounting

You are approached by your best friend, who asks you to lend her £1,000. She promises to give you back £1,200 in two years' time. Your money is in a building society and earns 6 %. Putting friendship aside, do you lend her the money?

To work this out, we need to compare like with like. We could either work forwards (i.e., multiplying £1,000 by the 6 % earned over two years (1.06^2) = £1, 123.60). £1,000 today is worth £1,123.60 in two years' time. Or more conventionally, we work back from the future using the time value of money, in this case 6 %.

Thus, £1,200 in one year's time = £1,200 × (100/106, i.e., 0.9434)

$$= £1,132.08 \text{ today}$$

While £1,200 in two years' time = £1,200 × (100/112.36, i.e., 106 × 1.06)

$$= £1,200 × 0.8900$$

$$= £1,068 \text{ today}$$

Therefore, as £1,200 in two year's time is the equivalent of £1,068 today you should accept your friend's offer as this is £68 more than you currently have.

Fortunately, we do not have to calculate discount rates all the time! We use discount tables (see Appendix 8.1 at the end of this chapter). So to obtain a 10 % interest rate in two year's time, we look up the number of years (two) and the discount rate (10 %). We then find a discount factor of 0.8264!

As Definition 8.3 shows, net present value uses the discounting principle to work out the value in today's money of future expected cash flows. It uses the cost of capital as the discount rate. Conventionally, the cost of capital is taken as the rate at which the business can borrow money. However, the estimation of the cost of capital can be quite difficult. In Chapter 9 we look in more detail at how companies can derive their cost of capital. Cost of capital is a key element of capital investment appraisal. Essentially, a business is seeking to earn a higher return from new projects than its cost of capital. If this is achieved, the projects will be viable. If not, they are unviable.

DEFINITION 8.3

Net Present Value

Net present value is a capital investment appraisal technique which discounts future expected cash flows to today's monetary values using an appropriate cost of capital.

Specific advantages

1 Looks at all the cash flows.
2 Takes into account the value of money.

Specific disadvantages

1 Estimation of cost of capital may be difficult.
2 Assumes all cash flows occur at end of year.
3 Can be complex.

Behavioural factors can also play their part in making a decision. This is shown in Real-Life Nugget 8.4.

REAL-LIFE NUGGET 8.4

Behavioural Implications of Cost of Capital

If a company decides it will only go ahead with projects that show a discounted return on investment of better than 15 per cent, anyone putting forward a project will ensure that the accompanying figures indicate a better than 15 per cent return. If the criterion is raised to 20 per cent, the figures will be improved accordingly. And there is no way in which the person analysing the project can contest those figures – unless he can find a flaw in the performance of the projection rituals.

Source: Graham Cleverly (1971), *Managers and Magic*, Longman Group Ltd, London, p. 86

Figure 8.6 applies net present value to the Everfriendly Building Society.

Figure 8.6 Net Present Value as Applied to the Everfriendly Building Society

| | Project Cash Flows | | | Discount Rate | Discounted Cash Flows | | |
	A	B	C	10%	A	B	C
Year	£	£	£		£	£	£
0 (i.e. now)	(20,000)	(20,000)	(20,000)	1	(20,000)	(20,000)	(20,000)
1	4,000	8,000	8,000	0.9091	3,636	7,273	7,273
2	4,000	6,000	8,000	0.8264	3,306	4,958	6,611
3	8,000	6,000	6,000	0.7513	6,010	4,508	4,508
4	6,000	3,000	6,000	0.6830	4,098	2,049	4,098
5	6,000	2,000	3,000	0.6209	3,725	1,242	1,863
Total discounted cash flows					20,775	20,030	24,353
Net Present Value (NPV)					775	30	4,353

All three projects have a positive net present value and, therefore, are worth carrying out. However, project C has the highest NPV and thus should be chosen if funds are limited.

When using the net present value, it is useful to follow the steps laid out in Helpnote 8.1.

HELPNOTE 8.1

Calculating Net Present Value

1. Calculate initial cash flows.

2. Choose a discount rate (usually given), normally based on the company's cost of capital.

3. Discount original cash flows using discount rate.

4. Match discounted cash flows against initial investment to arrive at net present value.

5. Positive net present values are good investments. Negative ones are poor investments.

6. Choose the highest net present value. This is the project that will most increase the shareholders' wealth.

PAUSE FOR THOUGHT 8.6°

Discount Tables

Using the discount tables given in Appendix 8.1, what are the following discount factors:

(i) 8% at 5 years, (ii) 12% at 8 years, (iii) 15% at 10 years, (iv) 20% at 6 years, and (v) 9% at 9 years.

....

From Appendix 8.1, we have
(i) 0.6806; (ii) 0.4039; (iii) 0.2472; (iv) 0.3349; (v) 0.4604.

In practice, calculating net present values becomes very complicated. For example, you have to take into account taxation, inflation, etc. However, net present value is a very versatile technique, allowing you to determine which projects are worth investing in and to choose between competing projects.

Internal Rate of Return (IRR)

The internal rate of return is a more sophisticated discounting technique than net present value. As Definition 8.4 shows, it can be defined as the rate of discount required to give a net present value of zero. Another way of looking at this is the maximum rate of interest that a company can afford to pay without suffering a loss on the project. Projects are accepted if the company's cost of capital is less than the IRR. Similarly, projects are rejected if the company's cost of capital is higher than the IRR. The advantages of the internal rate of return are that it takes into account the time value of money and calculates a break-even rate of return. However, it is complex and difficult to understand.

DEFINITION 8.4

The Internal Rate of Return

The internal rate of return represents the discount rate required to give a net present value of zero. It pays a company to invest in a project if it can borrow money for less than the IRR.

Specific advantages
1 Uses time value of money.
2 Determines the break-even rate of return.
3 Looks at all the cash flows.

Specific disadvantages
1 Difficult to understand.
2 No need to select a specific discount rate.
3 Complex, often needing a computer.
4 In certain situations, gives misleading results (for example, where there are unconventional cash flows).

The relationship of the internal rate of return to net present value is shown in Figure 8.7 and the internal rate of return is then applied to the Everfriendly Building Society in Figure 8.8.

Figure 8.7   Relationship Between the Net Present Value and Internal Rate of Return

A project has the following net present values (NPVs).

£2,000 NPV at 10% discount rate.
(£1,000) NPV at 15% discount rate.
What is the internal rate of return?

We can find the internal rate of return either (i) *diagrammatically* or (ii) *mathematically* by a process called interpolation.

(i) Diagrammatically

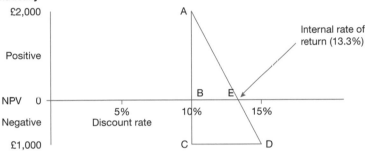

A = Discount rate 10%, £2,000 NPV
D = Discount rate 15%, (£1,000) NPV
E = Internal rate of return (13.3%)

(ii) Mathematically

We need to find point E. To do this, we can find the distance from B to E using the principles of similar triangles from mathematics: $\dfrac{BE}{CD} = \dfrac{AB}{AC}$

$$\therefore \quad \frac{BE}{5} = \frac{2,000}{3,000}$$

$$\therefore \quad \frac{BE}{5} = \frac{10,000}{3,000} = 3.3\%$$

$\therefore$ IRR = 10% + 3.33% = 13.3%

This can be re-written as follows:

IRR	=	Lowest discount rate	+	difference in discount rates	×	lowest discount rate NPV / difference in NPVs
13.3%	=	10%	+	5%	×	2,000 / 3,000

It is this formula that we will use from now on.

Figure 8.8   Internal Rate of Return as Applied to the Everfriendly Building Society

From Figure 21.6, we know that at 10% our net present values are all positive, A £775, B £30 and C £4,353. To solve the problem mathematically, we need to ascertain a negative present value for each project. So, first of all, we try 15%.

Year	Project Cash Flows			Discount Rate 15%	Discounted Cash Flows (DCF)			Discount Rate 20%	DCF C
	A	B	C		A	B	C		
	£	£	£		£	£	£		£
0	(20,000)	(20,000)	(20,000)	1	(20,000)	(20,000)	(20,000)	1	(20,000)
1	4,000	8,000	8,000	0.8696	3,478	6,957	6,957	0.8333	6,666
2	4,000	6,000	8,000	0.7561	3,024	4,537	6,049	0,6944	5,555
3	8,000	6,000	6,000	0.6575	5,260	3,945	3,945	0.5787	3,472
4	6,000	3,000	6,000	0.5718	3,431	1,715	3,431	0.4823	2,894
5	6,000	2,000	3,000	0.4972	2,983	994	1,492	0.4019	1,206
Total discounted cash inflows					18,176	18,148	21,874		19,793
Net Present Value (NPV)					(1,824)	(1,852)	1,874		(207)

15% produced A (£1,824), B (£1,852) and C £1,874 in net present values. We still need a negative value for C. So above we also ran a higher discount rate 20% for C. This gives us a negative NPV of (£207).

To solve this we can now use our formula.

$$\text{IRR} = \text{Lowest discount rate} + \text{difference in discount rates} \times \frac{\text{lowest discount rate NPV}}{\text{difference in NPVs}}$$

$$\text{A. } 10\% + (15 - 10\%) \times \frac{£775}{£775 + £1,824} = 10\% + (5\% \times 0.2982) = 11.5\%$$

$$\text{B. } 10\% + (15 - 10\%) \times \frac{£30}{£30 + £1,852} = 10\% + (5\% \times 0.01594) = 10.1\%$$

$$\text{C. } 10\% + (20 - 10\%) \times \frac{£4,353}{£4,353 + £207} = 10\% + (10\% \times 0.9546) = 19.6\%$$

Our ranking for the IRR method is thus project C, then A and, finally, B. As all projects have IRRs which exceed our cost of capital of 10% all three projects are potentially viable. However, for project B the IRR is only marginally greater than the cost of capital.

When calculating the IRR, there are four main steps. These are shown in Helpnote 8.2.

The IRR can be a very useful technique. However, the complexity is often off-putting. In practice, students will be pleased to learn that the calculations to arrive at the IRR are generally done using a computer program. Normally, the results from NPV and IRR will be consistent. However, in some cases, such as projects with unconventional cash flows (e.g., alternating cash inflows and outflows), the NPV and IRR may give different results. In these cases, NPV is probably the most reliable.

If there was a clash between the results from the different methods then it would be difficult to choose. Different businesses will prefer different methods depending on their priorities. I would probably choose net present value as the superior method. This is because it takes into account the time value of money, is more reliable, and is easier to understand and use than the internal rate of return.

Now that we have calculated the results for the Everfriendly Building Society using all four methods, we can compare them (see Figure 8.9). Project C is clearly the superior method.

> ## HELPNOTE 8.2
>
> ## Calculating the Internal Rate of Return (IRR)
>
> 1. Calculate a positive NPV for all projects.
> 2. Calculate a negative NPV for all projects. Use trial and error. The higher the discount rate, the lower the NPV.
> 3. Calculate out the IRR using the formula:
>   IRR = Lowest discount rate + difference in discount rates $\times \dfrac{\text{lowest discount rate NPV}}{\text{difference in NPVs}}$
> 4. Choose the project with the highest IRR. When evaluating a single project, the project will be chosen when its IRR is higher than the company's cost of capital.

Figure 8.9   Comparison of the Projects for Everfriendly Building Society Using the Four Capital Appraisal Methods

	Projects		
	A	**B**	**C**
Payback Period	3.67 years	3 years	2.67 years
Ranking	3	2	1
Accounting Rate of Return	28%	25%	31%
Ranking	2	3	1
Net Present Value	£775	£30	£4,353
Ranking	2	3	1
Internal Rate of Return	11.5%	10.1%	19.6%
Ranking	2	3	1

Project C is the superior project using all methods, so we could choose project C.

Before we leave the capital investment appraisal techniques, it is important to reiterate that the results achieved will only be as good as the assumptions that underpin them. This is powerfully expressed in Real-Life Nugget 8.5.

REAL-LIFE NUGGET 8.5

Investment Appraisal Techniques

But where the very existence of angels is in doubt, debating how many of them can dance on a pin seems a sterile exercise. Where the validity of one's original information is suspect, performing ever more sophisticated calculations seems pointless. Nonetheless, there can hardly be a company in which new projects are not required to be subjected to a ritual calculation of the 'internal rate of return', 'net present value', 'payback period' or some other criterion of profitability. And yet most of the time the performers themselves are not convinced of the validity of the material information they are manipulating.

Source: Graham Cleverly (1971), *Managers and Magic*, Longman Group Ltd, London, p. 86

Other Factors

There are many other factors that affect capital investment appraisal. Below we discuss three of the most important: sensitivity analysis, inflation and taxation.

1. Sensitivity analysis

The assumptions underpinning the capital investment decision mean that it is often sensible to undertake some form of **sensitivity analysis**. Sensitivity analysis involves modelling the future to see if alternative scenarios will change the investment decision. For example, a project's estimated cash outflow might be £10 million, its estimated inflows might be £6 million and its cost of capital might be 10 %. All three of these parameters would be altered to assess any impact upon the overall results.

2. Inflation

The effects of inflation should also be included in any future capital investment model. Inflation means that a pound in a year's time will not buy as much as a pound today, as the price of goods will have risen. Therefore, we need to adjust for inflation. This can be done in two ways.

1 *By adjusting future cash flow*. Under this method, we increase the future cash flows by the expected rate of inflation. If inflation was 3 % over a year we would, therefore, increase an expected cash flow of £100 million by 3 % to £103 million. We would then discount these adjusted flows as normal.

2 *By adjusting the discount rate*. If we were using a discount rate of 10 %, we would deduct the inflation rate. If inflation was 3 %, we would then discount the future cash flows at 7 %.

3. Taxation

As we saw in Chapter 8 cash flow and profit are distinctly different. Discounted cash flows are based on cash flows not on accounting profit. In order to arrive at forecast cash flows from forecast profit we must, therefore, adjust the profit for non cash-flow items. In particular, we need to add back depreciation (disallowed by taxation authorities) and deduct any capital allowances. Capital allowances are allowed by the taxation authorities as a replacement for depreciation. They can be set off against taxable profits. Capital allowances, thus, reduce cash outflows. Normally, companies will pay their taxation nine months after their year end.

Conclusion

Capital investment appraisal methods are used to assess the viability of long-term investment decisions. Capital investment projects might be a football club building a new stadium or a company building a new factory. Capital investment decisions are long-term and often very expensive. It is, therefore, very important to test their viability. Four capital investment appraisal methods are commonly used: payback period; accounting rate of return; net present value; and internal rate of return. Unlike the last two, the first two do not take into account the time value of money. The payback period simply assesses how long it takes a company's cumulative cash inflows to outstrip its initial investment. The accounting rate of return assesses the profitability of a project using average annual profit over initial capital investment. Net present value discounts back estimated future cash flows to today's values using cost of capital as a discount rate. Finally, internal rate of return establishes the discount rate at which a project breaks even. All four appraisal methods are based on many assumptions about future cash flows. These assumptions are often tested using sensitivity analysis.

Q&A   Discussion Questions

Questions with numbers in blue have answers at the back of the book.

Q1 (a) Why do you think capital investment is necessary for companies?
    (b) What sort of possible capital investment might there be in:
     (i) the shipping industry?
     (ii) the hotel and catering industry?
     (iii) manufacturing industry?

Q2 Discuss the general assumptions that underpin capital investment appraisal.

Q3 Briefly outline the four main capital investment appraisal techniques and then discuss the specific advantages and disadvantages of each technique.

Q4 Why is time money?

Q5 State whether the following statements are true or false. If false, explain why.
    (a) The four main capital investment appraisal techniques are payback period, accounting rate of return, net present value and internal rate of return.
    (b) The payback period and net present value techniques generally use discounted cash flows.
    (c) The accounting rate of return is the only investment appraisal technique that focuses on profits not cash flows.
    (d) The discount rate normally used to discount cash flows is the interest rate charged by the Bank of England.
    (e) Sensitivity analysis involves modelling future alternative scenarios and assessing their impact upon the results of capital investment appraisal techniques.

Q&A   Numerical Questions

Questions with numbers in blue have answers at the back of the book.

These questions gradually increase in difficulty. Students may find question 6, in particular, testing.

Q1 What are the appropriate discount factors for the following:

    (i)   5 years at 10 % cost of capital   (iv) 4 years at 12 % cost of capital
    (ii) 6 years at 9 % cost of capital   (v) 3 years at 14 % cost of capital
    (iii) 8 years at 13 % cost of capital   (vi) 10 years at 20 % cost of capital

Q2   A company, Fairground, has a choice between investing in one of three projects: the Rocket, the Carousel or the Dipper. The cost of capital is 8 %. There are the following cash flows.

	Rocket £	Carousel £	Dipper £
Initial outlay	(18,000)	(18,000)	(18,000)
Cash inflow			
Year 1	8,000	6,000	10,000
Year 2	8,000	4,000	6,000
Year 3	8,000	14,000	5,000

Required: An evaluation of Fairground using:
  (i) the payback period
  (ii) the accounting rate of return (assume cash flows are equivalent to profits)
  (iii) net present value
  (iv) the internal rate of return.

Q3   Wetday is evaluating three projects: the Storm, the Cloud, and the Downpour. The company's cost of capital is 12 %. These projects have the following cash flows.

Year	Storm £	Cloud £	Downpour £
0 (Initial outlay)	(18,000)	(12,000)	(13,000)
Cash inflow			
1	4,000	5,000	4,000
2	5,000	2,000	4,000
3	6,000	3,000	4,000
4	7,000	2,500	4,000
5	8,000	3,000	4,000

Required: Calculate
  (i) the payback period
  (ii) the accounting rate of return (assume cash flows equal profits)
  (iii) the net present value
  (iv) the internal rate of return.

Q4 A company, Choosewell, has £30,000 to spend on capital investment projects. It is currently evaluating three projects. The initial capital outlay is on a piece of machinery that has a four-year life. Its cost of capital is 9 %.

	Ready		Steady		Go	
	£		£		£	
Initial capital outlay	(30,000)		(15,000)		(15,000)	
	Inflows	Outflows	Inflows	Outflows	Inflows	Outflows
Year	£	£	£	£	£	£
1	36,000	24,000	25,000	16,000	16,000	8,000
2	36,000	14,000	18,000	11,000	13,000	6,500
3	32,000	26,000	17,000	12,000	12,000	6,000
4	4,000	5,000	3,000	4,000	6,000	6,000

Required: Calculate
 (i) the payback period
 (ii) the accounting rate of return
 (iii) the net present value
 (iv) the internal rate of return.

Q5 A football club, Manpool, is considering investing in a new stadium. There are the following expected capital outlays and cash inflows for two prospective stadiums.

Year	Bowl £000	Superbowl £000
Outlays		
0	(1,000)	(1,000)
1	(1,000)	(1,000)
Net inflows		
1	50	300
2	100	300
3	150	300
4	200	300
5	250	300
6	300	300
7	350	300
8	400	300
9	450	300
10	500	300

Assume the football club can borrow money at respectively

(a) 5 %   (b) 8 %   (c) 10 %

Required:

(i) Calculate which stadium should be built and at which rate using net present value?

(ii) What is the internal rate of return for the two stadiums?

Q6   A company, Myopia, has the following details for its new potential product, the Telescope.

Year	Capital Outlay	Capital Inflow	Sales	Interest	Expenses (Excludes Depreciation)	Taxation
	£	£	£	£	£	£
0	(700,000)	–	–	–	–	–
1			340,000	20,000	(40,000)	–
2			270,000	20,000	(130,000)	(4,500)
3			320,000	20,000	(160,000)	(18,375)
4			345,000	20,000	(185,000)	(24,281)
5			430,500	20,000	(205,000)	(48,361)
6			330,300	20,000	(160,300)	(35,033)
7			200,600	20,000	(100,100)	(16,825)
8			145,300	20,000	(46,500)	(18,034)
9			85,200	20,000	(28,100)	(6,925)
10		5,000	38,600	20,000	(8,300)	–

Myopia's cost of capital is 10 %. The capital outlay is for the Jodrell machine which will last 10 years. The capital inflow of £5,000 is the scrap value after 10 years.

Required: Calculate

(i) the payback period

(ii) the accounting rate of return

(iii) the net present value

(iv) the internal rate of return.

Helpnote. In this question, which has a different format from those encountered so far, it is first necessary to calculate *profit before interest and tax* (i.e., sales less expenses and depreciation). After this we need to adjust for interest, taxation, depreciation (based on the initial capital outlay) and other cash flows to arrive at a final cash flow figure.

Appendix 8.1 Present Value of £1 at Compound Interest Rate (1 + r)

Years (n)	Interest rates (r)									
	1 %	2 %	3 %	4 %	5 %	6 %	7 %	8 %	9 %	10 %
1	0.9901	0.9804	0.9709	0.9615	0.9524	0.9434	0.9346	0.9259	0.9174	0.9091
2	0.9803	0.9612	0.9426	0.9246	0.9070	0.8900	0.8734	0.8573	0.8417	0.8264
3	0.9706	0.9423	0.9151	0.8990	0.8638	0.8396	0.8163	0.7938	0.7722	0.7513
4	0.9610	0.9238	0.8885	0.8548	0.8227	0.7921	0.7629	0.7350	0.7084	0.6830
5	0.9515	0.9057	0.8626	0.8219	0.7835	0.7473	0.7130	0.6806	0.6499	0.6209
6	0.9420	0.8880	0.8375	0.7903	0.7462	0.7050	0.6663	0.6302	0.5963	0.5645
7	0.9327	0.8706	0.8131	0.7599	0.7107	0.6651	0.6227	0.5835	0.5470	0.5132
8	0.9235	0.8535	0.7894	0.7307	0.6768	0.6274	0.5820	0.5403	0.5019	0.4665
9	0.9143	0.8368	0.7664	0.7026	0.6446	0.5919	0.5439	0.5002	0.4604	0.4241
10	0.9053	0.8203	0.7441	0.6756	0.6139	0.5584	0.5083	0.4632	0.4224	0.3855

Years (n)	Interest rates (r)									
	11 %	12 %	13 %	14 %	15 %	16 %	17 %	18 %	19 %	20 %
1	0.9009	0.8929	0.8850	0.8772	0.8696	0.8621	0.8547	0.8475	0.8403	0.8333
2	0.8116	0.7972	0.7831	0.7695	0.7561	0.7432	0.7305	0.7182	0.7062	0.6944
3	0.7312	0.7118	0.6931	0.6750	0.6575	0.6407	0.6244	0.6086	0.5934	0.5787
4	0.6587	0.6355	0.6133	0.5921	0.5718	0.5523	0.5337	0.5158	0.4987	0.4823
5	0.5935	0.5674	0.5428	0.5194	0.4972	0.4761	0.4561	0.4371	0.4190	0.4019
6	0.5346	0.5066	0.4803	0.4556	0.4323	0.4104	0.3898	0.3704	0.3521	0.3349
7	0.4817	0.4523	0.4251	0.3996	0.3759	0.3538	0.3332	0.3139	0.2959	0.2791
8	0.4339	0.4039	0.3762	0.3506	0.3269	0.3050	0.2848	0.2660	0.2487	0.2326
9	0.3909	0.3606	0.3329	0.3075	0.2843	0.2630	0.2434	0.2255	0.2090	0.1938
10	0.3522	0.3220	0.2946	0.2697	0.2472	0.2267	0.2080	0.1911	0.1756	0.1615

Helpnote: This table shows what the value of £1 today will be in the future, assuming different interest rates. Therefore, £1 today will be worth 90.91 pence in one year's time if the interest rate is 10 %. If you are given cash flows at a future time you need to use the interest rates in the table to adjust them to today's monetary value. Thus, if we have £5,000 in five years' time and our interest rate is 10 %, then, using the table, this will be worth £5,000 × 0.6209 or £3,104 in today's money.

Chapter 9

"It doesn't take very long to screw up a company. Two, three months should do it. All it takes is some excess inventory [stock], some negligence in collecting, and some ignorance about where you are."

Mary Baechler in *Inc.*, October (1994) quoted in *The Wiley Book of Business Quotations* (1998), p. 86

Learning Outcomes

After completing this chapter you should be able to:

✔ **Explain the nature and importance of sources of finance.**

✔ **Discuss the nature of short-term financing.**

✔ **Analyse the ways in which the long-term finance of a company may be provided.**

✔ **Understand the concept of the cost of capital.**

The Management of Working Capital and Sources of Finance

In a Nutshell

■ *Sources of finance are vital to the survival and growth of a business.*

■ *There are internally and externally generated sources of finance.*

■ *Sources of finance can be short-term or long-term.*

■ *Short-term and long-term sources of finance are normally matched with current assets and long-term, infrastructure assets, respectively.*

■ *Short-term internal sources of finance concern the more efficient use of cash, debtors and stock.*

■ *Techniques for the internal management of working capital involve the debtors collection model, the economic order quantity and just-in-time stock management.*

■ *Short-term external sources of finance include a bank overdraft, a bank loan, debt factoring, invoice discounting, and the sale and buy back of stock.*

■ *Retained profits are where a company finances itself from internal funds.*

■ *Three major sources of external long-term financing are leasing, share capital and long-term loans.*

■ *Leasing involves a company using, but not owning, an asset.*

■ *Share capital is provided by shareholders who own the company and receive dividends.*

■ *Loan capital providers do not own the company and receive interest.*

■ *Cost of capital is the effective rate at which a company can raise finance.*

Introduction

Sources of finance are vital to a business. They allow it to survive and grow. Sources of finance may be raised internally and externally. The efficient use of working capital is an important internal, short-term source of funds, while retained profits can be an important internal, long-term source. External funds may also be short-term or long-term. Bank loans and debt factoring are examples of external short-term finance. External long-term sources allow businesses to carry out their long-term strategic aims. Share capital and loan capital are examples of long-term finance. Every business aims to optimise its use of funds. This involves minimising short-term borrowings and financing long-term infrastructure investments as cheaply as possible.

Nature of Sources of Finance

Sources of finance may be generated internally or raised externally. These sources of finance may be short-term or long-term. If short-term, they will typically be associated with operational activities involving the financing of working capital (such as stock, debtors or cash). If long-term, they will typically be associated with funding longer-term infrastructure assets, such as the purchase of land and buildings.

Normally, it is considered a mistake to borrow short and use long (e.g., use bank overdrafts for long-term purposes). For instance, if a bank overdraft was used to finance a new building, then the company would be in trouble if the bank suddenly withdrew the overdraft facility.

As Figure 9.1 shows, *internal* sources of finance may be generated over the *short term* through the efficient management of working capital, or over the *long term* by reinvesting retained profits.

Figure 9.1   Overview of Sources of Finance

	Short-term (less than 2 years)	*Long-term (over 2 years)*
Internal (within firm)	(a) Efficient cash management (b) Efficient debtors management (c) Efficient stock management	(a) Retained profits
External (outside firm)	(a) Bank overdraft (b) Bank loans (c) Invoice discounting (d) Debt factoring (e) Sale and leaseback	(a) Leasing (b) Share capital (c) Long-term borrowing

External sources of capital may be raised in the *short term* by cash overdrafts, bank loans, invoice discounting, debt factoring or sale and leaseback. Over the *longer term* the three most important external sources of finance are leasing, share capital and long-term borrowing. Although 'short-term' is defined as less than two years, this is, in fact, very arbitrary. For example, some leases may be for less than two years while bank overdrafts and bank loans will sometimes be for more than two years. However, this division provides a useful and convenient simplification.

Short-Term Financing

Short-term financing is often called the management of working capital (current assets less current liabilities). One of the main aims is to reduce the amount of short-term finance that companies need to borrow for their day-to-day operations. The more money that is tied up in current assets, the more capital is needed to finance those current assets. Essentially, as well as using its working capital as efficiently as possible, a company may use short-term borrowings to finance its stock, debtors or cash needs.

Figure 9.2 provides an overview of a company's short-term sources of finance. This includes *internal* management techniques for the efficient management of working capital (for example, debtor collection model and economic order quantity) and the main *external* sources of funds.

Figure 9.2   Overview of Short-Term Sources of Finance

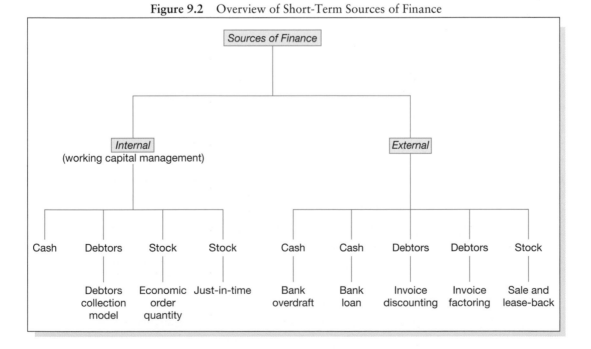

Internal Financing

Companies will try to minimise their levels of working capital so as to avoid short-term borrowings. In this section, we look at the main elements of efficient working capital management and three important techniques used to control working capital levels.

(a) Cash

Cash is the lifeblood of a business. Companies need cash to survive. Businesses will try to keep enough cash to manage their day-to-day business operations (e.g., purchase stock and pay creditors), but not to maintain excessive amounts of cash. Businesses prepare cash budgets (see Chapter 4), which enable them to forecast the levels of cash that they will need to finance their operations. They may also use the liquidity and quick ratio to assess their level of cash. If despite careful cash management the business's short-term cash requirements are insufficient then the business will have to borrow.

(b) Debtors

Debtors management is a key activity within a firm. It is often called credit control. Debtors result from the sale of goods on credit. There is, therefore, the need to monitor carefully the receipts from debtors to see that they are in full and on time.

There will often be a separate department of a business concerned with credit control. The credit control department will, for example, establish credit limits for new customers, monitor the age of debts and chase up bad debts. In particular, they may draw up a debtors age schedule. This will profile the age of the debts and allow old debts to be quickly identified.

Debtors Collection Model   A useful technique designed to maintain the most efficient level of debtors for a company is the debtors collection model. A debtors collection model balances the extra revenue generated by increased sales with the increased costs associated with extra sales (i.e., credit control costs, bad debts and the delay in receiving money). The model assumes that the more credit granted the greater the sales. However, these extra sales are offset by increased bad debts as the business sells to less trustworthy customers. Whether the delay in receipts means that the business receives less interest or pays out more interest depends on whether or not the bank account is overdrawn. Usually, the cost of capital (i.e., effectively, the company's borrowing rate: see later in this chapter) is used to calculate the financial costs of the delayed receipts. Figure 9.3 illustrates the debtors collection model.

Figure 9.3   Debtors Collection Model

Bruce Bowhill is the finance director of a business with current sales of £240,000. If credit rises, so do bad debts. The contribution is 20%, the cost of capital is 15%, the credit control costs are £10,000 per annum at all levels of sales.

Credit	Annual sales	Bad Debts
Nil	£240,000	–
1 month	£320,000	1%
2 months	£500,000	5%
3 months	£650,000	10%

What is the most favourable level of sales?

We need to balance the increased contribution earned by increased sales with the increased costs of easier credit (i.e., credit control, bad debts and cost of capital).

	Nil credit £	1 month £	2 months £	3 months £
Sales	240,000	320,000	500,000	650,000
Contribution 20%	48,000	64,000	100,000	130,000
Cost of credit control		(10,000)	(10,000)	(10,000)
Bad debts 1% sales		(3,200)		
5% sales			(25,000)	
10% sales				(65,000)
Cost of capital relating to delay in payment: 15% of average debtors*		(4,000)	(12,500)	(24,375)
Revised Contribution	48,000	46,800	52,500**	30,625

*Average debtors per month
= £26,667   (£320,000 ÷ 12) (1 month)
= £83,333   (£500,000 ÷ 6)   (2 months)
= £162,500 (£650,000 ÷ 4)   (3 months)

**The optimal level is thus two months as it has the highest revised contribution.

(c) Stock

For many businesses, especially for manufacturing businesses, stock is often an extremely important asset. Stock is needed to create a buffer against excess demand, to protect against rising prices or against a potential shortage of raw materials and to balance sales and production.

Stock control is concerned not primarily with valuing stock (see Chapter 3), but with protecting the stock physically and ensuring that the optimal level is held. Stock may be stolen or may deteriorate. For many businesses such as supermarkets the battle against theft and deterioration is never-ending. A week-old lettuce in a supermarket is not a pleasant asset!! For supermarkets, stock can also be a competitive advantage (see Real-Life Nugget 9.1).

REAL-LIFE NUGGET 9.1

Stock

A Way to Look at It

When F.W. Woolworth opened his first store, a merchant on the same street tried to fight the new competition. He hung out a big sign: 'Doing business in this same spot for over fifty years'. The next day Woolworth also put out a sign. It read: 'Established a week ago; no old stock'.

Source: Peter Hay (1988), *The Book of Business Anecdotes*, Harrap Ltd, London, p. 275

Two common techniques associated with efficient stock control are the economic order quantity model and just-in-time stock management.

(i) Economic Order Quantity (EOQ)   The EOQ model seeks to determine the optimal order quantity needed to minimise the costs of ordering and holding stock. These costs are the costs of placing the order and the carrying costs. Carrying costs are those costs incurred in keeping an item in stock, such as insurance, obsolescence, interest on borrowed money or clerical/security costs. The costs of ordering stock are mainly the clerical costs. The EOQ can be determined either graphically or algebraically. Figure 9.4 on the next page demonstrates both methods. A key assumption underpinning the EOQ model is that the stock is used in production at a steady rate.

Figure 9.4   Economic Order Quantity

Tree plc has the following information about the Twig, one of its stock items. The Twig has an average yearly use in production of 5,000 items. Each Twig costs £1 and the company's cost of capital is 10% per annum. For each Twig, insurance costs are 2p per annum, storage costs are 2p per annum and the cost of obsolescence is 1p. The ordering costs are £60 per order.

i. Graphical Solution
We must first compile a table of costs at various order levels. For example, at an order quantity of 500, Tree needs 10 orders per annum (i.e., to buy 5,000 Twigs) which would give a total order cost of £600. The average quantity in stock (250) will be half the order quantity (500). If it costs 15 pence to carry an item, the total carrying cost will be £37.50 (i.e., 250 × 15p). Finally, the total cost will be £637.50 (total order cost £600 plus total carrying cost £37.50).

Order quantity (Q)	Average number or orders per annum	Order cost	Total order cost	Average quantity in stock	Carrying cost per item of stock	Total carrying cost	Total cost
			(1)	(2)	(3)	(4)	(5)
		£	£		£	£	£
500	10	60	600	250	0.15	37.50	637.50
1,000	5	60	300	500	0.15	75.00	375.00
2,000	2.5	60	150	1,000	0.15	150.00	300.00
2,500	2	60	120	1,250	0.15	187.50	307.50
5,000	1	60	60	2,500	0.15	375.00	435.00

Notes from table:
(1) Number of orders per annum multiplied by order cost.
(2) This represents half the order quantity. It assumes steady usage and instant delivery of stock.
(3) Cost of capital 10p (10% × £1), insurance 2p, storage 2p, obsolescence 1p. All per item.
(4) Average quantity in stock (2) multiplied by the carrying cost of £0.15 (3).
(5) Total order cost (1) and total carrying cost (4).

The graph can now be drawn with order quantity on the horizontal axis and annual costs along the vertical axis. The intersection of carrying cost and ordering cost represents the optimal re-order level. The optimal order quantity is thus close to 2,000.

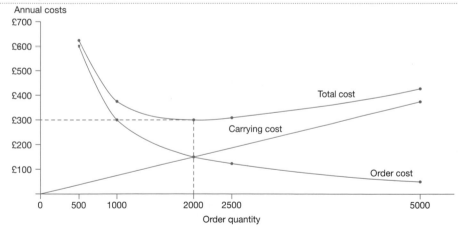

ii. Algebraic Solution
Fortunately, there is no need to know how to derive this formula, just apply it.

$$Q = \sqrt{\frac{2AC}{i}} \quad \text{where} \quad \begin{aligned} Q &= \text{economic order quantity} \\ A &= \text{average annual usage} \\ C &= \text{cost of each order being placed} \\ i &= \text{carrying cost per unit per annum} \end{aligned} \qquad \therefore Q = \sqrt{\frac{2 \times 5,000 \times 60}{0.15}} = 2,000 \text{ Twigs}$$

(ii) Just-in-Time   Just-in-time was developed in Japan, where it has proved an effective method of stock control. It seeks to minimise stock holding costs by the careful timing of deliveries and efficient organisation of production schedules. At its best, just-in-time works by delivering stock just before it is used. The amount of stock is thus kept to a minimum and stock holding costs are also minimised. In order to do this, there is a need for a very streamlined and efficient production and delivery service. The concept behind just-in-time has been borrowed by many UK and US firms. Taken to its logical extreme, just-in-time means that no stocks of raw materials are needed at all. One potential problem with just-in-time is that if stock levels are kept at a minimum there is no stock buffer to deal with unexpected emergencies. For example, in the fuel blockade of Autumn 2000 in the UK, many supermarkets ran out of food because they had kept low levels of stock in their stores.

External Financing

(a) Cash

If a company is not generating enough cash from trading it may need to borrow. The most common method of borrowing is via a bank overdraft or a bank loan. Bank overdrafts are very flexible. Most major banks will set up an overdraft facility for a business as long as they are sure the business is viable. A bank overdraft is a good way to tackle the fluctuating cash flows experienced by many businesses.

PAUSE FOR THOUGHT 9.1

Bank Overdrafts

A bank overdraft represents a flexible way for a business to raise money. Can you think of drawbacks?

. . . .

Overdrafts usually carry relatively high rates of interest. Overdrafts often carry variable rates of interest and are subject to a limit, which should not be exceeded without authorisation from the bank. They can be withdrawn at very short notice and are normally repayable on demand. Generally, interest is determined by time period and security. The shorter the time period, the higher the interest rate typically paid. In addition, if the loan is not secured on an asset (i.e., is unsecured) the rate of interest charged will once again be higher. Small businesses without a track record may often find it difficult to get a bank overdraft. Even when an overdraft is granted, the bank may insist that it is secured against the company's assets.

An alternative to a bank overdraft is a bank loan. The exact terms of individual bank loans will vary. However, essentially a loan is for a set period of years and this may well be more than two years. The rate of interest on a loan will normally be lower than on a bank overdraft. Loans may be secured on business assets, for example specific assets, such as stock or motor vehicles.

(b) Debtors

Since debtors are an asset, it is possible to raise money against them. This is done by debt factoring or invoice discounting.

(i) Debt factoring Debt factoring is, in effect, the subcontracting of debtors. Many department stores, for example, find it convenient to subcontract their credit sales to debt factoring companies. The advantage to the business is twofold. First, it does not have to employ staff to chase up the debtors. Second, it receives an advance of money from the factoring organisation. There are, however, potential problems with factoring. The debt factoring company is not a charity and will charge a fee, for example 4 % of sales, for its services. In addition, the debt factoring company

> **SOUNDBITE 9.1**
>
> # Debt Factoring
>
> 'Handing over your sales ledger to a factor was once viewed in the same league as Dr Faustus flogging his soul off to the devil – a path of illusory rides that would lead only to inevitable business ruin and damnation.'
>
> Jerry Frank, *No Longer a Deal with the Devil*
>
> Source: *Accountancy Age*, 18 May 2000, p. 27

will charge interest on any cash advances to the company. Finally, the company will lose the management of its customer database to an external party. As Soundbite 9.1 shows, debt factoring has traditionally been viewed with some suspicion.

(ii) Invoice discounting Invoice discounting, in effect, is a loan secured on debtors. The financial institution will grant an advance (for example, 75 %) on outstanding sales invoices (i.e., debtors). Invoice discounting can be a one-off, or a continuing, arrangement. An important advantage of invoice discounting over debt factoring is that the credit control function is not contracted out. The company, therefore, keeps control over its records of debtors. Figure 9.5 compares debt factoring with invoice discounting.

Figure 9.5   Comparison of Debt Factoring and Invoice Discounting

Element	Debt Factoring	Invoice Discounting
Loan from financial institution	Yes	Yes
Sales ledger (i.e., keeping records of debtors)	Management by financial institution	Managed by company
Time period	Continuing	Usually one-off, but can be continuing

The aim of debtors management is simply to collect money from debtors as soon as possible. For an optimal cash balance, with no considerations of fairness, a business will benefit if it can accelerate its receipts and delay its payments. Receipts from customers and payments to suppliers are measured using the debtors/creditors collection period ratio.

(c) Stock

As with debtors, it is sometimes possible to borrow against stock. However, the time period is longer. Stock needs to be sold, then the debtors need to pay. Stock is not, therefore, such an attractive basis for lending for the financial institutions. However, in certain circumstances, financial institutions may be prepared to buy the stock now and then sell it back to the company at a later date.

PAUSE FOR THOUGHT 9.2

Sale and Buy Back of Stock

Can you think of any businesses where it may take such a long time for stock to convert to cash that businesses may sell their stock to third parties?

....

The classic example of sale and buy back occurs in the wine and spirit business. It takes a long time for a good whisky to mature. A finance company may, therefore, be prepared to buy the stock from the whisky distillery and then sell it back at a higher price at a future time. In effect, there is a loan secured against the whisky.

Another example might be in the construction industry. Here the financial institution may be prepared to loan the construction company money in advance. The money is secured on the work-in-progress which the construction company has already completed. The construction company repays the loan when it receives money from the customers.

Long-Term Financing

There are potentially four main sources of long-term finance: retained profits; leasing; share capital; and loan capital (see Figures 9.6 and 9.7).

Figure 9.6   Overview of Sources of Long-Term Finance

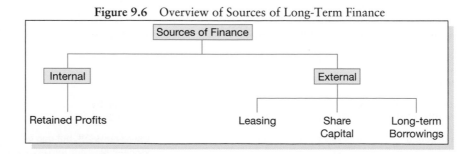

Figure 9.7   Sources of Long-Term Finance

(i) Internal Sources	Main Features
Retained profits	The company reinvests the profits it has made back into the business. It does not have to pay interest.
(ii) External Sources	
Leasing	A lessor leases specific assets to a company, such as a train or a plane. The company makes lease payments to the lessor.
Share capital	Money is raised from shareholders. Company pays dividends.
Long-term loan	Money is borrowed from banks or debt holder. Company repays interest.

For long-term finance, there is a need to raise money as cheaply and effectively as possible. Long-term finance is usually used to fund long-term infrastructure projects and can often be daunting, given the huge sums involved (see Soundbite 9.2).

Internal Sources

Retained Profits

Retained profits (or revenue reserves) represent an alternative to external financing. In effect, the business is financing itself from its past successes. Instead of distributing its profits as dividends, the company invests them for the future. Shareholders thus lose out today, but hope to gain tomorrow. As the company grows using its retained profits, it will in the future make more profits, distribute more dividends and then have a higher share price. In theory, that is!

In many businesses, retained profits represent the main source of long-term finance. It is important to realise that retained profits, themselves, are not directly equivalent to cash. However, indirectly they represent the cash dividends that the company could have paid out to shareholders. Retained profits are particularly useful in times when interest rates are high.

> **SOUNDBITE 9.2**
>
> # Finance
>
> 'What is high finance? It's knowing the difference between one and ten, multiplying, subtracting and adding. You just add noughts. It's no more than that.'
>
> John Bentley, *Sunday Mirror*, 8 April 1973
>
> *Source*: The Book of Business Quotations (1991), p. 156

PAUSE FOR THOUGHT 9.3

Retained Profits

What might be a limitation of using only retained funds as a source of long-term finance?

....

Retained profits are an easy resource for a company to draw upon. There is, however, one major limitation: a company can only grow by its own efforts and when funds are available. Therefore, growth may be very slow. The situation is similar to buying a house, you could save up for 25 years and then buy a house. Or you could buy one immediately by taking out a mortgage. Most people, understandably, prefer not to wait.

External Sources

(a) Leasing

In principle, the leasing of a company's assets is no different to an individual hiring a car or a television for personal usage. The property, initially at least, remains the property of the lessor. The lessee pays for the lease over a period of time. Depending on the nature of the property, the asset may eventually become the property of the lessee or remain, forever, the property of the lessor.

The main advantage of leasing is that the company leasing the asset does not immediately need to find the capital investment. The company can use the asset without buying it. This is particularly useful where the leased asset will directly generate revenue which is then used to pay the leasing company. Many of the tax benefits of leasing assets have now been curtailed. However, leasing remains an attractive way of financing assets such as cars, buses, trains or planes. Normally, leasing is tied to specific assets.

In the end, the company leasing the assets will pay more for them than buying them outright. The additional payments are how the leasing companies make their money. Leases are usually used for medium or long-term asset financing. Hire purchase or credit sales, which share many of the general principles of leases, are sometimes used for medium to short-term financing.

Strictly, leasing is a source of assets rather than a source of finance. It does not result in an inflow of money. However, it is treated as a source of finance because if the asset had been bought outright, not leased, the business would have needed to fund the original purchase. Long-term leasing can be considered equivalent to debt. The asset is purchased by the lessor, but used and paid for by the lessee, including an interest payment. Long-term leases must be disclosed on the balance sheet. There is a recent trend where businesses that own property portfolios sell them for cash. They then lease back the original properties. This is the strategy being considered by Marks & Spencer in Real-Life Nugget 9.2.

REAL-LIFE NUGGET 9.2

Sale and Leaseback

Marks & Spencer, the troubled retail group, is poised to sell up to 40 of its high street stores across the country in a bid to raise up to £250 m.

M&S, whose chief executive Peter Salsbury is conducting a strategy review to reverse the group's slump in profits, is said to be in talks with a select band of property investors. Under the proposals being considered, M&S would lease back the stores which are all understood to be prime sites and could include Oxford Circus, one of the retailer's larger London flagship stores.

Source: M&S £250 m Stores Sale, Doug Morrison, *The Sunday Telegraph*, 21 March 1999

(b) Share Capital

Apart from reserves, there are two main types of corporate long-term capital: share capital and loan capital. Share capital is divided into ordinary shares and preference shares. Both sets of shareholders are paid dividends. However, while ordinary shareholders are owners, preference shareholders are not (Chapter 9 provides a fuller discussion of these issues).

When a company wishes to raise substantial sums of new money, the normal choice is either raising share capital or loan capital. Freeserve, the Internet service provider, for example, chose a stock market flotation raising an anticipated £1.9 billion from shares (see Real-Life Nugget 9.3).

REAL-LIFE NUGGET 9.3

Stock Market Flotations

Freeserve, the free internet access service launched last September by Dixons Group, the electrical retailer, is likely to be valued at £1.9 billion or £1,500 per subscriber, when it comes to the stock market. A flotation is likely to take place next month.

Details of the float, disclosed yesterday, emerged at a turbulent time for Internet stocks in the US, and are likely to cause controversy in the City.

Freeserve's value on a 'per subscriber' basis will be similar to that of BSkyB, the satellite broadcaster, 40 per cent owned by News International.

Source: Freeserve plans £1.9bn float, Chris Ayres, *The Times*, 16 June 1999, p. 25

There are three main methods by which a company may raise share capital: rights issue, public issue and placing. The main features of these alternatives are listed in Figure 9.8.

Figure 9.8   Types of Share Issue

Type	Main Feature
Rights Issue	Existing shareholders can buy more shares in proportion to their existing holdings.
Public Issue	Company itself directly offers shares to the public. A prospectus containing the company's details is issued. The shares may be issued at a fixed price or open to tender (i.e., bidding). A variation on the public issue is the offer for sale. The company sells the new issue of shares to a financial institution which then issues them on the company's behalf.
Placing	A company coming to the market for the first time may allow underwriters to 'place' shares with certain financial institutions. These institutions will then hold them or sell them.

A **rights issue** is therefore an issue to existing shareholders. In June 2001, for example, British Telecom asked its *existing* shareholders for £5.9 billion extra cash. By contrast, **public issues** and **placings** involve new shareholders. The public issue is distinguished from the placing chiefly by the fact that the shares are 'open' to public purchase rather than being privately allocated. In all three types of share issue, the company receives the amount that the shareholders pay for the shares. This money can then be used to finance expansion or on any other corporate activity. Stock market issues can make entrepreneurs potentially very rich, as happened to the creators of Lastminute.com (see Real-Life Nugget 9.4), although this wealth is dependent upon them selling their shares!

REAL-LIFE NUGGET 9.4

Getting Rich Quick

Yesterday's frenzied debut for Lastminute.com once again raises a question that may never be properly answered: how much is an internet company really worth?

To many people a share is worth what the financial markets think it is, no more and no less. That would make Lastminute 'worth' every penny of the £800 m at which the total value of its shares were trading at one point yesterday. And no one can say investors were hoodwinked. They flocked to buy the shares despite the descant sung by analysts that they were overvalued.

Source: Watch out for those last minute lemmings, Victor Keegan, *The Guardian*, 15 March 2000, p. 26. © Guardian Newspapers Limited 2000

(c) Loan Capital

Loan capital is long-term borrowing. The holders of the loans are paid loan interest. Loan capital can chiefly be distinguished from ordinary share capital by four features. First, loan interest is a *deduction* from profits *not*, like dividends, a *distribution* of profits. Second, loan capital, unlike ordinary share capital, is commonly repaid. Third, unlike ordinary shareholders, the holders of loan capital do not own the company. And, finally, most loans will be secured either on the general assets of the company or on specific assets, such as land and buildings. In other words, if the company fails, the loan holders have first call on the company's assets. They will be able to sell the assets of the company to recover their loans. Sometimes convertible loans are issued which may be converted into ordinary shares at a specified future date. Loans and debt have always attracted humorists, as Real-Life Nuggets 9.5 and 9.6 show.

REAL-LIFE NUGGET 9.5

Loans
The Importance of Being Seen

Around the turn of the century a speculator by the name of Charles Flint got into financial difficulties. He had a slight acquaintance with J.P. Morgan, Sr., and decided to touch him for a loan. Morgan asked him to come for a stroll around the Battery in lower Manhattan. The two men discussed the weather in some detail, and other pressing matters, when finally, after about an hour or so, the exasperated Flint burst out: 'But Mr. Morgan, how about the million dollars I need to borrow?'

Morgan held out his hand to say goodbye: 'Oh, I don't think you'll have any trouble getting it now that we have been seen together.'

Peter Hay (1988), *The Book of Business Anecdotes*, Harrap Ltd, London, p. 5

REAL-LIFE NUGGET 9.6

Debt
Stratagem

A moneylender complained to Baron Rothschild that he had lent 10,000 francs to a man who had gone off to Constantinople without a written acknowledgement of his debt.

'Write to him and demand back 50,000 francs,' advised the baron.

'But he only owes me 10,000,' said the moneylender.

'Exactly, and he will write and tell you so in a hurry. And that's how you will have acknowledgement of his debt.'

Peter Hay (1988), *The Book of Business Anecdotes*, Harrap Ltd, London, p. 5

The relationship between ordinary share capital and a company's fixed interest funds (long-term loans and preference shares) is known as gearing. Gearing is particularly important when assessing the viability of a company's capital structure.

Cost of Capital

From the details of a company's different sources of finance, it is possible to determine its cost of capital. In essence, the cost of capital is simply the cost at which a business raises funds. The two main sources of funds are debt (from long-term loans) and equity (from share capital). Normally, debt finance will be cheaper than equity. As Soundbite 9.3 below shows, it is an important business concept. Each source of finance will have an associated cost of capital. However, it is important to calculate the business's overall cost of capital (known as the **weighted average cost of capital** or WACC). WACC is the cost of capital normally used as the discount rate in capital investment appraisal (see Chapter 8).

SOUNDBITE 9.3

Cost of Capital

'Business is the most important engine for social change in our society . . . And you're not going to transform society until you transform business. But you're not going to transform business by pretending it's not a business. Business means profit. You've got to earn your cost of capital. They didn't do it in the former Soviet Union, that's why it's former.'

Lawrence Perlman, *Twin Cities Business Monthly* (November 1994)

Source: *The Wiley Book of Business Quotations* (1998), p. 69

The same principles can be adopted for personal finance and for business. We take the examples of Deborah Ebt, a student, in Figure 9.9 and Costco plc in Figure 9.10 (both overleaf).

Figure 9.9   Calculation of Cost of Capital for a Student, D. Ebt

D. Ebt finances her college course as follows:

General expenses, by credit card	£3,000 at 25% interest per annum
Accommodation, by bank loan	£4,000 at 10% interest per annum
Car, by loan from uncle	£3,000 at 5% interest per annum

What is D. Ebt's overall weighted average cost of capital?

Source of Finance	Proportion	Cost of Capital	Weighted Average Cost of Capital (WACC)
	£	%	%	%
Credit card	3,000	30	25	7.5
Bank loan	4,000	40	10	4.0
Personal loan	3,000	30	5	1.5
	10,000	100		13.0

Helpnote
The weighted average cost of capital is the proportion of total debt financed by loan source multiplied by interest rate. Therefore, for credit cards (£3,000/£10,000) × 25% = 7.5%. The cost of capital for each source of finance is simply the interest rate.

Figure 9.9 thus shows that overall the weighted average cost of capital is 13% for D. Ebt. The most expensive source of finance was the credit card and the cheapest was the personal loan.

Figure 9.10   Example of a Company's Cost of Capital

Costco plc has 800,000 £1 ordinary shares currently quoted on the stock market at £2.50 each. It pays a dividend of 20p per share. Costco also has £200,000 worth of debt capital currently worth £1,000,000 on the stock market. The loan interest payable is 60,000.

Calculate Costco plc's weighted average cost of capital.

Source of Finance	Market Value	Proportion %	Cost of capital	Weighted Average Cost of Capital (WACC)
Equity	£2,000,000	66.67	8% (£0.20 ÷ £2.50)	5.3%
Debt	£1,000,000	33.33	6% (£60,000 ÷ £1,000,000)	2.0%
	£3,000,000	100.00		7.3%

The cost of capital is thus 7.3%.

Helpnote
We need to take the *market value* of the capital, not the original nominal value of the capital, as this is the value that the capital is *currently worth*. The cost of equity capital is simply the dividend divided by the share price and the cost of debt capital is the interest payable divided by the market price of the debt.

Figure 9.10 thus indicates that overall the weighted average cost of capital is 7.3 %. The equity capital constitutes most of this (i.e. 5.3 %).

The cost of capital is a potentially complex and difficult subject. However, the basic idea is simple, the company is trying to find the optimal mix of debt and equity which will enable it to fund its business at the lowest possible cost. Investors show great interest in a company's cost of capital (see Real-Life Nugget 9.7).

REAL-LIFE NUGGET 9.7

Railtrack's Cost of Capital

As for cost of capital, it's a matter of guesswork – or the capital-asset pricing model – to calculate the figure in the first place. However, the rail regulator reckons that Railtrack's cost of capital is close to 7.5 per cent before both tax and inflation. For investors, that figure looks pretty generous. Here's why: Railtrack will pay little tax in the coming years so, assuming inflation averages 2.5 per cent a year, the regulator is allowing Railtrack a post-tax return on its capital of nearly 10 per cent. That's approaching growth stock status and – using another branch of the capital-asset pricing model – means that investors could expect a total return from owning Railtrack shares of 10 per cent plus their current dividend yield, which is 2.8 per cent.

Source: Playing Monopoly, Bearbull, *The Investors Chronicle*, 4 August 2000, p. 18

Conclusion

Sources of finance are essential to a business if it is going to grow and survive. We can distinguish between short-term and long-term sources of finance. Short-term financing concerns the management of working capital: cash, debtors and stock. This may involve the more efficient use of working capital using various techniques such as the debtors collection model and the economic order quantity model. Alternatively, it may involve raising loans from the bank by an overdraft, or loans secured on debtors by debt factoring, or by the sale and leaseback of stock. Long-term sources of capital are used to fund the long-term activities of a business. The four main sources are an internal source (retained profits) and three external sources (leasing, share capital and loan capital). Retained profits are not borrowings but, in effect, represent undistributed profits ploughed back into the business. Leasing involves a company using an asset, but not owning it. Shareholders own the company and are paid dividends. Loan capital providers do not own the company and are paid loan interest. A key function of managing long-term finance is to minimise a company's cost of capital which is the effective rate at which a company can raise funds.

Q&A Discussion Questions

Questions with numbers in blue have answers at the back of the book.

Q1 Why are the sources of finance available to a firm so important? What are the main sources of finance and which activities of a business might they finance?

Q2 What is working capital and how might a company try to manage it?

Q3 What are the advantages and disadvantages of retained funds, debt and equity as methods of funding a business?

Q4 What is the weighted average cost of capital and why is it an important concept in business finance?

Q5 State whether the following statements are true or false. If false, explain why.
   (a) Long-term sources of finance are usually used to finance working capital.
   (b) A debtors collection model seeks the efficient management of debtors by balancing the benefits of extra credit sales against the extra costs of those sales.
   (c) Two common techniques of stock control are the economic order quantity model and the just-in-time approach.
   (d) There are four external long-term sources of finance: retained profits, leasing, share capital and loan capital.
   (e) A rights issue, a public issue and a placing are three major ways in which a company can raise share capital.

Q&A Numerical Questions

Questions with numbers in blue have answers at the back of the book.

Q1 Lathe plc is a small manufacturing firm. It buys in a subcomponent, the Tweak, for £1.50. The cost of insurance and storage per Tweak are £0.40, and £0.50 per item per year, respectively. It costs £25 for each order. The annual quantity purchased is 20,000.

   Required:
   (i) What is the economic order quantity? Solve this (a) graphically and (b) algebraically.
   (ii) What are the total costs per annum at this level?

Q2   A bookshop, Bookworm, buys 2,500 copies of the book, *Deep Heat*, per year. It costs the bookshop £0.80 per annum to carry the book in stock and £20 to prepare a new order.

Required:
(i) The total costs if orders are 1, 2, 5, 10 and 20 times per year.
(ii) The economic order quantity. An algebraic solution only is required.

Q3   Winter Brollies wishes to revise its credit collection policy. Currently it has £500,000 sales, a credit policy of 25 days and an average collection period of 20 days. 1 % of debtors default. Credit control costs are £5,000 for 25 days and 30 days; £6,000 for 60 days and 90 days. There is the following potential sales forecast.

Credit Period (Days)	Average Collection Period (Days)	New Annual Sales (£)	Bad Debts (%)
30	25	600,000	2
60	55	700,000	4
90	85	800,000	8

The cost of capital is 10 % and the average contribution is 20 % on selling price. Assume 360 days in year.

Required: Advise Winter Brollies whether or not it should revise its credit policy.

Q4   Albatross plc has the following information about its capital.

Source of Finance	Current Market Value £million	Present Cost of Capital %
Ordinary shares	4	12
Preference shares	1	10
Long-term loan	3	8

Required: What is Albatross's weighted average cost of capital?

Q5   Nebula plc is looking at its sources of finance. It collects the following details. Currently, there are 500,000 ordinary shares in issue, with a market price of £1.50 and a current dividend of £0.30. The number of preference shares in issue is 300,000, with a market price of £1.00 and a dividend of 15p. There are £200,000 of long-term debentures carrying 12 % interest. These are currently trading at £220,000.

Required: Calculate Nebula's weighted average cost of capital.

Further Reading

In this book, I have tried to give readers a comprehensive introduction to accounting. Most accounting textbooks are designed for accounting students and, therefore, often focus on demonstrating and explaining technical issues. These books must, therefore, be used by with care.

Section A: Financial Accounting

I list below some further reading which students may find useful to develop their knowledge of management accounting.

Arnold, J. and S. Turley (1996) *Accounting for Management Decisions*, Prentice Hall.
Provides a reasonable coverage of many of the key issues. At times may be too complex for non-specialist, first year students.

Drury C. (2005) *Management and Cost Accounting*, Thomson Business Press.
Provides a comprehensive coverage of management accounting for those who have grasped the basics.

Horngren C.T., G.L. Sundem and W.O. Stratton (2004) *Introduction to Management Accounting*, Prentice Hall.
A heavy-weight US text which mirrors the similar text on financial accounting. The in-depth approach and use of US terminology may make this book less accessible to UK students.

Weetman P. (2002) *Financial and Management Accounting: An Introduction*, Financial Times/Prentice Hall.
An accessible text for students who wish to rehearse their knowledge of the basics.

Glossary of Key Accounting Terms

This glossary contains most of the key accounting terms that students are likely to encounter. Words highlighted in bold are explained elsewhere in the glossary.

Absorption costing
The form of costing used for valuing stock for external financial reporting. All the overheads which can be attributed to a product are recovered. Unlike **marginal costing** which can sometimes be used for stock valuation, absorption costing includes both fixed and variable production overheads.

Acid test ratio
See **quick ratio**

Accounting
The provision of information to managers and owners so they can make business decisions.

Accounting concept
A principle underpinning the preparation of accounting information.

Accounting period
The time period for which the accounts are prepared. Audited financial statements are usually prepared for a year.

Accounting policies
The specific accounting methods selected and followed by a company in areas such as sales, foreign currencies, stocks, goodwill and pensions.

Accounting rate of return
A method of **capital investment appraisal** which assesses the viability of a project using annual profit and initial capital invested.

Accounting standards
Accounting pronouncements which set out the disclosure and measurement rules businesses must follow to give a **true and fair view** when drawing up accounts.

Accruals

The amounts owed to the suppliers of services at the balance sheet date, for expenses such as telephone or light and heat.

Accruals concept

See **matching concept**

Accumulated depreciation

The total depreciation on **tangible fixed assets** including this year's and prior years' depreciation.

Activity-based costing

A cost recovery technique which identifies key activities and key activity **cost drivers**

Annual report

A report produced annually by **companies** comprising both financial and non-financial information.

Assets

Essentially, items owned or leased by a business. Assets may be tangible or intangible, current or fixed. Assets bring economic benefits through either sale (for example, stock) or use (for example, a car).

Attainable standard cost

A **standard cost** which can be reached with effort.

Auditors

A team of professionally qualified accountants *independent* of a company. Appointed by the **shareholders** on the recommendation of the **directors**, the auditors check and report on the accounts prepared by the directors.

Auditors' report

A statement in a company's **annual report** which states whether the financial statements present a 'true and fair view' of the company's activities over the previous financial year.

Average cost (AVCO)

A method of stock valuation where stock is valued at the average purchase price (see also **first-in-first-out** and **last-in-first-out**).

Bad debts

Those debts that will definitely not be paid. They are an **expense** in the **profit and loss account** and are written off **debtors** in the **balance sheet**.

Balance sheet

A financial statement which is a snapshot of a business at a particular point in time. It records the **assets, liabilities** and **capital** of a business. Assets less liabilities equals capital. Capital is the owners' interest in the business.

Balanced scorecard

In **management accounting**, the balanced scorecard looks at a business from multiple perspectives such as financial, customer, internal business, and innovation and learning perspectives.

Bank overdraft

A business or individual owes the bank money.

Batch costing

A number of items of a similar nature are processed and costed together (e.g., baking bread).

Benchmarking

In **management accounting**, benchmarking measures a business against its competitors across a series of performance indicators (e.g., customer service or number of complaints).

Bookkeeping

The preparation of the basic accounts. Monetary transactions are entered into the books of account. A **trial balance** is then extracted, and a **profit and loss account** and a **balance sheet** are prepared.

Break-even analysis

Break-even analysis involves calculating the point at which a product or service makes neither a profit nor a loss. **Fixed costs** are divided by the contribution per unit giving the **break-even point**.

Break-even point

The point at which a firm makes neither a profit nor a loss. A firm's break-even point can be expressed as: Sales – variable costs – fixed costs = 0.

Budget

A future plan which sets out a business's financial targets.

Budgeting

Budgeting involves setting future targets. Actual results are then compared with budgeted results. Any **variances** are then investigated.

Called-up share capital

The amount of **issued share capital** that is fully paid up by **shareholders**. For example, a share may be issued for £1.50 and paid in three equal instalments. After two instalments the called-up share capital is £1.

Capital

Capital represents the owner's interest in the business. In effect, capital is a liability as it is owed by the business to the owner (e.g., **sole trader**, partner or **shareholder**). Capital is the assets of a business less its liabilities to third parties. Capital is accumulated wealth and is increased by profit, but reduced by losses. For listed companies capital is known as **equity**.

Capital expenditure

A payment to purchase an **asset** with a long life such as a **fixed asset**.

Capital investment appraisal

A method of evaluating long-term **capital expenditure decisions**.

Capital investment decisions

Usually long-term decisions (such as building a new factory).

Capital reserves

Reserves not distributable to shareholders as dividends (e.g., the **share premium account** or **revaluation reserve**).

Carrying costs

Costs such as insurance, obsolescence, interest on borrowed money or clerical/security costs incurred in holding stock.

Cash and bank

The actual money held by the business either at the business as cash or at the bank.

Cash at bank

Money deposited with a bank.

Cash budget

This budget records the projected inflows and outflows of cash.

Cash cows

An element in the **product portfolio matrix**. Cash cows are a company's dream product. They are well-established, require little capital expenditure, but generate high returns.

Cash flow statement

A financial statement which shows the cash inflows and outflows of a business.

Companies Acts

Acts of Parliament which lay down the legal requirements for companies including accounting regulations.

Company
A business enterprise where the **shareholders** have **limited liability**.

Consistency concept
An accounting principle which states similar items should be treated similarly from year to year.

Contract costing
A form of **costing** in which costs are allocated to contracts (i.e., usually big jobs which occur in construction industries such as shipbuilding). A long-term contract extends over more than one year and creates the problem of when to take profit.

Contribution
Contribution to fixed overheads, or contribution in short, is **sales** less **variable costs**.

Contribution analysis
A technique for short-term decision making where **fixed costs, variable costs** and **contribution** are analysed. The objective is to maximise a company's contribution (and thus profit) when choosing between different operating decisions.

Contribution graph
A graph which plots cumulative contribution against cumulative sales. Also called a profit/volume graph.

Controllable cost
A cost that a manager can influence and that a manager can be held responsible for.

Corporate governance
The system by which companies are directed and controlled. The financial aspects of corporate governance relate principally to internal control and the way in which the board of directors functions and reports to the shareholders on the activities and progress of the company.

Cost
An item of expenditure (planned or actually incurred).

Cost accounting
Essentially, **costing** and **planning and control**.

Cost allocation
The process by which **indirect costs** are recovered into total cost or into stock.

Cost centre
In **responsibility accounting**, where a manager is held responsible for costs.

Cost driver
In **activity-based costing**, a factor causing a change in an activity's costs.

Cost minimisation
Minimising cost either by tight budgetary control or cutting back on expenditure.

Cost recovery
The process by which costs are recovered into a product or service to form the basis of pricing or stock valuation.

Cost of capital
The interest rate at which a business raises funds.

Cost of sales
Essentially the cost of directly providing the sales.

Cost-volume-profit analysis
A **management accounting** technique which looks at the effect of changes in fixed costs, variable costs and sales on profit. Also called **contribution analysis**.

Costing
Recovering **costs** as a basis for pricing and stock valuation.

Credit
An entry on the right-hand side of a 'T' account. Records principally increases in **liabilities, capital** or **income**. May also record decreases in **assets** or **expenses**.

Credit control
Controlling **debtors** by establishing credit limits for new customers, monitoring the age of debts and chasing up **bad debts**.

Creditors
Amounts owed to trade suppliers for goods supplied on credit, but not yet paid. Known as **trade payables** for listed companies.

Creditors budget
This **budget** forecasts the level of future creditors. It keeps a running balance of creditors by adding purchases and deducting cash payments.

Creditors collection period
Measures how long a business takes to pay its **creditors** by relating creditors to cost of sales.

Current assets
Those **assets** (e.g., **stocks, debtors** and cash) that a company uses in its day-to-day operations.

Current liabilities
The liabilities that a business uses in its day-to-day operations (e.g., **creditors (trade payables)**).

Debenture
Another name for a **long-term loan**. Debentures may be **secured** or **unsecured loans**.

Debit
An entry on the left-hand side of a 'T' **account**. Records principally increases in either **assets** or **expenses**. May also record decreases in **liabilities, capital** or **income**.

Debt factoring
Where the **debtors** are subcontracted to a third party who are paid to manage them.

Debtors
When sales are made on credit, but the customers have not yet paid. Known as **trade receivables** for **listed companies**.

Debtors age schedule
A credit control technique which profiles the age of the debts and allow old debts to be quickly identified.

Debtors budget
This **budget** forecasts the level of future debtors. It keeps a running balance of debtors by adding sales and deducting cash received.

Debtors collection model
A technique for managing **working capital** which seeks to maintain the most efficient level of debtors for a company. It balances the extra revenue generated by increased sales with the increased costs associated with extra sales (e.g., credit control costs, bad debts and the delay in receiving money).

Debtors collection period
A ratio which measures how long customers take to pay their debts by relating debtors to sales.

Decision making in management accounting
The choice between alternatives. Only **relevant costs and revenues** should be considered.

Decision-making objective of financial reporting
Providing users, especially shareholders, with financial information so that they can make decisions such as whether to buy or sell shares.

Depreciation
Depreciation attempts to match a proportion of the original cost of the **fixed assets** to the **accounting period** in which the fixed assets were used up as an annual expense.

Direct costs
Costs directly identifiable and attributable to a product or service (e.g., the amount of direct labour or direct materials incurred). Sometimes called *product costs*.

Direct labour overall variance
Standard cost of labour for actual production less actual cost of labour used in production.

Direct labour price variance
(Standard price per hour – actual price per hour) × actual quantity of labour used.

Direct labour quantity variance
(Standard quantity of labour hours for actual production – actual quantity of labour hours used) × standard labour price per hour.

Direct materials overall variance
Standard cost of materials for actual production less actual cost of materials used in production.

Direct materials price variance
(Standard price per unit of material – actual price per unit of material) × actual quantity of materials used.

Direct materials quantity variance
(Standard price per unit of material – actual price per unit of material) × actual quantity of materials used.

Direct method of preparing cash flow statement
Classifies *operating* cash flows by function or type of activity (e.g., receipts from customers).

Directors
Those responsible for running the business. Accountable to the **shareholders** who, in theory, appoint and dismiss them.

Discount allowed
A reduction in the selling price of a good or service allowed by the business to customers for prompt payment. Treated as an **expense**.

Discount factor
A factor by which future cash flows are discounted to arrive at today's monetary value.

Discount received

A reduction in the purchase price of a good or service granted to a business from the supplier for paying promptly. Treated as an **income**.

Discounted cash flow

The future expected cash inflows and outflows of a potential project discounted back to their present value today to see whether or not proposed projects are viable.

Dividends

A cash payment to shareholders rewarding them for investing money in a company.

Dogs

An element in the **product portfolio matrix**. Dogs are cash traps with low market growth and low market share.

Double-entry bookkeeping

A way of systematically recording the financial transactions of a company so that each transaction is recorded twice.

Doubtful debts

Debts which may or may not be paid. Usually, businesses estimate a certain proportion of their debts as doubtful.

Earnings per share (EPS)

A key ratio by which investors measure the performance of a company.

Economic order quantity (EOQ)

A technique for managing **working capital**. The optimal EOQ is calculated so as to minimise the costs of ordering and holding stock.

Efficiency ratios

Ratios which show how efficiently a business uses its assets.

Entity concept

A business has a distinct and separate identity from its owner. This is obvious in the case of a large limited company where **shareholders** own the company and managers manage the company. However, there is also a distinction between a **sole trader's** or **partnership's** personal and business assets.

Equity

The term used for **capital** for a listed company.

Equivalent units
In **process costing**, partially finished units are converted to fully completed equivalent units by estimating the percentage of completion.

Expenses
The day-to-day **costs** incurred in running a business, e.g., telephone, business rates and wages. Expenses are expenses even if goods and services are consumed, but not yet paid. Expenses are, therefore, different from cash paid.

Financial accounting
The provision of financial information on a business's financial performance targeted at external users, such as shareholders. It includes not only **double-entry bookkeeping**, but also the preparation and interpretation of the financial accounts.

Finished goods stock
The final stock after the manufacturing process is completed, for example, finished tables. The cost includes materials and other manufacturing costs (e.g., labour and manufacturing overheads).

First-in-first-out (FIFO)
A method of stock valuation where the stock bought first is the first to be sold. See also **average cost** and **last-in-first-out**.

Fixed assets
Infrastructure assets used to run the business long-term and *not* used in day-to-day production. Includes **tangible fixed assets** (e.g., motor vehicles, land and buildings, fixtures and fittings, plant and machinery) and **intangible fixed assets** (e.g., goodwill). Fixed assets are known as **property, plant and equipment** for a listed company.

Fixed costs
Costs that *do not vary* with production or sales (for example, insurance) in an **accounting period** and are not affected by short-term decisions. Often called fixed overheads.

Fixed overheads
See **fixed costs**.

Fixed overheads quantity variance
(Standard fixed overheads – actual fixed overheads).

Flexing the budget
Adjusting the **budget** to account for the *actual quantity produced*.

Gearing
The relationship between a company's ordinary shareholders' funds and the debt capital.

General reserve
A **revenue reserve** created to deal with general, unspecified contingencies such as inflation.

Gross profit
Sales less **cost of sales**.

Historical cost
A **measurement system** where monetary amounts are recorded at the date of original transaction.

Ideal standards
In **standard costing**, standards attained in an ideal world.

Income
The revenue earned by a business, e.g., **sales**. Income is income, even if goods and services have been delivered but customers have yet to pay. Income thus differs from cash received.

Income statement
The term used in **listed companies** for the **profit and loss account**.

Indirect costs
Those costs *not* directly identifiable *nor* attributable to a product or service, e.g., administrative, and selling and distribution costs. These costs are totalled and then recovered indirectly into the product or service. Also called *indirect overheads* or *period costs*.

Indirect method of preparing cash flow statement
Operating cash flow is derived from the **profit and loss account** and **balance sheet** and not classified directly by function (such as receipts from sales).

Indirect overheads
See **indirect costs**.

Intangible assets
Fixed assets one cannot touch, unlike **tangible fixed assets** (such as land and buildings). Most common in **companies**.

Internal rate of return (IRR)
A **capital investment appraisal** technique. The internal rate of return represents the discount rate required to give a **net present value** of zero. It pays a company to invest in a project if it can borrow money for less than the IRR.

International Accounting Standards Board (IASB)
An international body founded in 1973 to work for the improvement and harmonisation of accounting standards worldwide. Originally called the International Accounting Standards Committee.

Inventory
The term used for **stock** in a **listed company**.

Investment Centre
In **responsibility accounting**, where a manager is held responsible for the revenues, costs (i.e., profits) and investment.

Investments
Assets such as stocks and **shares**.

Invoice discounting
The sale of debts to a third party for immediate cash.

Issued share capital
The share capital *actually* issued by a **company**.

Job costing
The recovery of costs into a specific product or service.

Just-in-time
A method of stock control developed in Japan. It seeks to minimise stock holding costs by the careful timing of deliveries and efficient organisation of production schedules. At its best, just-in-time delivers stock just before it is used.

Last-in-first-out (LIFO)
A method of stock valuation where the last stock purchased is the first sold. See also **average cost** and **first-in-first-out**.

Leasing
Where the **assets** are owned by a third party which the business pays to use them.

Liabilities
Amounts the business owes (e.g., creditors, bank loan). They can be short-term or long-term, third party liabilities or capital (i.e., liability owed by the business to the owner).

Limiting factor
Where production is constrained by a particular shortage of a key element, e.g., a restricted number of labour hours.

Limited liability
Shareholders are only liable to lose the amount of money they initially invested.

Listed company
A **company** quoted on a stock exchange.

Loan capital
Money loaned to a company by third parties who do not own the company and are entitled to interest *not* dividends.

Loans
Amounts borrowed from third parties, such as a bank.

Long-term creditors
Amounts borrowed from third parties and repayable after a year. The most common are **long-term loans**. Known as **non-current liabilities** for **listed companies**.

Long-term loan
A loan, such as a bank loan, not repayable within a year. Sometimes called a **debenture**.

Management accounting
The provision of both financial and non-financial information to managers for **cost accounting, planning, control and performance, and decision making**. It is thus concerned with the internal accounting of a business.

Management accounting control system
An assemblage of management control techniques which enable a business to plan, monitor and control ongoing financial activities. In addition, management control systems facilitate performance evaluation. **Budgeting** and **standard costing** are examples of management accounting control systems.

Margin of safety
In **break-even analysis,** the difference between current sales and break-even sales.

Marginal costing
Marginal costing excludes fixed overheads from the costing process. It focuses on **sales, variable costs** and **contribution. Fixed costs** are written off against contribution. It can be used for decision making or for valuing stock. When valuing stock only variable production overheads are included in the stock valuation.

Market value
The value shares fetch on the open market, i.e., their trading value. This may differ significantly from their **nominal value**.

Master budget
The overall budgeted **balance sheet** and **profit and loss account** prepared from the individual **budgets**.

Matching concept
Recognises **income** and **expenses** when accrued (i.e., earned or incurred) rather than when money is received or paid. Income is matched with any associated expenses to determine the appropriate profit or loss. Also known as the accruals concept.

Materials requirement planning (MRP) system
An MRP system is based on sales demand and coordinates production and purchasing to ensure the optimal flow of raw materials and optimal levels of **raw material stocks**.

Net assets
Total assets less **long-term loans** and **current liabilities**.

Net book value
The cost of **tangible fixed assets** less accumulated depreciation.

Net present value
A **capital investment appraisal** technique which discounts future expected cash flows to today's monetary values using an appropriate cost of capital.

Net profit
Sales less **cost of sales** less **expenses**.

Nominal value
The face value of the shares when originally issued.

Non-current liabilities
The term used for **long-term creditors** in a **listed company**.

Normal standards
In **standard costing**, standards which a business usually attains.

Objective of financial statements
To provide information about the financial position, performance and changes in financial position of an enterprise useful to a wide range of **users** in making decisions.

Opportunity cost
The potential benefit lost by rejecting the best alternative course of action.

Ordinary (equity) share capital
Share capital issued to the **shareholders,** who own the company and are entitled to ordinary **dividends.**

Overall variances
In **standard costing,** the budgeted cost of the actual items produced (*standard cost of actual production*) is compared with the actual cost of items produced (*actual cost of production*).

Overheads
See **indirect costs.**

Padding the budget
In **budget** setting, where individuals try to create slack to give themselves some room for manoeuvre.

Partnership
Business enterprises run by more than one person, whose liability is normally unlimited.

Payback method
A method of **capital investment appraisal** which measures the cumulative cash inflows against the cumulative cash outflows to determine when a project will pay for itself.

Performance evaluation
The monitoring and motivation of individuals often in **responsibility accounting** systems.

Period costs
See **indirect costs.**

Planning, control and performance
The planning and control of future costs as well as the evaluation of performance using **budgeting** and **standard costing.** An abbreviated form of planning, control and performance evaluation.

Preference share capital
Share capital issued to **shareholders** who are *not* owners of the company and who are entitled to fixed dividends.

Prepayment
The amount paid in advance to the suppliers of services, e.g., prepaid insurance.

Present value
A **measurement system** where future cash inflows are discounted back to present-day values.

Price variances
In **standard costing,** the *standard* price for the *actual* quantity used or sold is compared with the *actual* price for the *actual* quantity used or sold.

Prime cost
Direct materials, direct labour and direct expenses totalled.

Private limited company
A company where trading in shares is restricted.

Process costing
Used in industries with a continuous production process (e.g., beer brewing) where products progress from one department to another.

Product costs
See **direct costs.**

Product life cycle analysis
In **management accounting,** the analysis of product life cycles. The five stages of birth (known as introduction), growth, maturity, decline and senility (known as withdrawal) are associated with a certain level of sales and profit.

Product portfolio matrix
A strategic way of looking at a company's products and dividing them into **cash cows, dogs, question marks** and **stars.**

Production cost budget
This **budget** estimates the future cost of production, incorporating direct labour, direct materials and production overheads.

Production departments
Where products are manufactured.

Profit
Sales less purchases and **expenses.**

Profit and loss account
A financial statement which records the **income** and **expenses** of a business over the **accounting period,** normally a year. **Income** less **expenses** equals **profit.** By contrast, where expenses are greater than income, losses will occur. The balance from the profit and loss account is transferred annually to the **balance sheet** where it becomes part of **revenue reserves.** The term **income statement** is used for a listed company.

Profit centre
In **responsibility accounting,** where a manager is held responsible for the revenues and costs and thus profits.

Profitability ratios
They establish how profitably a business is performing.

Profit/volume chart
See **contribution graph.**

Property, plant and equipment
The term used for **fixed assets** in a **listed company.**

Provision for doubtful debts
Those debts a business is dubious of collecting. Deducted from **debtors** in the **balance sheet.** Only *increases* or *decreases* in the provision are entered in the **profit and loss account.**

Public limited company
A **company** where shares are bought and sold by the general public.

Quantity variances
The budgeted cost of the actual items produced or sold (*standard cost of actual production* or *standard quantity sold*) is compared with the actual quantity produced or sold (*actual quantity used or sold*).

Question marks
An element of the **product portfolio matrix.** Question marks have low market share, but high market growth.

Quick ratio
Measures extreme short-term liquidity, i.e., **current assets** (excluding stock) against **current liabilities.** Sometimes called the 'acid test ratio'.

Ratio analysis
See **interpretation of accounts.**

Raw material stock
Stock purchased and ready for use, e.g., a carpenter with wood awaiting manufacture into tables.

Raw materials budget
This **budget** forecasts the future quantities of raw materials required. May supply the purchases figure for the **creditors budget.**

Realisable value
A **measurement system** where assets are valued at what they would fetch in an orderly sale. Also known as net realisable value.

Relevant costs and revenues
Costs that will affect a decision (as opposed to non-relevant costs, which will not).

Reserves
The accumulated profits (**revenue reserves**) or capital gains (**capital reserves**) to shareholders.

Residual Income
A ratio often used in **performance evaluation** in which a required rate of return on investment is deducted from income.

Responsibility accounting systems
Where an organisation is divided into budgetary areas for which individuals are held responsible. The budgetary areas may be known as **revenue centres, cost centres, profit centres,** or **investment centres.**

Retained profits
The **profit** a company has not distributed via **dividends**. An alternative to external financing. In effect, the business finances itself from its past successes.

Return on capital employed
A ratio looking at how effectively a company uses its capital. It compares **net profit** to capital employed. The most common definition measures **profit** before tax and **debenture** interest against long-term capital (i.e., **ordinary share capital** and **reserves, preference share capital, long-term loans**).

Return on investment
A ratio often used in **performance evaluation** which relates income to investment.

Return on sales
A ratio often used in **performance evaluation** which relates operating profit to sales.

Revaluation reserve
A **capital reserve** created when **fixed assets** are revalued to more than the original amount for which they were purchased. The revaluation is a gain to the shareholders.

Revenue centre
In **responsibility accounting**, where a manager is held responsible for the revenues.

Revenue expenditure
Payments for a current year's good or service such as purchases for resale or telephone expenses.

Revenue reserves
Reserves potentially distributable to shareholders as **dividends**, e.g., the **profit and loss account, general reserve**.

Rights issue
Current **shareholders** are given the right to subscribe to new shares in proportion to their current holdings.

Sale and leaseback
Companies sell their **tangible fixed assets** to a third party and then lease them back.

Sales
Income earned from selling goods.

Sales budget
This **budget** estimates the future quantity of sales.

Sales price variance
(Standard price per unit – actual price per unit) × actual quantity of units sold.

Sales quantity variance
(Standard quantity of units sold – actual quantity of units sold) × standard contribution per unit.

Secured loans
Loans guaranteed (i.e., secured) by the **assets** of the company.

Sensitivity analysis
Involves modelling the future to see if alternative scenarios will change an investment decision.

Service costing
Service costing concerns specific services such as canteens run as independent operations. The cost of a particular service is the total costs for the service divided by the number of service units.

Service delivery departments
Departments in service industries that deliver the final service to customers.

Service support departments
Departments that supply support activities such as catering, administration, or selling and distribution.

Share capital
The total capital of the business is divided into shares. Literally a 'share' in the capital of the business.

Share options
Directors or employees are allowed to buy shares at a set price. They can then sell them for a higher price at a future date if the share price rises.

Shareholders
The owners of the company who provide share capital by way of shares.

Sole trader
A business enterprise run by a sole owner whose liability is unlimited.

Spending to budget
Departments ensure they spend their allocated **budgets**. If they do not the department may lose the money.

Standard cost
A standard cost is the individual cost elements of a product or service (such as direct materials, direct labour and variable overheads) that are estimated in advance. Normally, the quantity and the price of each cost element are estimated separately. Actual costs are then compared with standard costs to determine **variances**.

Standard costing
A standardised version of **budgeting**. Standard costing uses preset costs for direct labour, direct materials and overheads. Actual costs are then compared with the standard costs. Any **variances** are then investigated.

Stars
An element of the **product portfolio matrix**. Stars are characterised by high market growth and high market share. Stars may be cash earners or cash drains requiring heavy capital expenditure.

Stewardship
Making individuals accountable for **assets** and **liabilities**. Stewardship focuses on the physical monitoring of assets and the prevention of loss and fraud rather than evaluating how efficiently the assets are used.

Stock
Goods purchased and awaiting use (**raw materials**) or produced and awaiting sale (**finished goods**). **Inventory** is the term used for stock in a **listed company**.

Strategic management accounting

A form of **management accounting** which considers an organisation's internal and external environments.

Sunk cost

A past cost with no ongoing implications for the future. It should thus be *excluded from decision making* as it is a non-relevant cost.

SWOT analysis

A strategic way of critically assessing a business's strengths and weaknesses, opportunities and threats.

Tangible fixed assets

Fixed assets one can touch (e.g., land and buildings, plant and machinery, motor vehicles, fixtures and fittings). Tangible fixed assets are known as **property, plant and equipment** in **listed companies**.

Target costing

A price is set with reference to market conditions and customer purchasing patterns. A target profit is then deducted to arrive at a target cost.

Third party liabilities

Amounts owing to third parties. They can be short-term (e.g., **creditors,** bank overdraft) or long-term (e.g., a bank loan).

Throughput accounting

This uses a variant of contribution per limiting factor to determine a production system's main bottlenecks (e.g., shortage of machine hours in a certain department).

Total absorption costing

Both **direct costs** and **indirect costs** are absorbed into a product or service so as to recover the total costs in the final selling price.

Total shareholders' funds

The **share capital** and **reserves** owned by both the ordinary and preference shareholders.

Trade payables

The term used for **creditors** in a **listed company.**

Trading and profit and loss account

The formal name for the full profit and loss account prepared by a **sole trader**.

Trading and profit and loss and appropriation account

The formal name for the profit and loss account prepared by a **company** or a **partnership**.

Trial balance

A listing of debit and credit balances to check the correctness of the **double-entry bookkeeping** system.

True and fair view

Difficult to define but, essentially, a set of financial statements which faithfully, accurately and truly reflect the underlying economic transactions of the organisation.

Uncontrollable cost

A cost that a manager cannot influence and that the manager cannot be held responsible for.

Unsecured loans

Loans which are not guaranteed (i.e., secured) by a company's **assets**.

Users

Those with an interest in using accounting information, such as shareholders, lenders, suppliers and other trade creditors, customers, government, the public, management and employees.

Value chain analysis

In **management accounting**, a strategic way of determining a value chain for a business consisting of primary activities (e.g., receiving goods) and support activities (e.g., technology development).

Variable costs

These costs vary with production and sales (for example, the metered cost of electricity). Short-term decision making is primarily concerned with variable costs.

Variable overheads overall variance

Standard cost of variable overheads for actual production less actual cost of variable overheads for production.

Variable overheads price variance

(Standard variable overheads price per hour – actual variable overheads price per hour) × actual quantity of labour hours used.

Variable overheads quantity variance

(Standard quantity of labour hours for actual production – actual quantity of labour hours used) × standard variable overheads price per hour.

Variance

The difference between the budgeted costs and the actual costs in both **budgeting** and **standard costing**.

Work-in-progress stock
Partially completed stock (sometimes called stock in process) which is neither **raw materials** nor **finished goods**.

Working capital
Current assets less **current liabilities** (in effect, the operating capital of a business).

Zero-based budgeting
A **budget** based on the premise that the activities are being incurred for the first time.

Appendix: Answers

Chapter 1: Discussion *Answers*

The answers provide some outline points for discussion.

A1 Accounting is important because it is the language of business and provides a means of effective and understandable business communication. The general terminology of business is thus accounting-driven. Concepts such as profit and cash flow are accounting terms. In addition, accounting provides the backbone of a business's information system. It provides figures for performance measurement, for monitoring, planning and control and gives an infrastructure for decision making. It enables businesses to answer key questions about past business performance and future business policy.

A3 There are many differences. The six listed below will do for starters!
(a) Financial accounting is designed to provide information on a business's recent financial performance and is targeted at external users such as shareholders. However, the information is also often used by managers. By contrast, management accounting is much more internally focused and is used solely by managers.
(b) Financial accounting operates within a regulatory framework set out by accounting standards and the Companies Acts. There is no such framework for management accounting.
(c) The main work of financial accounting is preparing financial statements such as the balance sheet and profit and loss account (income statement). By contrast, management accounting uses a wider range of techniques for planning, control and performance, and for decision making.
(d) Financial accounting is based upon double-entry bookkeeping, while management accounting is not.
(e) Financial accounting looks backwards, while management accounting is forward-looking.
(f) The end product of financial accounting is a standardised set of financial statements. By contrast, management accounting is very varied. Its output depends on the needs of its users.

Chapter 2: Discussion *Answers*

The answers provide some outline points for discussion.

A1

Branches	Functions
(1) Cost Accounting	
(i) Costing	To recover costs as a basis for pricing and for stock valuation.
(ii) Planning, Control and Performance	
(a) Budgeting	To plan and control future costs and engage in performance evaluation through budgeting.
(b) Standard costing	To plan and control future costs and engage in performance evaluation through standard costing.
(2) Decision Making	
(i) Short-term Decisions	To make short-term decisions (such as whether to make a product) using techniques such as contribution analysis and break-even analysis. In addition, to minimise the cost of working capital.
(ii) Long-term Decisions	
(a) Strategic management	To make decisions of a strategic nature such as whether or not to diversify the business.
(b) Capital budgeting	To make decisions about whether or not to invest in long-term projects such as a new product or service.
(c) Sources of finance	To make decisions about whether to raise new finance via share or loan capital.

A6 True or False?
(a) *True.*
(b) *False.* Total absorption costing is where all the costs incurred by a company are totalled so that they can be recovered into the product or service's final selling price.
(c) *True.*
(d) *False.* Strategic management accounting is concerned with the long-term strategic direction of a firm.
(e) *True.*

Chapter 3: Discussion *Answers*

The answers provide some outline points for discussion.

A1 Costing is the process of recording, classifying, allocating and then absorbing costs into individual products and services. Costing is particularly important for two main reasons: stock valuation and pricing. In stock valuation, the aim is to recover the costs incurred in producing a good. The costs of stock valuation thus include direct materials, direct labour, direct expenses and appropriate production overheads. In absorption costing, we include all production overheads, both fixed and variable. In marginal costing, we include only variable production overheads. In effect, financial accounting drives the stock valuation process. This is because external reporting regulations allow attributable production overheads (i.e., allow absorption costing) to be included in stock. For pricing, all the overheads (i.e., total absorption costing) are included in the cost before a percentage is added for profit. Thus the total cost may include direct materials, direct labour, direct expenses, production and non-production overheads. Nowadays, with the decline of manufacturing industry, there has been a decline in the importance of direct costs and an increase in the importance of indirect costs or overheads.

A5 True or False?
  (a) *False.* It is true that a cost can be an actual past expenditure. However, it is important to appreciate that a cost can also be an estimated, future expenditure.
  (b) *True.*
  (c) *False.* We identify activity cost drivers in activity-based costing.
  (d) *True.*
  (e) *False.* No, in financial reporting we use absorption costing.

Chapter 3: Numerical *Answers*

A1 *Sorter*

(i) Direct materials	*c* (purchase of raw materials)
(ii) Direct labour	*a* (machine workers' wages)
(iii) Production overheads	*b* (cost clerk's wages)* Assumes cost clerks are based in factory, *d* (machine repairs), *m* (depreciation on machinery), *o* (electricity for machines)
(iv) Administrative expenses	*e* (finance director's salary), *f* (office cleaners), *h* (managing director's car expenses), *i* (depreciation on office furniture), *j* (computer running expenses for office), *k* (loan interest), *l* (auditors' fees), *p* (bank charges)
(v) Selling and distribution costs	*g* (delivery van staff's wages), *n* (advertising costs)

A2 Costa

Costa
Costing Statement for Costa

	£	£	£
Direct materials			320,000
Direct labour			200,000
Royalties			3,600
(i) Prime Cost			523,600
Production Overheads			
Factory supervisors' wages		120,000	
Depreciation (£8,000 + £5,000)		13,000	
Computer overheads		6,000	
Other overheads		70,000	209,000
(ii) Production Cost			732,600
Other Costs			
Administrative Expenses			
Administrative salaries	90,800		
Depreciation (£4,200 + £2,500)	6,700		
Computer overheads	3,000		
Interest on loans	3,000	103,500	
Selling and Distribution Costs			
Wages	18,300		
Marketing salaries	25,000		
Commission	1,200		
Depreciation (£3,500 + £2,500)	6,000	50,500	154,000
(iii) Total Cost			886,600

A3 Makemore

Makemore
Overhead Allocation Statement

	Total £	Ratio Split	A £	B £	C £
Supervisors' salaries	25,000	1,000:2,000:500	7,143	14,286	3,571
Computer advisory	18,000	1,000:2,000:500	5,143	10,286	2,571
Rent and business rates	20,000	10,000:6,000:4,000	10,000	6,000	4,000
Depreciation	21,000	30,000:15,000	14,000	7,000	–
Repairs	4,000		2,800	1,100	100
Allocated	88,000		39,086	38,672	10,242
Reallocation of service support department C's costs			60 %	40 %	(100 %)
			6,145	4,097	(10,242)
Total Allocation	88,000		45,231	42,769	–
			80,000	40,000	
(i) Labour hours					
Rate per hour			£0.57	£1.07	
(ii) Machine hours			100,000	200,000	
Rate per hour			£0.45	£0.21	

A8 Serveco

Calculate activity-cost driver rates

Activity	Spare Parts Installed	Technical Support	Service Documentation
Cost	£100,000	£125,000	£300,000
Cost driver	150,000 parts	175,000 minutes	125,000 units
Cost per unit of Cost driver	£0.667	£0.7143	£2.4

Costs absorbed to services				Total cost
Basic	50,000 × £0.667 = £33,333	75,000 × £0.7143 = £53,572	100,000 × £2.4 = £240,000	£326,905
Enhanced	100,000 × £0.667 = £66,667	100,000 × £0.7143 = £71,428	25,000 × £2.4 = £60,000	£198,095
Total costs	£100,000	£125,000	£300,000	£525,000

Total overhead costs	Total overheads	Call outs	Overheads per call out
Basic	£326,905	50,000	£6.54
Enhanced	£198,095	10,000	£19.81

Call Out Cost/Charge

	Basic £		Enhanced £	
Labour hours (including travelling time)	20.00	$\dfrac{(25,000 + 25,000) \times £20}{50,000 \text{ call outs}}$	106.25	$\dfrac{(37,500 + 5,000) \times £25}{10,000 \text{ call outs}}$
Overheads	6.54		19.81	
Total Cost	26.54		126.06	
Profit: 25 % mark-up on cost	6.63		31.51	
Call out Charge	33.17		157.57	

Note: Some of the calculations have been rounded in this answer.

Chapter 4: Discussion *Answers*

The answers provide some outline points for discussion.

A1 A major advantage of budgeting is that it requires you to predict the future in economic terms. You can plan ahead and buy in extra resources and schedule workloads. In addition, budgeting enables you to predict your future performance. You can then tell how well or how badly you are actually doing against your predicted budget. Finally, budgeting has an important responsibility and control function. You can put somebody in charge of the budget, make them responsible and so control future activities. Variances from budget can thus be investigated.

The major disadvantages of budgets are that they may be constraining and dysfunctional to the organisation. The constraint is caused by the budget perhaps setting a straitjacket which inhibits innovation and the adoption of flexible business policies. The dysfunctional nature of budgeting is that the objectives of the individual may not necessarily be the same as that of the organisation. Individuals may, therefore, seek to 'pad' their budgets or manage them to their own personal advantage.

A4 True or False?
(a) *True.*
(b) *False.* Although sometimes production is a limiting factor, the commonest limiting factor is sales.
(c) *True.*
(d) *False.* Depreciation is never found in a cash budget as it does not represent a cash flow.
(e) *True.*

Chapter 4: Numerical *Answers*

A1 Jill Lee

Jill Lee
Cash Budget for Six Months Ending June

	Jan. £	Feb. £	March £	April £	May £	June £	Total £
Opening cash	15,000	28,200	21,100	8,280	(5,942)	1,389	15,000
Add *Receipts*							
Sales	25,200	27,100	21,200	20,250	48,300	37,500	179,550
	25,200	27,100	21,200	20,250	48,300	37,500	179,550
Less Payments							
Goods	–	21,000	19,500	18,500	23,400	25,900	108,300
Expenses	12,000	13,200	14,520	15,972	17,569	19,326	92,587
	12,000	34,200	34,020	34,472	40,969	45,226	200,887
Cash flow	13,200	(7,100)	(12,820)	(14,222)	7,331	(7,726)	(21,337)
Closing cash	28,200	21,100	8,280	(5,942)	1,389	(6,337)	(6,337)

A3 Fly-by-Night

Fly-by-Night
Sales Budget for Six Months Ending June

	Jan. £	Feb. £	March £	April £	May £	June £	Total £
Moon (1)	20,000	21,000	22,000	28,750	30,000	31,250	153,000
Star (2)	20,000	21,000	22,000	23,000	24,000	25,000	135,000
	40,000	42,000	44,000	51,750	54,000	56,250	288,000
(1) Moon (units)	1,000	1,050	1,100	1,150	1,200	1,250	6,750
(2) Star (units)	2,000	2,100	2,200	2,300	2,400	2,500	13,500

Helpnote: Multiply the units by the price per unit.

A4 D. Ingo

D. Ingo
Debtors Budget for Six Months Ending June

	Jan. £	Feb. £	March £	April £	May £	June £	Total £
Opening debtors	2,400	2,000	2,100	2,310	2,541	2,795	2,400
Credit sales	1,000	1,100	1,210	1,331	1,464	1,610	7,715
	3,400	3,100	3,310	3,641	4,005	4,405	10,115
Cash received	(1,400)	(1,000)	(1,000)	(1,100)	(1,210)	(1,331)	(7,041)
Closing debtors	2,000	2,100	2,310	2,541	2,795	3,074	3,074

A6 B. Ear

B. Ear
Production Cost Budget Six Months Ending June

	Jan. £	Feb. £	March £	April £	May £	June £	Total £
Raw materials	3,500	3,750	4,000	4,250	4,500	4,750	24,750
Direct labour	3,850	4,125	4,400	4,675	4,950	5,225	27,225
Variable overheads	1,400	1,500	1,600	1,700	1,800	1,900	9,900
	8,750	9,375	10,000	10,625	11,250	11,875	61,875
Units	700	750	800	850	900	950	4,950

A7 R. Abbit

R. Abbit
Raw Materials Budget Six Months Ending June

	Jan. £	Feb. £	March £	April £	May £	June £	Total £
Opening stock	1,000	940	1,080	1,420	1,670	2,120	1,000
Purchases	900	1,100	1,300	1,500	1,700	1,900	8,400
	1,900	2,040	2,380	2,920	3,370	4,020	9,400
Used in production	(960)	(960)	(960)	(1,250)	(1,250)	(1,250)	(6,630)
Closing stock	940	1,080	1,420	1,670	2,120	2,770	2,770

A11 All Sunshine Enterprises

	London	Oslo	Stockholm
i, Return on Investment			
$\dfrac{\text{Income}}{\text{Investment}}$	$\dfrac{£700,000}{£2,000,000} = 35\,\%$	$\dfrac{£400,000}{£1,000,000} = 40\,\%$	$\dfrac{£165,000}{£500,000} = 33\,\%$
ii, Residual Income			
Income − (Required rates of return × investment)	£700,000 − (12 % × £2,000,000)	£400,000 − (12 % × £1,000,000)	£165,000− (12 % × £500,000)
	= £460,000	= £280,000	= £105,000
iii, Return on Sales			
$\dfrac{\text{Operating profit}}{\text{Sales}}$	$\dfrac{£700,000}{£1,500,000}$	$\dfrac{£400,000}{£800,000}$	$\dfrac{£165,000}{£300,000}$
	= 46.7 %	= 50 %	= 55 %

Therefore, Return on Investment gives Oslo 40 % and is its best relative measure. Residual Income gives Madrid £460,000 and is its best relative measure. Return on Sales gives Stockholm 55 % and is its best relative measure.

Chapter 5: Discussion *Answers*

The answers provide some outline points for discussion.

A1 Setting the standards involves first of all making a decision about whether one is aiming for ideal, attainable or normal standards. Ideal standards are those that can be reached if everything goes perfectly. Attainable standards are those that can be reached with a little effort. Normal standards are those that are based on past experience and that the business normally meets. Attainable standards are probably the best because they include a motivational element.

The two main elements of a standard are quantity (i.e., hours, materials) and price (i.e., hourly rate, price per kilo). It follows, therefore, that we need to consider the factors that influence quantity and price. These might be based on past experience, prevailing market conditions and future expectations. For instance, if a firm were setting labour standards it might base its labour quantity standard on the hours taken in the past less an improvement element. The labour price standard might be based on the prevailing wage rate with an amount built in for any wage increases.

A5 True or False?
(a) *True.*
(b) *False.* Flexing the budget means adjusting the budget to take into account the actual quantity produced.
(c) *True.*
(d) *True.*
(e) *False.* The direct labour quantity variance is: (standard *quantity* of labour hours for actual production – actual *quantity* of labour hours used) × standard labour price per hour.

Chapter 5: Numerical *Answers*

A1 Stuffed
(i–iii)

	Budget	Flexed Budget	Actual	Sales Price and Overall Cost Variances*	
Number of customers	10,000	12,000	12,000		
	£	£	£	£	
Sales	100,000	120,000	127,200	7,200	Fav.
Food cost					
(i.e., materials cost)	(30,000)	(36,000)	(37,200)	(1,200)	Unfav.
Labour cost	(35,000)	(42,000)	(36,000)	6,000	Fav.
Variable overheads	(5,000)	(6,000)	(6,000)	–	
Contribution	30,000	36,000	48,000	12,000	Fav.
Fixed overheads	(3,000)	(3,000)**	(3,100)	(100)	Unfav.
Profit	27,000	33,000	44,900	11,900	Fav.

Helpnotes
*The sales price variance is £7,200 Fav. The overall cost variances are food cost (i.e., direct materials) variance £1,200 Unfav., labour cost variance £6,000 Fav., zero overall variable overheads cost variance, and £100 Unfav. fixed overhead variance.
**Remember, fixed costs remain unchanged whatever the level of activity. We do not, therefore, flex these.

A1 Stuffed (*continued*)

(iv) *Sales Quantity Variance* = (standard quantity of meals sold – actual quantity of meals sold) × standard   contribution   per unit = 10,000 – 12,000 × (£30,000 ÷ 10,000) = £6,000 Fav.

Note this is simply the flexed profit (£33,000) less the original budget (£27,000) = £6,000 Fav.

(v) (a) *Sales Variances*. Both are favourable. 2,000 more customers visited the restaurant than anticipated. They paid £0.60 more per meal than expected.

(b) *Material Cost*. We paid £1,200 more than expected. This may be due to increased prices or increased quantity used. We need more information on this.

(c) *Labour Cost*. We paid £6,000 less than expected. Either we paid less per hour or we used fewer hours than expected. We need more information.

(d) *Variable Overheads*. These were as budgeted.

(e) *Fixed Overheads*. These were slightly more (£100 more) than expected.

A3 Birch Manufacturing

	£
(i) Overall Direct Materials Variance	
Standard cost of materials for actual production	
(10 metres of wood* at 50p × 11,000)	55,000
Actual cost of materials used in production	
(120,000 metres × 0.49 pence)	58,800
	(3,800) Unfav.

*Each bookcase is estimated to take 10 metres of wood (100,000 metres ÷ 10,000 bookcases)

	£
(ii) Direct Materials Price Variance	
(standard price per unit of material – actual price	
per unit of material) × actual quantity of materials used	
= (50p – 49p) × 120,000 metres	1,200 Fav.

(iii) Direct Materials Quantity Variance	
(standard quantity of materials for actual production –	
actual quantity of materials used) × standard	
material price per unit	
= (11,000 × 10 metres – 120,000 metres) × 0.50p	(5,000) Unfav.
	(3,800) Unfav.

A4 Sweatshop

	£
(i) Overall Direct Labour Variance	
Standard cost of labour for actual production	
(500 sweatshirts at 2 hours) × £5.50	5,500
Actual cost of labour used in production	5,880
	(380) Unfav.

A4 Sweatshop (*continued*)

(ii) Direct Labour Price Variance   £

(standard labour price per hour − actual price per hour)
   × actual quantity of labour used
   = (£5.50 − £5.60*) × 1,050 hours   (105)   Unfav.
*£3,780 labour cost divided by 1,050 hours

(iii) Direct Labour Quantity Variance

(Standard quantity of labour hours for actual production −
   actual quantity of labour hours used)
   × standard labour price per hour
   = (2 hours × 500 sweatshirts − 1,050 hours) × £5.50 per hour   (275)   Unfav.
                                                                         (380)   Unfav.

A6 Wonderworld

(i) Overall Variable Overheads Cost Variance

Standard cost of variable overheads for actual production   £
(110,000 teleporters at 2 labour hours at £2.50)   550,000
Actual cost of variable overheads for production   517,500
                                                                         32,500   Fav.

(ii) Variable Overheads Price Variance

(standard variable overheads price per hour −
   actual variable overheads price per hour) ×
   actual quantity of labour hours used   £
   = (£2.50 − £2.25)* × 230,000   57,500   Fav.
*variable overheads £517,500 ÷ 230,000 actual labour hours

(iii) Variable Overheads Quantity Variance

(standard quantity of labour hours for actual production −
   actual quantity of labour hours used) × standard variable
   overheads price per hour
   = (110,000 × 2 hours − 230,000 hours) × £2.50   (25,000) Unfav.
                                                                         32,500   Fav.

(iv) Fixed Overheads Variance

Standard fixed overheads less actual fixed overheads   £
   = £10,000 − £9,800   200   Fav.

A8 Peter Peacock plc
August's results

(i) Flexed budget

	Budget (i.e., standard)	Flexed Budget (i.e., standard quantity of actual production)	Actual	Sales Price and Overall Cost Variances	
Volume	200,000	220,000	220,000		
	£	£	£	£	
Sales	560,000	616,000	611,600	(4,400)	Unfav.
Direct materials	(125,000)	(137,500)	(150,000)	(12,500)	Unfav.
Direct labour	(290,000)	(319,000)	(317,550)	1,450	Fav.
Variable overheads	(40,000)	(44,000)	(42,500)	1,500	Fav.
Contribution	105,000	115,500	101,550	(13,950)	Unfav.
Fixed overheads	(68,000)	(68,000)	(67,000)	1,000	Fav.
Profit	37,000	47,500	34,550	(12,950)	Unfav.

(ii) Individual Variances: Sales

Sales Quantity Variance

(Standard quantity of units sold – actual quantity of units sold) × standard contribution

$$£$$
$$(200,000 - 220,000) \times 0.525* = 10,500 \text{ Fav.}**$$

$$\frac{\text{*Contribution}}{\text{Budgeted sales volume}} = \frac{105,000}{200,000}$$

**Represents budgeted profit £37,000 – flexed budget profit £47,500

Sales Price Variance

This can be taken direct from the flexed budget, or it can be calculated as follows:
(standard selling price – actual selling price per unit) × actual quantity of units sold
(£2.80 – £2.78) × 220,000 = (£4,400) Unfav.

A8 Peter Peacock plc (*continued*)
   Costs

Price	Quantity
(standard price − actual price per unit) × actual quantity	*(standard quantity of actual production − actual quantity) × standard price*

Direct Material Variances

(£1.25 per sheet − £1.20 per sheet) × 125,000 sheets = £6,250 Fav.

(220,000 subcomponents × 0.50 sheets per subcomponent* gives 110,000 sheets − 125,000 sheets) × £1.25 = (£18,750) Unfav.
*100,000 sheets ÷ 200,000 subcomponents. This gives the amount of material per subcomponent.

Direct Labour Variances

(£7.25 per hour − £7.30 per hour) × 43,500 hours = (£2,175) Unfav.

(220,000 subcomponents × 0.20 hours* gives 44,000 hours − 43,500 hours) × £7.25 = £3,625 Fav.
*40,000 hours : 200,000 subcomponents. This gives the amount of the labour per subcomponent

Variable Overhead Variances

(£1.00 per hour − £0.977 per hour)* × 43,500 hours = £1,000 Fav.
*£42,500 variable overheads ÷ 43,500 hours

(220,000 subcomponents × 0.20 hours* gives 44,000 hours − 43,500 hours) × £1.00 = £500 Fav.
*40,000 hours ÷ 200,000 subcomponents. This gives the amount of labour per subcomponent and we are recovering our variable overheads on the labour hours.

Fixed Overheads

£68,000 standard fixed overheads − £67,000 actual fixed overheads = £1,000 Fav.

(iii)
Peter Peacock plc
Standard Cost Reconciliation Statement for August

	£	£	£	
Budgeted Profit			37,000	
Sales quantity variance			10,500	Fav.
Budgeted profit at actual sales			47,500	
Variances	*Fav.*	*Unfav.*		
Sales price		4,400		
Direct materials price	6,250			
Direct materials quantity		18,750		
Direct labour price		2,175		
Direct labour quantity	3,625			
Variable overheads price	1,000			
Variable overheads quantity	500			
Fixed overheads variance	1,000			
	12,375	25,325	(12,950)	
Actual Profit			34,550	

(iv) The actual profit for Peacock is £2,450 less than budgeted (£37,000 − £34,550). Peacock has actually sold 20,000 more units than anticipated, creating a favourable sales quantity variance of £10,500. However, it has done this by reducing the price slightly so there is an unfavourable sales price variance.

On the cost variances, there is a favourable direct materials price variance (£6,250) as the sheets are cheaper than anticipated. However, more sheets were used than anticipated, possibly because they were poorer quality. There is thus an unfavourable quantity variance of £18,750. The labour price variance of £2,175 is unfavourable since Peacock paid £7.30 per hour rather than the budgeted £7.25. However, perhaps because a better quality of labour was used, less hours were used creating a favourable quantity variance of £3,625. For variable overheads, less overheads than anticipated were incurred creating a favourable price variance of £1,000. Also because of the fewer hours used, less overheads were recovered into the product causing a favourable quantity variance. Finally, fixed overheads were less than anticipated.

Chapter 6: Discussion *Answers*

The answers provide some outline points for discussion.

A1 Fixed costs are those costs, like depreciation or insurance, which do not vary with production or sales. They remain fixed whatever the level of production or sales. This is not universally true as at a certain point, such as acquiring a new machine, fixed costs will vary. However, it is a reasonable working assumption.

Variable costs, by contrast, are those costs that do vary with production or sales. If we make more products or provide more services, then our variable costs will increase. Conversely, if we make fewer products or provide fewer services, then our variable costs will decrease.

Fixed costs are irrelevant for decision making because they will be incurred whatever the decision. They are fixed within the relevant range of activity. For example, insurance and depreciation will not vary whether we choose to produce more of product A or more of product B. We should, therefore, ignore these costs when making decisions.

A4 **True or False?**
  (a) *False*. Wrong time horizon. Fixed costs do *not* vary with short-term changes in the level of sales or production.
  (b) *True*.
  (c) *False*. Wrong numerator. Break-even point is $\dfrac{\text{Fixed costs}}{\text{Contribution per unit}}$
  (d) *False*. Contribution/sales ratio is $\dfrac{\text{Contribution}}{\text{Sales}}$
  (e) *False*. Non-financial items do not feature directly in the calculations, but they are extremely important.

Chapter 6: Numerical *Answers*

A1 Jungle Animals

(i), (ii)	Selling Price £	Variable Costs £	Contribution £	Contribution/ Sales Ratio %
Alligators	1.00	1.05	(0.05)	(5.0)
Bears	1.20	1.00	0.20	16.7
Cougars	1.10	1.14	(0.04)	(3.6)
Donkeys	1.15	1.08	0.07	6.1
Eagles	1.20	0.96	0.24	20.0
Foxes	0.90	0.85	0.05	5.6
Giraffes	1.05	0.85	0.20	19.0
Hyenas	1.25	0.94	0.31	24.8
Iguanas	0.95	0.72	0.23	24.2
Jackals	0.80	0.73	0.07	8.8

(iii) The two toys with the highest contribution are Hyenas (£0.31 contribution) and Eagles (£0.24 contribution).

(iv) The three toys with the highest contribution/sales ratio are Hyenas (24.8 %), Iguanas (24.2 %) and Eagles (20 %).

(v) Alligators and Cougars have a negative contribution so we would not make them.

A3 Scrooge

Internal bid:	£
Clerical labour	60,000
Supervisory labour	60,000
Direct materials	15,000
Variable overheads	30,000
	165,000
External bid	(160,000)
Thus saving by buying in	5,000

So on the straight accounting calculation Scrooge would outsource. The chief assumption is that all the labour is indeed variable and can be laid off or redeployed easily. Other factors are the impact upon industrial relations, long-term implications and confidentiality. The outside bid is marginally superior. However, when these other factors are taken into account it may be better to go with the status quo.

A6 Freya

(i) Contribution per hammer

	£	£
Sales		10
Less: *Variable Costs*		
Direct materials	4	
Variable expenses	3	7
Contribution		3

$$\text{Break-even point: } \frac{\text{Fixed costs}}{\text{Contribution per unit}} = \frac{£30,000}{£3} = 10,000 \text{ hammers}$$

(ii) (a) If 4,000 sold

Contribution (4,000 × £3) =		£12,000
Fixed costs		(£30,000)
Loss		(£18,000)

(b) If 14,000 sold

Contribution (14,000 × £3) =		£42,000
Fixed costs		(£30,000)
Profit		£12,000

(iii) Current margin of safety

(a) Units (i.e. Hammers):

$$\frac{\text{Actual hammers sold} - \text{hammers at break-even}}{\text{Hammers at break-even}}$$

$$= \frac{20,000 - 10,000}{10,000} = 100\,\%$$

(b) £s:

$$\frac{\text{Actual sales} - \text{sales at break-even}}{\text{Sales at break-even}}$$

$$= \frac{200,000 - 100,000}{100,000} = 100\,\%$$

(iv) Break-even chart

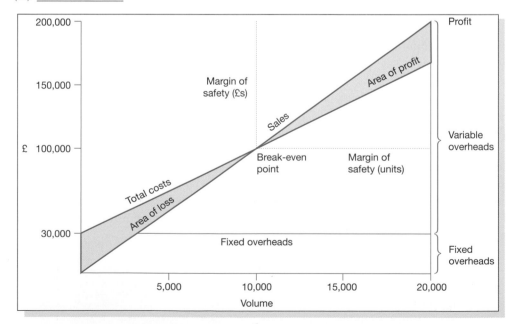

A8 Modem

(i)

Branch	Sales £	Variable Costs £	Contribution £	Contribution/ Sales Ratio %	Ranking
Cardiff	200,000	165,000	35,000	17.5 (£35,000/£200,000)	2
Edinburgh	300,000	230,000	70,000	23.3 (£70,000/£300,000)	1
London	1,000,000	870,000	130,000	13.0 (£130,000/£1,000,000)	3
	1,500,000	1,265,000	235,000		
Fixed costs			(150,000)		
Net Profit			85,000		

(ii) Cumulative profit table in contribution/sales ratio ranking:

	Cumulative Sales £	Cumulative Contribution £	Cumulative Profit/Loss £
Fixed costs			(150,000)
Edinburgh	300,000	70,000	(80,000)
Cardiff	500,000	105,000	(45,000)
London	1,500,000	235,000	85,000

Modem's Contribution/Sales Graph

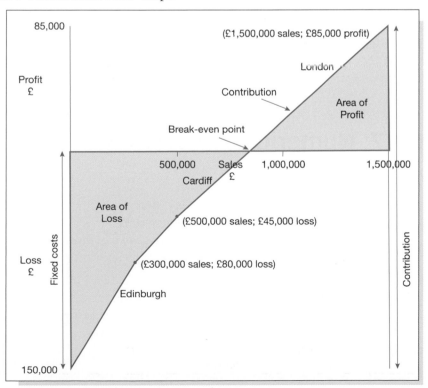

Chapter 7: Discussion *Answers*

The answers provide some outline points for discussion.

A1 Strategic management accounting is a relatively new branch of management accounting. It is concerned with a business's strategic future, long-term direction. A working definition of strategic management accounting is a form of management accounting which considers both an organisation's internal and external environments. Strategic management accounting comprises three main stages. First, an assessment of the current position of a business, which seeks to establish the internal and external elements of the business's environment. Second, an appraisal of the current position of the business. This establishes the current strengths and weaknesses. Finally, strategic management accounting looks at the possible strategic choices of the business, such as product diversification or mergers/acquisitions.

Strategic management accounting grows out of a concern with the traditional role of the management accountant. Traditionally, management accounting has been criticised as inward-looking and failing to respond to the external environment. Strategic management accounting attempts to lift management accountants out of this, traditionally fairly narrow, functional specialism. There is an emphasis on long-term strategic thinking embracing the whole business.

A5 True or False?
  (a) *True.*
  (b) *True.*
  (c) *False.* No, the four components are stars, question marks, cash cows and dogs.
  (d) *False.* The balanced scorecard uses a mixture of financial and non-financial performance indicators.
  (e) *False.* Almost right. SWOT analysis stands for strengths, weaknesses, *opportunities* and threats.

Chapter 7: Numerical *Answers*

A1 Maxi, Mini, Midi

In year 3		
Maxi – high sales, high profitability, thus	**Maturity**
Mini – sales declining, profits declining thus	**Decline**
Midi – sales growing fast, profitability growing, thus	**Growth**

A2 Apple, Orange, Pear and Banana

Apple:	Star (high market share; high market growth)
Orange:	Question mark (low market share; high market growth)
Pear:	Cash cow (high market share; low market growth)
Banana:	Dog (low market share; low market growth)

The pears are cash cows and likely to be profitable, whereas the bananas are dogs and probably unprofitable. The situation with apples and oranges is more complex. The apples are stars and it depends on the current capital expenditure. If low they would be profitable, but if high they might not be. The oranges are question marks and are probably unprofitable at the moment. They leave the company with the difficult question of whether to invest more resources or whether to pull out of the market.

Chapter 8: Discussion *Answers*

The answers provide some outline points for discussion.

A1 (a) Capital investment is necessary for the development of a company's infrastructure. Companies also expand or reorientate their strategic direction. Therefore, they need to invest in infrastructure assets, such as factories or plant and machinery. Essentially, in a competitive business world companies will either grow or stagnate. If they stagnate they will be likely to be taken over.

(b) (i) Ships or equipment for making ships such as dry docks, cranes, heavy equipment etc.

(ii) New hotels or refurbishment of old ones.

(iii) New factories, plant and machinery, computer technology.

A5 True or False?

(a) *True.*

(b) *False.* Net present value and the internal rate of return use discounted cash flows. The payback period generally does not use discounted cash flows. It is, however, possible to incorporate them into payback models.

(c) *True.*

(d) *False.* The discount rate normally used for discounting cash flows is the company's weighted average cost of capital.

(e) *True.*

Chapter 8: Numerical *Answers*

A1 (i) 0.6209   (iv) 0.6355

(ii) 0.5983   (v) 0.6750

(iii) 0.3762   (vi) 0.1615

A2 Fairground

	Rocket	Carousel	Dipper
(i) Payback	£16,000 + (£2,000/£8,000) = 2.25 years	£10,000 + (£8,000/£14,000) = 2.57 years	£16,000 + (£2,000/£5,000) = 2.4 years

(ii) Accounting rate of return

	Rocket	Carousel	Dipper
Annual average profit/ Initial investment	(£24,000 ÷ 3)/ £18,000 = 44.4 %	(£24,000 ÷ 3)/ £18,000 = 44.4%	(£21,000 ÷ 3)/ £18,000 = 38.9%

(iii) Net present value

Year	Rocket £	Carousel £	Dipper £	Discount Rate 8 %	Rocket £	Carousel £	Dipper £
0	(18,000)	(18,000)	(18,000)	1	(18,000)	(18,000)	(18,000)
1	8,000	6,000	10,000	0.9259	7,407	5,555	9,259
2	8,000	4,000	6,000	0.8573	6,858	3,429	5,144
3	8,000	14,000	5,000	0.7938	6,350	11,113	3,969
Net Present Value (NPV)					2,615	2,097	372

So on (i)–(iii) we would choose the Rocket on all criteria as our project.

(iv) Internal rate of return (IRR): choose 18 % to achieve a negative NPV

Net present value Year	Rocket £	Carousel £	Dipper £	Discount Rate 18 %	Rocket £	Carousel £	Dipper £
0	(18,000)	(18,000)	(18,000)	1	(18,000)	(18,000)	(18,000)
1	8,000	6,000	10,000	0.8475	6,780	5,085	8,475
2	8,000	4,000	6,000	0.7182	5,746	2,873	4,309
3	8,000	14,000	5,000	0.6086	4,869	8,520	3,043
Net Present Value (NPV)					(605)	(1,522)	(2,173)

Therefore, calculate IRR using formula:

$$\text{IRR} = \text{Lowest discount rate} + \text{difference in discount rates} \times \frac{\text{lowest discount rate NPV}}{\text{difference in NPVs}}$$

$$\text{Rocket} = 8\% + \left(10\% \times \frac{£2,615}{£2,615 + £605}\right) = 16.1\%$$

$$\text{Carousel} = 8\% + \left(10\% \times \frac{£2,097}{£2,097 + £1,522}\right) = 13.8\%$$

$$\text{Dipper} = 8\% + \left(10\% \times \frac{£372}{£372 + £2,173}\right) = 9.5\%$$

A2 Fairground (*continued*)

Therefore, as our cost of capital (8 %) is less than the IRR, we could potentially undertake all the projects. We would choose to invest in Rocket because it has the highest IRR. Rocket is the preferred project under all four methods.

A3 Wetday

	Storm	Cloud	Downpour
(i) **Payback**	£15,000 +	£10,000 +	£12,000 +
	(£3,000/£7,000)	(£2,000/£2,500)	(£1,000/£4,000)
	= 3.43 years	= 3.8 years	= 3.25 years

(ii) Accounting rate of return

	Storm	Cloud	Downpour
Average annual profit/	£6,000/£18,000	£3,100/£12,000	£4,000/£13,000
Initial investment	= 33.3 %	= 25.8%	= 30.8%

(iii) Net present value

Year	Storm £	Cloud £	Downpour £	Discount Rate 12 %	Storm £	Cloud £	Downpour £
0	(18,000)	(12,000)	(13,000)	1	(18,000)	(12,000)	(13,000)
1	4,000	5,000	4,000	0.8929	3,572	4,464	3,572
2	5,000	2,000	4,000	0.7972	3,986	1,594	3,189
3	6,000	3,000	4,000	0.7118	4,271	2,135	2,847
4	7,000	2,500	4,000	0.6355	4,449	1,589	2,542
5	8,000	3,000	4,000	0.5674	4,539	1,702	2,270
Net Present Value (NPV)					2,817	(516)	1,420

Therefore, depending upon the criteria, we will choose a different project. Downpour has the quickest payback; Storm the highest accounting rate of return and NPV. Probably, therefore, we will choose Storm. We will definitely not choose Cloud, because of its negative NPV.

(iv) Internal rate of return (IRR).

Choose 20 % for Storm and Downpour to get a negative NPV. However, choose 8 % for Cloud to get a positive NPV.

Year	Storm £	Cloud £	Downpour £	Discount Rate 20 % £	Discount Rate 8 % £	Storm (20 %) £	Cloud (8 %) £	Downpour (20 %) £
0	(18,000)	(12,000)	(13,000)	1	1	(18,000)	(12,000)	(13,000)
1	4,000	5,000	4,000	0.8333	0.9259	3,333	4,629	3,333
2	5,000	2,000	4,000	0.6944	0.8573	3,472	1,715	2,778
3	6,000	3,000	4,000	0.5787	0.7938	3,472	2,381	2,315
4	7,000	2,500	4,000	0.4823	0.7350	3,376	1,837	1,929
5	8,000	3,000	4,000	0.4019	0.6806	3,215	2,042	1,608
Net Present Value (NPV)						(1,132)	604	(1,037)

A3 Wetday (*continued*)

Calculate IRR, using formula

$$\text{IRR} = \text{Lowest discount rate} + \text{difference in discount rates} \times \frac{\text{lowest discount rate NPV}}{\text{difference in NPVs}}$$

$$\text{Storm} \quad = \quad 12\% \quad + \quad \left(8\% \times \frac{£2,817}{£2,817 + £1,132}\right) \quad = \quad 17.7\%$$

$$\text{Cloud} \quad = \quad 8\% \quad + \quad \left(4\% \times \frac{£604}{£604 + £516}\right) \quad = \quad 10.2\%$$

$$\text{Downpour} \quad = \quad 12\% \quad + \quad \left(8\% \times \frac{£1,420}{£1,420 + £1,037}\right) \quad = \quad 16.6\%$$

As our cost of capital is 12%, we could potentially undertake Storm or Downpour. Storm has the highest IRR and we would choose this project if funds were limited. As Storm has the highest accounting rate of return, NPV and IRR, this is our preferred project.

Chapter 9: Discussion *Answers*

The answers provide some outline points for discussion.

A1 Firms are in some ways like living things. They need energy to survive and grow. In the case of living things, the energy is provided by sunlight. For firms, the energy is supplied by sources of finance. These may be short-term, like a bank overdraft, or long-term, like a long-term loan. These sources of finance enable a firm to buy stock, carry out day-to-day operations and expand by the purchase of new fixed assets. In essence, short-term finance should be used to sustain the firm's working capital, while long-term finance should fund the company's infrastructure. Some of the major sources of finance and the activities financed are outlined below:

Source of finance	*Activities financed*
Bank overdraft	Working capital, day-to-day operations
Debt factoring	Debtors
Invoice discounting	Debtors
Sale and buy back of stock	Stock
Leasing	Leased assets
Retained profits	Infrastructure assets, e.g., fixed assets
Share capital	Infrastructure assets, e.g., fixed assets
Long-term loan	Infrastructure assets, e.g., fixed assets

A5 True or False?

(a) *False*. They are normally used to finance long-term infrastructure assets.
(b) *True*.
(c) *True*.
(d) *False*. Retained profits is an internal, not an external, source of long-term finance.
(e) *True*.

Chapter 9: Numerical *Answers*

A1 Lathe

(i) (a) **Graphical Solution**

Order Quantity Q	Number of Orders per annum	Order Cost	Total Order Cost	Average Quantity in Stock	Carrying Cost	Total Carrying Cost	Total Cost
		£	£	£	£	£	£
250	80	25	2,000	125	0.90	112.50	2,112.50
500	40	25	1,000	250	0.90	225.00	1,225.00
1,000	20	25	500	500	0.90	450.00	950.00
1,500	13.33	25	333	750	0.90	675.00	1,008.00
2,000	10	25	250	1,000	0.90	900.00	1,150.00

Graphical solution: Optimal order quantity about 1,000

A1 Lathe (*continued*)

   (i) (b) Algebraic solution:

Economic order quantity formula

$$Q = \sqrt{\frac{2AC}{i}}$$

where:

Q = Economic order quantity
A = Average annual usage
C = Cost of each order being placed
i = Carrying cost per unit per annum

$$Q = \sqrt{\frac{2 \times 20,000 \times 25}{0.90}} = 1,054 \text{ Tweaks}$$

  (ii) Total costs per annum

		£
Costs of purchase	£1.50 × 1,054	1,581
Order costs	$\dfrac{20,000}{1,054} \times £25$	474
Holding costs	$\dfrac{1,054}{2} \times 0.90$	474
Total costs		2,529

A4 Albatross

Source of Finance	Current Market Value		Present Cost of Capital	Weighted Average Cost of Capital
	£ million	%	%	%
Ordinary shares	4	50.0	12	6.00
Preference shares	1	12.5	10	1.25
Long-term loan	3	37.5	8	3.00
	8	100.0		10.25

Index